Do Think Tanks Matter?
Assessing the Impact of
Public Policy Institutes

DONALD E. ABELSON

McGill-Queen's University Press
Montreal & Kingston · London · Ithaca

© McGill-Queen's University Press 2002
ISBN 0-7735-2316-2 (cloth)
ISBN 0-7735-2317-0 (paper)

Legal deposit first quarter 2002
Bibliothèque nationale du Québec

Printed in Canada on acid-free paper

This book has been published with the help of a grant
from the Humanities and Social Sciences Federation
of Canada, using funds provided by the Social Sciences
and Humanities Research Council of Canada, and
with a grant from the J.B. Smallman Publication
Fund, Faculty of Social Science, The University
of Western Ontario.

McGill-Queen's University Press acknowledges the
financial support of the Government of Canada
through the Book Publishing Industry Development
Program (BPIDP) for its publishing activities. It also
acknowledges the support of the Canada Council for
the Arts for its publishing program.

The author and publisher are grateful to the following
for permission to draw on previously published
material: Donald E. Abelson, "Do Think Tanks
Matter? Opportunities, Constraints and Incentives
for Think Tanks in Canada and the United States,"
Global Society, vol. 14, no. 2, 2000, 213–36; Donald E.
Abelson, "Public Visibility and Policy Relevance:
Assessing the Impact and Influence of Canadian Policy
Institutes," *Canadian Public Administration*, vol. 42,
no. 2, (summer 1999), 240–70; and Donald E. Abelson
and Christine M. Carberry, "Following Suit or Falling
Behind? A Comparative Analysis of Think Tanks in
Canada and the United States," *Canadian Journal of
Political Science*, vol. 31, no. 3, 1998, 525–55.

National Library of Canada Cataloguing
in Publication Data

Abelson, Donald E.
    Do think tanks matter? : assessing the impact of public
policy institutes
    Includes bibliographical references and index.
    ISBN 0-7735-2316-2 (bound). –
    ISBN 0-7735-2317-0 (pbk.)
    1. Research institutes. 2. Policy sciences.
    3. Research institutes – United States.
    4. Research institutes – Canada. I. Title.
    H97.A24 2002   320'.6   C2001-901592-5

Typeset in Sabon 10/12
by Caractéra inc., Quebec City

For Stephanie, Rebecca, and Seth
A constant reminder of what matters most

Contents

Tables

Acknowledgments

Aware of the risk of being overconfident or unduly pessimistic, legendary New York Yankees catcher Yogi Berra often remarked, "It ain't over till it's over." Taking my cue from Yogi, one of baseball's truly great philosophers, I am pleased that the lengthy process of researching and writing this book is finally over. I can now take this opportunity to thank the many individuals who assisted me in this endeavour.

First and foremost, I would like to express my gratitude to Evert Lindquist for helping me sharpen the focus of my manuscript and for the many insightful comments he made throughout this project. As in the past, he went out of his way to ensure that I asked the right questions and provided appropriate responses. I am also grateful to several of my other colleagues in the academic community who read various chapters of the book and passed along many valuable suggestions. They include Ian Brodie, Christine Carberry, Michael Lusztig, James McGann, Diane Stone, Richard Vernon, Kent Weaver, and Robert Young. I would also like to thank the anonymous reviewers of the manuscript for their important input.

Over the course of researching this book, I was able to draw on the expertise of several staff members from think tanks in Canada and the United States. Always willing to oblige, they shared their insights and experiences about how their institutions seek to convey ideas to policymakers and the difficulties they often encounter in assessing their policy impact. This book could not have been completed without their cooperation, nor could it have come to fruition without the tremendous research assistance of Julie Beeton, Vida Brodie, Mark Raymond, Adrian Smith, Laura Stephenson, David Vernon, Kimberly Wilhelm, and Walter Zimmerman.

A debt of gratitude must also be paid to Penelope Lister for proofreading and editing an earlier version of the manuscript. She significantly improved the readability of the book. In addition, I would like to thank Philip Cercone of McGill-Queen's University Press for his support and encouragement of this project, as well as members of his staff, including Brenda Prince and Joan McGilvray, for navigating the book through the publication process. Their hard work on my behalf is greatly appreciated.

Finally, I am forever indebted to my wife and our two wonderful and spirited children, who have witnessed firsthand the joy and frustration that come with this profession. This book is dedicated to them.

Acronyms

PRI   Policy Research Initiative
RIIA   Royal Institute of International Affairs
SCC   Science Council of Canada

Do Think Tanks Matter?

Introduction

According to a recent survey conducted for the National Institute for Research Advancement (NIRA), a Tokyo-based research institute, over thirty-five hundred public policy institutes, or think tanks, as they are more commonly referred to, exist worldwide. Of these, more than half are located in the United States: think tanks such as the world-renowned Brookings Institution, the Hoover Institution on War, Revolution and Peace, and RAND.[1] For many scholars and journalists studying the so-called think tank phenomenon, the explosion of policy institutes in the latter part of the twentieth century is indicative of their growing importance in the policy-making process, a perception reinforced by directors of think tanks, who often credit their institutes with influencing major policy debates and government legislation. Yet, despite their more visible presence in many advanced and developing countries, few studies to date have assessed the influence or impact of think tanks on policy-making. Acknowledging that such an assessment would be notoriously difficult, many scholars have consciously avoided discussing how to measure their effectiveness; others have simply asserted that think tanks exercise influence, without demonstrating how they actually achieve it.

The purpose of this book is to go beyond much of the descriptive and anecdotal literature in the field by addressing one critical, though frequently ignored, question – Do think tanks matter? To answer this seemingly straightforward but, in fact, highly problematic question, I will study the experiences of think tanks in the United States, a country where these organizations have become an integral feature of the political landscape, and in Canada, where think tanks have become far more visible but have enjoyed less prominence in policy-making. My central argument is that think tanks in both countries have at times played an important role in shaping the political dialogue and the policy preferences and choices of policymakers, but often in different ways and during different stages of the policy cycle. For instance, several American think tanks, including the Hoover Institution, the Heritage Foundation, and the Brookings Institution, have undertaken active roles in several presidential campaigns and in the transition periods that followed. Conversely, think tanks in Canada are rarely important repositories of policy expertise during federal and provincial elections and tend to maintain a modest presence during a new government's transition to power. Nonetheless, a handful of Canadian think tanks, including the Fraser Institute, the C.D. Howe Institute, and the North-South Institute, are often active at other stages of the policy cycle. To market their ideas, these and other think tanks pursue a range of strategies, including seeking access to the print and broadcast media, distributing publications to policymakers and journalists, and testifying before parliamentary committees. As will become clear in the chapters that follow, while think tanks in the United States and Canada share a common desire to influence public policy, how and under what circumstances they seek to do so ultimately depends on a wide range of internal and external factors.

Much of the literature that compares think tanks in the United States to those in parliamentary systems such as Canada and Great Britain, sparse as it is,[2] suggests that the "distinctive characteristic of think tanks in the United States is not their size or, for that matter, the considerable funding of some institutions ... What makes think tanks in the United States unique, besides their sheer number, is the extent to which they have become involved actively in various stages of the policy-making process."[3] Implicit in this observation is the idea that think tanks tend to play a more significant role in the United States. That country has a more decentralized and fragmented political system than Canada, where the principles of strong party unity and cabinet solidarity and the presence of a permanent senior civil service entrusted with advising policymakers are thought to limit opportunities for think tanks and other nongovernmental organizations to influence policy-making. In short, differences in the institutional structures of the two countries may account for Canadian think tanks playing a less active role in policy-making than think tanks in the United States. The perception that think tanks in the United States have had a more discernible impact on policy-making and in shaping specific policy issues than think tanks in Canada has generally been supported by scholars in the field. Indeed, the limited number of case studies available on the subject have concluded that while several U.S. think tanks have played a decisive role in shaping key policy debates and some important pieces of government legislation, Canadian think tanks, with a few exceptions,[4] have made only modest contributions to public discussions on issues ranging from pension reform and tax policy to the public debt.[5] As I will demonstrate, however, while individual case studies help to shed light on their involvement in particular policy areas or during different stages of the policy-making process, scholars and journalists must resist the temptation to generalize about the impact of think tanks.

Think tanks in the United States may have more opportunities, or access points, to directly and indirectly influence public policy than their Canadian counterparts, and they may face fewer constraints in conveying ideas to policymakers.[6] However, at times several Canadian think tanks have contributed both to policy-making and to shaping the policy- or decision-making environment.[7] The importance of distinguishing between influencing policy-making and the policy-making environment will become clearer in the case studies included here. Some institutional constraints or political structures, as well as a host of other factors have, indeed, limited the potential impact of Canadian think tanks at some stages of the policy cycle.[8] Still, parliamentary systems, parliamentarians, and public servants do not pose a barrier to think tanks or to their leaders, as some have suggested.[9] The ability of think tanks in parliamentary systems to convey their ideas effectively is constrained less by their political environment and more by their limited funding and staff. Interestingly enough, although they have more opportunities to influence public policy, modest institutional resources also plague the majority of American think tanks.

How much impact or influence think tanks have both in policy-making and in shaping the policy-making environment is a question scholars continue to struggle with. One major methodological problem in assessing influence is that think tanks and policymakers, not to mention the scholars themselves, have different perceptions of what constitutes influence and how it can best be measured.[10] Moreover, as the policy-making community becomes increasingly crowded, tracing the origin of a policy to a particular individual or organization can prove futile in all but the most exceptional cases. Every successful policy idea, as many have claimed, has a hundred mothers and fathers; every bad policy idea is always an orphan.

Although some effort has been made to track how often think tanks in Canada and the United States are referred to by the media and how often their staff testify before parliamentary and congressional committees, few definitive conclusions have been reached regarding their impact in policy-making.[11] The amount of media coverage think tanks generate may indicate how much influence they have placing issues on the political agenda; several journalists and directors of think tanks in both countries have made such claims. Yet, as will be discussed, media exposure cannot be used as the sole indicator or, indeed, even a reliable indicator of policy influence even at the most preliminary stages of the policy-making process. Several factors explain why some think tanks in Canada and in the United States appear to have more impact on the policy-making community than others. As Monique Jérôme-Forget, former president of the Montreal-based Institute for Research on Public Policy observes, "quantitative measures, such as the number of media citations, show only that ideas are being talked about, as opposed to genuinely influencing the thinking of observers of an issue."[12]

Two central paths of inquiry will be followed in order to explain how and to what extent think tanks shape the policy-making environment and the policy-making process. First, consideration must be given to the stage or stages in the policy cycle at which think tanks are most actively engaged. While in both Canada and the United States they rely on similar strategies to convey their ideas to policymakers and to the general public, they often take advantage of different opportunities to achieve their goals. As noted, providing advice to u.s. presidential candidates or to an incoming president and his staff is an opportunity they cannot afford to miss. It is not surprising, therefore, that during the presidential election of 2000 a select group of scholars at the Hoover Institution, the American Enterprise Institute, and other think tanks discussed several policy ideas with Republican presidential candidate George W. Bush. As will be discussed in chapter 6, it is not uncommon for American think tanks to devote considerable resources to providing presidential candidates and new administrations with detailed blueprints on how to manage the nation's affairs. Often released with considerable fanfare, several of these studies have hit the bestseller list.

In Canada, by contrast, think tanks rarely regard elections and transition periods as the most opportune time to convey their ideas to policymakers. Far less conscious of the electoral cycle than their u.s. counterparts, many Canadian think tanks place a higher priority on working closely with senior and middle-level public servants and members of the cabinet on an ongoing or ad hoc basis to advance their interests, a strategy pursued by such think tanks as the Caledon Institute, the Public Policy Forum and the Canadian Policy Research Networks, Inc. (CPRN). Canadian think tanks may not enjoy the stature and visibility of some think tanks in the United States, but their less noticeable presence does not necessarily indicate a limited policy influence. As Judith Maxwell, president of the CPRN recently stated, "the most important type of influence is never documented."[13]

By determining where in the policy cycle think tanks in the two countries are most actively engaged, we can explore several factors that may help to explain why think tanks in the United States are thought to play a more significant role in the policy-making process than those in Canada. As this study will reveal, while think tanks in Canada and the United States function in very different political systems, their ability or inability to establish and maintain a strong presence in the policy-making community may have as much to do with how these institutions define their missions and with the directors who lead them and the resources and strategies they employ to achieve their stated goals as with the political environments they inhabit. In other words, the structure of the political system may at times frustrate or facilitate the efforts of think tanks to influence public policy, but this factor alone cannot account for their success or failure.

In addition to considering how various institutional, political, economic, and cultural factors facilitate or constrain think tank development, it is important to think more critically about how to measure their relative performance in what has become, particularly in the United States, an increasingly competitive marketplace of ideas. Should the influence of think tanks be measured by media citations, number of appearances before legislative committees, and total number of publications released in a given year? Or should other performance indicators be taken into consideration? This second and more difficult avenue of inquiry may not produce definitive conclusions about the influence of think tanks, but it will, nonetheless, provide tangible and some intangible indicators that can be considered in evaluating the strengths, limitations, and priorities of policy institutes.

CLASSIFYING THINK TANKS

Several scholars who have studied think tanks have made important contributions to our understanding of how they have evolved and the many political, economic, and social factors that have influenced their development. James Smith's exploration of American think tanks, *The Idea Brokers: Think Tanks and the Rise of the New Policy Elite*, and an edited volume that focuses on think tanks in several different countries, *Think Tanks across Nations*, are but two examples of studies that have assisted both students and practitioners of public policy and public administration to better understand the role of think tanks in the policy-making process.[14] But some basic questions remain unanswered. To begin with, what are the defining characteristics of think tanks, and how do they differ from the multitude of other organizations, including interest groups, that populate the policy-making community? What is their primary function? And what conceptual frameworks have been constructed to study their involvement in policy-making?

Defining a think tank has long posed problems for those seeking to accurately describe what has become an increasingly diverse set of organizations. As Kent Weaver and James McGann acknowledge, although originally employed in the United States during World War II to refer to a secure room or environment where defence scientists and military planners could meet to discuss strategy, the term think tank has since been used to describe several different types of organizations engaged in policy analysis.[15] Consequently, several classifications of think tanks have been developed.

These organizations elude simple definition, in large part because there is no consensus about what constitutes a think tank. While one has little difficulty identifying universities and trade unions, organizations that also engage actively in research and analysis, trying to agree on what a think tank is and what its primary goals are results in more questions than answers. For some, the term "think tank" should be reserved only for a handful of large well-funded organizations of high-powered intellectuals committed to studying critical political, social, and economic issues. The Brookings Institution, a Washington icon long heralded as the quintessential think tank, would likely be among the few institutes satisfying these rather restrictive conditions. If this usage of the term was adopted, however, dozens of other less visible institutes that also engage in serious research and analysis would be overlooked or identified as something other than what they are.

After struggling to define what a think tank is, most scholars have acknowledged that there *is* no typical think tank. As McGann concedes, in trying to describe a think tank, "I know one when I see one."[16] Think tanks may range in size from entities with as few as one or two people to ones with several hundred staff and researchers. They may possess budgets as low as one to two hundred thousand dollars or as high as several million dollars. In other words, a think tank could look like RAND, one of America's premier foreign and defence policy institutes, with an annual budget exceeding $100 million and an impressive building complex located on prime oceanfront property in Santa Monica, California, or like the Canadian Council for International Peace and Security, which, until it was disbanded in April 2001, paid for its rented office space in Ottawa's Byward Market with a modest $250,000 to $300,000 budget.

As much as think tanks vary in staff size and budget, they also vary tremendously in areas of specialization, research output and ideological orientation and greatly in terms of their institutional independence. Some are affiliated with university departments and must rely on their resources to sustain them. The various defence and foreign policy centres established at over a dozen Canadian universities under the Department of National Defence's Military and Strategic Studies

Program (MSSP), now called the Strategic Defence Forum (SDF), is a case in point. There are also think tanks that function inside government, including the Congressional Research Service and the Congressional Budget Office.[17] Of particular interest to this study, though, are independent public policy think tanks: organizations that function much like private corporations but whose bottom lines are measured not by profit margins but by their impact on policy ideas. Emphasis will be placed on these types of think tanks, in large part because their survival depends less on the willingness of legislators to sustain their operations (although many rely heavily on government funding) or on academic departments prepared to support their activities. Rather, their survival and success as independent centres of policy analysis depends, in large part, on how effective their directors and staff are in marketing and promoting their ideas.

Despite their considerable diversity, think tanks do have some characteristics in common: they are generally nonprofit, nonpartisan organizations engaged in the study of public policy. The majority in Canada and the United States are registered as nonprofit, tax-exempt organizations under the Income Tax Act and the Internal Revenue Code respectively. They qualify for nonprofit status by applying as educational organizations undertaking a commitment to increase public awareness about a host of policy issues. To obtain tax-exempt status, they must also remain nonpartisan. In other words, while think tanks in Canada and the United States are not prohibited from taking positions on various policy issues, as many frequently do, they cannot publicly endorse or oppose any political party or devote more than a legally prescribed percentage of their budget to lobbying government.[18] Think tanks can embrace whatever ideological orientation they desire and provide their expertise to any political candidate or office holder willing to take advantage of their advice. They must by law, however, refrain from engaging in certain overt political activities.

What has traditionally distinguished think tanks from the multitude of other organizations in the policy-making community is the emphasis they place on research and analysis. Not all think tanks share the same commitment to scholarly research or devote comparable resources to performing this function, yet it remains, for many, their raison d'être. However, the nostalgic vision of think tanks as idea factories, or brain trusts created to address society's most pressing social, economic, and political problems, must be reconsidered in any contemporary study.

THE ROLE OF THINK TANKS

During the progressive era of the early 1900s leading industrialists and philanthropists in the United States, including Pittsburgh steel baron

Andrew Carnegie and Robert Brookings, a St Louis businessman, recognized the importance of creating institutions composed of prominent economists, political scientists, and historians capable of bringing their scientific expertise to bear on important public policy issues. Carnegie and Brookings believed that by establishing an environment where academics would not be distracted by teaching responsibilities but could focus entirely on research relevant to public policy, think tanks could play an important and much-needed role in policy-making. In the absence of a permanent senior civil service that could advise elected officials in the United States, ample opportunities existed for think tanks to provide their insights and expertise.

The Carnegie Endowment for International Peace, the Brookings Institution, and a handful of other think tanks created during the first decades of the twentieth century to improve government decision making have contributed largely to the widely held perception of think tanks as objective and politically neutral organizations devoted to research and analysis. In recent years, however, as many policy institutes have placed a higher premium on marketing and recycling ideas than on generating them, this view of think tanks has come under closer scrutiny. In fact, as several think tanks, including the Heritage Foundation, the American Enterprise Institute, the Fraser Institute, and the Canadian Centre for Policy Alternatives, to name a few, have combined political advocacy with policy research, it has become increasingly difficult to differentiate between think tanks and other types of nongovernmental organizations like interest groups, which are also committed to improving public policy.

The comparison often drawn between think tanks, particularly those that are more advocacy-oriented, and interest or pressure groups is not entirely unwarranted. After all, many of the tactics interest groups use to convey their concerns to governments, including preparing and distributing studies, publishing articles in newspapers, giving interviews on television and on radio, arranging meetings with policymakers, and testifying before parliament, are also frequently employed by think tanks. As charitable organizations, think tanks, like interest groups, also try to recruit high-profile individuals to their organizations in an effort to attract more funding. The Hoover Institution, located on the picturesque campus of Stanford University, is but one think tank that has done this. Included on its roster are George Shultz, former secretary of state, Richard Allen, former national security adviser, Newt Gingrich, former speaker of the House of Representatives, and until recently, Condoleezza Rice, who has taken leave from the solitude of academic life to serve as national security adviser to President George W. Bush.

Still, despite the many similarities between think tanks and interest groups, there are some notable differences. To begin with, although some think tanks try to appeal to as large a segment of the electorate as possible, they do not, like most interest groups, speak on behalf of a particular constituency. For instance, although the conservative-leaning Heritage Foundation may in principle support the right of Americans to bear arms, a constitutional right protected by the second amendment, it does not, however, speak on behalf of gun owners in the United States. This function is performed by the National Rifle Association (NRA), one of America's most vocal interest groups, currently headed by actor Charlton Heston. Second, the main purpose of interest groups is not to advance social science research (although some do devote considerable resources to it), but to ensure that elected leaders pursue policies compatible with their interests. To this end, interest groups and political action committees donate to the campaign chests of political parties, incumbents, and challengers most likely to support their wishes. Think tanks, by contrast, are prohibited by law from endorsing or opposing candidates for office and are not allowed to make donations to political parties or candidates. They can, however, contribute in other valuable ways, including discussing various domestic and foreign policy issues with incumbents and aspiring office holders.

As think tanks place greater emphasis on marketing their ideas and as interest groups invest more resources in building a stronger research capacity, the characteristics distinguishing the two will become increasingly blurred. Nevertheless, it is important to keep in mind that think tanks do perform a range of functions that in many ways make them unique. It is to this that I now turn.

There has been much debate over what the motivations and priorities of think tanks are, but one of their primary functions is clearly to help educate policymakers and the public – not to mention the private and nonprofit, or third, sectors – on pressing social, economic, and political issues. As educators, think tanks draw on various sources of information and expertise to communicate their views and concerns to multiple target audiences. Just as teachers attempt to shape the minds of their students, think tanks actively seek to mould public opinion and the policy preferences and choices of leaders. Some, as will be discussed, have proven to be far more effective and engaging educators than others.

Think tanks perform their educational tasks frequently. At times they serve as research brokers by acting as a conduit between the scholarly community and policymakers.[19] In this role think tanks communicate their findings to government officials and their staff in a clear and easily understood form. At other times they provide a forum for policymakers, academics, and representatives of the private and non-profit sector to discuss issues of common concern. This function is performed well by a handful of think tanks, including two Ottawa-based organizations, the Public Policy Forum and CPRN, Inc. Outreach and consultation are other important, related functions performed by think tanks. To share their ideas with the public and with policymakers and to discover more about the concerns of particular stakeholders, think tanks frequently sponsor conferences and workshops. Several, as noted, also undertake contract research for government and for the private sector.

For many think tanks, serving in an educational or research capacity does not mean that they should, or must, avoid taking positions on policy issues or advocate a particular set of values, beliefs, or principles. On the contrary, as outlined in their mission statements, all are committed to carrying out a set of goals and objectives. These may range from supporting the preservation of free market principles – a goal embraced by the Heritage Foundation, the American Enterprise Institute, the Fraser Institute, and the C.D. Howe Institute, among others – to stimulating public discussion on poverty and social policy, the mandate of the Ottawa-based Caledon Institute. The question for scholars studying think tanks is not whether they are committed to policy research or to political advocacy but how much emphasis they place on each. By better understanding the priorities of think tanks, which can often be assessed by looking at how their budgets are allocated, it is possible to provide more informed insights into the strategies they rely on to convey their ideas, a subject that will be explored in some detail.

STUDYING THINK TANKS

In a 1987 study Joseph Peschek remarked correctly that little research had been conducted on think tanks and their role in the policy-making process. At the time, only a handful of institutional histories of some prominent American think tanks and a few academic articles had been written. Acknowledging this lack of scholarship, Peschek claimed that unless political scientists began to focus more on the "subtle levels of [policy-making where] identifying and defining problems, shaping public understanding of issues, and constructing a political agenda" occurred, the significance of think tanks and their impact would be overlooked.[20] Peschek's admonition has not been ignored. Since the publication of his study of elite policy planning organizations, several books, articles, and book chapters, not to mention hundreds of newspaper articles, have been written detailing the role of think tanks in various advanced and developing countries and their efforts to shape public opinion and public policy.[21] Directories of think tanks have even been produced to keep track of the hundreds of policy institutes established. [22] But as diverse as these publications are, so too are the various theoretical or conceptual approaches, or frameworks, employed to study think tanks.

As will be discussed in more detail in chapter 2, think tanks have been regarded by some, including Peschek, William Domhoff, Thomas Dye, and John Saloma, as organizations that often serve the economic and political interests of the corporate elite. The several-million-dollar endowments enjoyed by a select group in the United States, the number of prominent business leaders who serve on their boards of directors, and the steady pool of former and future high-level policymakers working at these organizations, provide elite theorists with evidence to support their theories.[23]

However, since the think tank population is so ideologically and economically diverse, some theorists, prefer to treat them not as instruments of the ruling elite but simply as one type of organization competing for attention in a pluralist political system. Like interest groups and trade unions, think tanks are seen as nongovernmental organizations that employ a wide range of resources to influence the content and outcome of public policy. Influenced to some extent by elite theory, however, even proponents of the pluralist approach acknowledge that some think tanks are better positioned to engage in policy-making than others.

Drawing on the literature on elite and pluralist theories of democracy, a handful of scholars have studied think tanks from a different perspective. For instance, Hugh Heclo and Evert Lindquist treat think tanks as part of larger epistemic or policy communities whose researchers are often called upon to help advise on particular policy matters.[25] In this sense, think tanks are regarded as sources of expertise that at times can help supplement the research capacity of government departments.

Many of these approaches are useful and can help to shed light on think tank development; this study of Canadian and American think tanks, however, will adopt a rather different perspective. Since the purpose of this book is to determine where and how think tanks have an impact on policy-making, more emphasis will be placed on trying to understand why some are far more effective at gaining access to some stages of the policy cycle than others. On this question the literature on think tanks and on other types of nongovernmental organizations has been noticeably silent. As previously mentioned, the differences in the institutional or political structures of the two countries may help in part to explain why think tanks in the United States appear to have more access to policymakers than those in Canada.[25] Nonetheless, differences in institutional structures tell us very little about why some think tanks in the same country are more visible at certain stages of policy-making than others. Explanations for different access to the executive, legislature, bureaucracy, and the media can be provided only by looking more closely at the priorities, resources, and strategies of think tanks.

In the following chapter (chapter 1), an overview of the think tank population in Canada and the United States will be provided. The chapter will trace their evolution in the two countries and will discuss some of the many factors that have contributed to their increasingly diverse nature. Among other things, it will become apparent that think tanks in Canada and in the United States have followed a similar path of development, albeit in Canada's case at a more staggered pace. In the process of tracing the evolution of think tanks, some of the more prominent institutes in both countries will be highlighted.

Chapter 3 will shift from a discussion of the think tank population in the two countries to an assessment of the competing conceptual approaches that have been employed to study think tanks. As noted, scholars have tended to treat think tanks as elite organizations with close and lasting ties to policymakers, as one of many nongovernmental organizations that seek to influence public policy, or as institutes composed of experts that frequently participate in policy or epistemic communities. While each of these approaches can yield and has yielded important insights about the behaviour of think tanks, this chapter argues that a different conceptual framework is needed to better assess the impact of think tanks, one more deeply rooted in the literature on agenda setting and policy formulation. Rather than trying to determine how much or how little influence think tanks have in shaping the policy-making environment and the policy-making process, an endeavour which, in most cases proves futile, I suggest that scholars more closely scrutinize how think tanks become engaged at different stages of the policy cycle. By focusing on how think tanks attempt to shape the political agenda, contribute to policy formulation, and assist in policy implementation, a clearer picture emerges of which think tanks may or may not have played an important role during critical stages of the policy-making process.

Building on the conceptual framework set out in chapter 2, chapter 3 will explain why think tanks in the United States appear to be more actively engaged at some stages of the policy cycle than their Canadian counterparts. By comparing the different political systems, we can begin to explain not only why think tanks in the United States appear to be in greater demand but where in the policy cycle think tanks make their presence strongly felt. Emphasis will be placed on evaluating the various internal and external constraints that might limit the involvement of Canadian and American think tanks in policy-making, as well as the incentives decision makers in the two countries might have to turn to think tanks for policy advice.

In chapter 5 I will discuss the various governmental and nongovernmental channels think tanks rely on to convey their ideas to policymakers and to the public, distinguishing between the public and private uses of influence. Particular emphasis will be placed on how think tanks in both Canada and the United States are relying increasingly on the media to shape the political dialogue and what some of the implications of this strategy are.

Documenting how think tanks attempt to influence policy is a reasonably straightforward exercise, but determining how to assess their impact at various stages of policy-making is not. In chapter 5 I will explore how scholars use various indicators such as media citations, parliamentary and congressional testimony, and consultations with government departments and agencies to evaluate the impact or relevance of think tanks at particular stages of the policy-making process. The many methodological obstacles that must be overcome before any useful conclusions about think tank performance can be reached will also be discussed.

The amount of media exposure think tanks generate and the number of appearances they make before legislative committees may provide some insight into how visible particular organizations are. Such indicators, however, tell us little about what impact think tanks have had either on specific policy issues or in assisting policymakers to formulate policy ideas. To acquire better insight into the relevance of think tanks, one must go beyond simple data sets. To this end, two case studies will be employed that highlight some of the many functions think tanks perform in the policy-making process: an analysis of the involvement of a select group of American think tanks in several recent u.s. presidential campaigns (chapter 6) and an evaluation of the role of Canadian think tanks in the constitutional conferences leading up to the Charlottetown Accord (chapter 7).

These case studies have been selected for several reasons. To begin with, they provide a unique opportunity to closely scrutinize think tanks in the public spotlight. In fact, it is difficult to think of many other instances where think tanks in Canada and the United States have assumed such notoriety. Second, identifying the key think tanks involved does not require monitoring the activities of dozens of organizations, a problem frequently encountered in studying u.s. think tanks. From newspaper accounts, government documents, and material from various presidential and think tank archives, a clear picture emerges of which think tanks played a critical role in advising various presidential candidates. Identifying the think tanks involved in the constitutional conferences is even easier: five think tanks were selected by the federal government in 1991–92 to organize a series of conferences on constitutional reform. Although these case studies provide valuable insights into how think tanks in Canada and in the United States can contribute to policy development in different ways, an obvious disadvantage is the temptation to draw general conclusions about the effectiveness or ineffectiveness of think tanks from such limited studies. As a result, these cases are simply offered as probes or snapshots of how think tanks have become involved in policy-making at specific times. They are not intended to serve as the basis for making sweeping judgments about the behaviour of these or other institutes.

In addition to discussing the many challenges confronting think tanks in Canada and in the United States in the future, including funding and recruitment, the concluding chapter will examine how policy institutes have come to play an increasingly active role on the world stage. The ongoing efforts of the World Bank and other international agencies to support the creation of think tank networks in newly emerging democracies is but one example of how these organizations have become more active participants in regional and global politics. As will become apparent, the World Bank, like Robert Brookings and Andrew Carnegie, clearly believes in the power of ideas.

CHAPTER ONE

Surveying the Think Tank Landscape in the United States and Canada

In the early 1900s policymakers in the United States and Canada did not require a directory to keep track of think tanks conducting research and analysis on domestic and foreign policy. Until the outbreak of World War II, less than two dozen policy institutes existed in the United States, and in Canada only a handful had been established. However, by the mid- to late 1970s and early 1980s, the think tank community in both countries had grown considerably. In his study of 1991 on the rise of American think tanks, James Smith estimated that more than twelve hundred private and university-based think tanks had sprung up throughout the United States, most notably in and around Washington, DC.[1] By the end of the twentieth century, this number exceeded sixteen hundred.[2]

Although much of the literature on think tanks has focused almost exclusively on the largest and most visible of the institutes in the United States, a typical American think tank more closely resembles the Acadia Institute of Bar Harbor, Maine, which has a full-time staff of ten and a budget between $250,000 and $500,000, than the world-renowned Brookings Institution. Indeed, the majority of American think tanks have little in common with the Brookings Institution, the Hoover Institution, the Heritage Foundation, and a select group of other prominent institutes that have budgets in excess of $18 to $20 million.[3] Most think tanks in the United States have even less in common with RAND, which has approximately one thousand staff and a budget exceeding $100 million. Interestingly enough, in size and resources the majority of think tanks in the United States resemble those in Canada, where there has also been a discernible increase in the think tank population. Evert Lindquist has estimated that more than one hundred policy institutes have been established in Canada, the largest concentration being in Ottawa and Toronto.[4]

The purpose of this chapter is not to chronicle the origin of the several hundred think tanks created over the last several decades but to illustrate their evolution and diversity in Canada and the United States. This will be done by focusing on four distinct periods, or waves, of think tank development: 1900–46, 1947–70, 1971–89, and 1990–98. The chapter begins by setting out a typology, or classification, of think tanks that can be employed to describe the different types of policy institutes in the two countries. This will help to identify the major types of think tanks associated with the four time periods outlined above. And finally, to further highlight the significant diversity among think tanks, a brief profile of some of the most prominent institutes in both countries will be provided. For comparative purposes, one think tank from the United States and one from Canada established during each of the periods under consideration will be profiled.

CLASSIFYING THINK TANKS
IN THE UNITED STATES AND CANADA

Since there is no consensus about what constitutes a think tank, several scholars have constructed various typologies to account for the diversity of policy institutes that comprise the policy research community.[5] They have also attempted to identify the key motivations and institutional traits associated with each generation, or wave, of think tanks. For instance, in studying the evolution of American think tanks, Weaver identifies three types of think tanks that populate the policy-making community: universities without students, government contractors, and advocacy tanks. McGann, on the other hand, contends that at least seven types of think tanks are necessary to account for the entire spectrum in the United States: academic diversified, academic specialized, contract/consulting, advocacy, policy enterprise, literary agent/publishing house, and state-based.

These and other typologies were originally intended to help identify the different types of think tanks in the United States, but they can, with appropriate modifications, also provide a useful framework for comparing American and Canadian think tanks. Before chronicling the different kinds of policy institutes associated with the four major waves of think tank development, I will set out a classification that highlights some of the similarities and differences between the major types of think tanks in the two countries.

Universities without Students

Universities without students are composed of dozens of academics hired to write scholarly studies, not to assume teaching and administrative responsibilities. They function like universities in the sense that their principal mission is to promote a greater understanding of important social, economic, and political issues confronting society. Unlike universities, however, the seminars and workshops they offer and the studies they produce are generally intended for policymakers, not students. Supported in large part "by funding from the private sector (with varying mixtures of foundation, corporate and individual funding)," scholars working at these institutions regard book-length studies as their primary research product.[6] The Brookings Institution and the Hoover Institution, two of the largest private research institutions in the United States, are among the few think tanks that would fall into this category.[7]

The Brookings Institution, the Hoover Institution, and other research-driven institutes have long been permanent fixtures in the United States, but these types of think tanks are noticeably absent in Canada. Despite recommendations made to the federal government in the late 1960s to create an independent interdisciplinary think tank on the scale of the Brookings Institution, Canada has yet to become home to a university without students. There are several think tanks that regard academic or policy-relevant research as one of their principal functions but none that come close to resembling the largest and most distinguished research-oriented think tanks in the United States. In the Canadian context, then, it might be more appropriate to refer to these types of think tanks simply as policy research institutions than as "universities without students." Institutions in this category are staffed by economists, political scientists, and other trained academics who conduct research on a diverse range of policy issues. The majority of their resources are devoted to research, although book-length studies are not regarded as their primary outputs. The Ottawa-based Conference Board of Canada, well known for its expertise in providing economic forecasting to policymakers and business leaders, would warrant this classification.

Government Contractors

What distinguishes government contractors from the preceding category is not so much the type of research they conduct (although some of what government contractors do is confidential) but their principal client and primary source of funding. Think tanks like RAND and the Urban Institute, two of the leading government contractors in the United States, rely primarily on government departments and agencies to sustain their operations. Similarly, there are several examples of think tanks in Canada whose work is, or was, almost entirely funded by government sources. In fact, during the 1960s a handful of think

tanks or "government councils" were created by the federal government to provide advice in specific policy areas. Many of these institutes, including the Economic Council of Canada, and the Science
Council of Canada were disbanded in the early 1990s.

Advocacy Think Tanks

Since the early 1970s the most common type of think tank to emerge
in both Canada and the United States has been what Weaver refers to
as the advocacy think tank. Advocacy think tanks, as the name implies,
"combine a strong policy, partisan or ideological bent with aggressive
salesmanship [in] an effort to influence current policy debates."[8]
Known more for marketing and repackaging ideas than for generating
them, advocacy think tanks have played a critical role in transforming
the complexion of the policy research community, a subject that will
be explored in more detail in chapter 4. Advocacy think tanks tend to
place greater emphasis on producing brief reports for policymakers
than on producing book-length studies. Moreover, to influence public
opinion and public policy, these types of institutes also place a high
premium on gaining access to the media. Their staff frequently appear
on network newscasts and political talk shows to share their insights
on a wide range of topical policy issues.

It is useful for comparative purposes to add a fourth and possibly
a fifth category – vanity, or legacy-based, think tanks and policy clubs.
Legacy-based think tanks are created by aspiring office holders (or
their supporters) and by former leaders intent on advancing their
political and ideological beliefs well after leaving office. Although far
more numerous in the United States, there are a few examples in
Canada of think tanks in this category.

The final category – policy clubs – may, according to Lindquist, best
describe the majority of think tanks in Canada. In his assessment of
the impact of Canadian policy institutes, he suggests that it may be
more appropriate to portray several think tanks in Canada as policy
clubs (where academics, policy analysts, and, occasionally, policymakers meet to discuss public policy issues) than as policy research
institutions capable of providing long-term strategic analysis.[9] Since
they are unable to compete with the institutional resources available
in several bureaucratic departments and large trade associations,
Lindquist contends that the nostalgic vision of think tanks as creators
of new and innovative ideas simply does not conform to the experience
of Canadian policy institutes. Although he bases his observations on
the work of several policy institutes created in the early 1970s, his
insights about think tanks as policy clubs can also account for the

activities of a handful of relatively small policy shops created in the
first decades of the twentieth century.

PROCEEDING WITH CAUTION: THE LIMITS OF THINK TANK TYPOLOGIES

Classifying generations, or waves, of think tanks according to specific
institutional criteria may allow scholars to distinguish one type of think
tank from another, and typologies can be useful in comparing think
tanks in different countries. Nonetheless, problems can arise in making
such classifications. To begin with, since some organizations possess
characteristics common to more than one type of think tank, they
could conceivably fall into several categories. For instance, while few
observers are likely to encounter difficulty distinguishing between the
work of the Conference Board of Canada and the Fraser Institute or
between the Brookings Institution and the Heritage Foundation, these
institutions engage in similar activities: they all conduct research and,
to varying degrees, market their findings. The main difference is in the
emphasis they place on pure research and political advocacy. To argue,
then, that the Conference Board of Canada and the Brookings Institution are policy research institutions and that the Fraser Institute and
Heritage Foundation are advocacy think tanks, would, on the surface,
be misleading. Each could conceivably be classified as both policy
research institutions and advocacy think tanks.

This potential problem cannot be understated. How scholars and
journalists classify institutes can have a profound impact on the way
different think tanks are perceived in the media and by the public.
Referring to the Brookings Institution as a world-renowned policy
research institution provides the organization with instant credibility.
It creates the impression, rightly or wrongly, that it produces objective
and balanced research. Conversely, indicating that the Heritage Foundation and the Fraser Institute are well-known advocacy think tanks
may imply that they are more committed to advancing their ideological
agenda than to pursuing scholarly research. The implication is that the
views and recommendations of "research institutions" should be taken
more seriously than those of "advocacy think tanks."

The problem of classifying think tanks incorrectly may become more
pronounced as these organizations adopt similar strategies to convey
their ideas. Like chameleons constantly changing their complexion to
suit new environments, think tanks frequently alter their behaviour to
become more competitive in the marketplace of ideas. To enhance their
profile, some think tanks that were created in the early decades of the
twentieth century now rely on strategies employed by newer generations

of institutes. Moreover, some newly created institutes have looked to older generations of think tanks for ideas on how to manage their operations. In short, despite the diverse nature of think tanks, it is becoming increasingly difficult to isolate their unique institutional traits.

In distinguishing between different types of think tanks, scholars may describe some institutes incorrectly. Unfortunately, given the methodological problems often encountered in their classification, this problem might be unavoidable; nevertheless, typologies can still be useful in identifying the kinds of think tanks that emerged during particular periods. As the section below illustrates, think tanks associated with each of the four waves of think tank development possessed certain defining characteristics. It is these characteristics that allow the identification of a new generation of think tanks.

THE EVOLUTION OF THINK TANKS IN THE UNITED STATES AND CANADA

The First Wave, 1900–45

The first decades of the twentieth century were a formidable period for think tank development in the United States. Although several prominent universities existed at the time, including Harvard University, Johns Hopkins University, and the University of Chicago, a handful of philanthropists and policymakers believed that what were needed were institutions whose primary focus was not teaching but research and analysis. Guided by the belief that modern science could be used to solve social, economic, and political problems, a philosophy that was widely embraced during the Progressive era,[10] a small group of philanthropists set out to establish privately funded research institutes dedicated ostensibly to serving the public interest.[11] With generous funding from Robert Brookings, Andrew Carnegie, Herbert Hoover, John D. Rockefeller, Sr. and Margaret Olivia Sage, among others, several of America's most venerable institutions were created. These included the Russell Sage Foundation (1907), the Carnegie Endowment for International Peace (1910), the Conference Board (1916), the Institute for Government Research (1916; it merged with the Institute of Economics and the Robert Brookings Graduate School of Economics and Government to form the Brookings Institution in 1927), the Hoover Institution on War, Revolution and Peace (1919), the National Bureau of Economic Research (1920), and the Council on Foreign Relations (1921).[12] Founded under different and often unusual circumstances, these institutions shared a commitment to debating and investigating a wide range of domestic and foreign policy issues in the hope of improving governmental decision making (for selected profiles, see table 1.1). Composed of scholars recruited primarily from the social sciences, think tanks created during this era placed a premium on producing objective and neutral policy research. However, as previous studies have revealed, their goals were not always entirely altruistic, nor were those of their generous benefactors.[13]

While many of the studies produced by these institutes meet the highest scholarly standards, the institutes themselves can rarely be regarded as value-neutral research bodies. The Brookings Institution is a case in point. One of America's oldest and most revered think tanks, Brookings has cultivated a reputation as an independent institute that assigns the highest priority to providing objective research and analysis. Preventing its board of directors from interfering in the research agendas of its scholars is just one way the institute has attempted to maintain its intellectual independence. Nonetheless, being independent and producing objective research are two different things. Few scholars studying think tanks have questioned Brookings institutional independence, but on several occasions its researchers have made their policy preferences well known. As early as 1920, a handful of scholars at the Institute for Government Research, one of the institutes from which Brookings evolved, engaged in an aggressive lobbying campaign to convince the federal government to adopt a national budget system. The result was the passage of the Budget and Accounting Act of 1921.[14] Since then, Brookings has been at the forefront of many other major policy debates. What distinguishes Brookings and other early twentieth-century policy institutes from more contemporary think tanks is not their reluctance to become involved in the political arena but the emphasis they continue to place on engaging in medium- and long-term research. In short, unlike such think tanks as the Heritage Foundation, which concentrates on providing policymakers with what it would like them to know now, many first-generation think tanks focus on issues policymakers may want to consider in years to come.

Despite gaining national prominence in the United States, major research-oriented think tanks were noticeably absent in Canada during the early 1900s.[15] There were a handful of relatively small organizations concerned about Canadian foreign policy, including the Round Table Movement, the Canadian Association for International Conciliation, the Institute of Pacific Relations, which enjoyed strong Canadian representation, and the Canadian Institute of International Affairs (CIIA), established in 1928 as the first off-shoot of the British Institute of International Affairs (BIIA, later the Royal Institute of International Affairs (RIIA)). Yet even the CIIA was created more as a "club" of

Table 1.1
Selected Profiles of American Think Tanks, in Chronological Order

Institution	Location	Date Founded	Staff	Budget Category 1999–2000 ($ millions)
Russell Sage Foundation	New York, NY	1907	31 s	2–5
Carnegie Endowment for International Peace	Washington, DC	1910	39 FTR, 43 s	over 10
The Brookings Institution	Washington, DC	1916	79 FTR, 161 s	over 20
Hoover Institution on War, Revolution and Peace	Stanford, CA	1919	80 FTR, 20 PTR, 130 s	over 20
The Twentieth Century Fund	New York, NY	1919	33 FTR, 1 PTR, 2 s	2–5
National Bureau of Economic Research	Cambridge, MA	1920	500 PTR, 45 s	2–5
Council of Foreign Relations	New York, NY	1921	100 FTR and PTR, 100 s	over 20
American Enterprise Institute for Public Policy Research	Washington, DC	1943	100 FTR, 65 s	over 10
RAND	Santa Monica, CA	1946	543 FTR, 80 PTR, 453 s	over 100
Foreign Policy Research Institute	Philadelphia, PA	1955	7 FTR, 13 PTR, 5 s	1–2
Hudson Institute	Indianapolis, IN	1961	54 FTR, 10 PTR, 13 s	over 10
Centre for Strategic and International Studies	Washington, DC	1962	50 FTR, 10 PTR, 62 s	over 10
Institute for Policy Studies	Washington, DC	1963	16 FTR, 3 PTR, 4 s	1–2
Urban Institute	Washington, DC	1968	212 FTR, 33 PTR, 134 s	over 10
Center for Defense Information	Washington, DC	1972	15 FTR, 4 s	1–2
Institute for Contemporary Studies	San Francisco, CA	1972	8 FTR and s	under 1
Heritage Foundation	Washington, DC	1973	134 FTR, 46 s	over 30
Worldwatch Institute	Washington, DC	1974	14 FTR, 16 s	2–5
Ethics and Public Policy Center	Washington, DC	1976	5 FTR, 10 PTR, 5 s	1–2
Rockford Institute	Rockford, IL	1976	4 FTR, 3 s	1–2
Cato Institute	Washington, DC	1977	42 FTR and PTR, 20 s	10–20
Northeast-Midwest Institute	Washington, DC	1977	11 FTR, 2 PTR, 5 s	2–3
Manhattan Institute for Policy Research	New York, NY	1978	25 FTR, 15 s	over 5

Table 1.1 (continued)

Institution	Location	Date Founded	Staff	Budget Category 1999–2000 ($ millions)
The Carter Center	Atlanta, GA	1982	35 FTR, 150 S	over 10
Citizens for a Sound Economy Foundation	Washington, DC	1984	98 FTR, 2 PTR, 10 S	over 20
United States Institute of Peace	Washington, DC	1984	50 FTR, PTR, and S	over 10
Economic Policy Institute	Washington, DC	1986	18 FTR, 20 S	2–5
Progressive Policy Institute	Washington, DC	1989	17 FTR, 3 S	1–2
Empower America	Washington, DC	1993	10 FTR, 25 S	5–10
The Progress and Freedom Foundation	Washington, DC	1993	4 FTR, 5 PTR	2–5
Nixon Center for Peace and Freedom	Washington, DC	1994	7 FTR, 3 S	–

Source: Several sources were used to compile the data, including personal correspondence and institute web sites. Additional information was obtained from Hellebust, *Think Tank Directory.*

Note: FTR = full-time researchers; PTR = part-time researchers; S = support staff.

Table 1.2
Selected Profiles of Canadian Think Tanks, in Chronological Order

Institution	Location	Date Founded	Staff	Budget Category 1999–2000 ($ millions)
Canadian Council on Social Development	Ottawa, ON	1920	24 FT	1.5–3
Canadian Institute of International Affairs	Toronto, ON	1928	9 FT	.5–1.5
Canadian Tax Foundation	Toronto, ON	1945	20 FT, 9 PT	2–5
Atlantic Provinces Economic Council	Halifax, NS	1954	5 FT	under 1
Conference Board of Canada	Ottawa, ON	1954	200 FT	over 10
Science Council of Canada (defunct, figures for 1992)	Ottawa, ON	1963	29	2–5
Economic Council of Canada (defunct, figures for 1992)	Ottawa, ON	1963	118	over 10
Vanier Institute of the Family	Nepean, ON	1965	6 FT	under 1
National Council of Welfare	Ottawa, ON	1968	4 FT	under 1
Parliamentary Centre	Ottawa, ON	1968	15 FT, 2 PT	.5–1.5
Canada West Foundation	Calgary, AB	1971	8 FT	.5–1.5
Institute for Research on Public Policy	Montreal, PQ	1972	14 FT, 4 PT	2–3
C.D. Howe Institute	Toronto, ON	1973	13 FT	1.5–3
The Fraser Institute	Vancouver, BC	1974	35 FT, 13 PT	1.5–3
Canadian Institute of Strategic Studies	Toronto, ON	1976	2 FT, 1 PT	under 1
The North-South Institute	Ottawa, ON	1976	18	1.5–3
Canadian Centre for Policy Alternatives	Ottawa, ON	1980	7	.5–1.5
Canadian Centre for Philanthropy	Toronto, ON	1981	24 FT, 1 PT	2–3
Canadian Institute for International Peace and Security (defunct, figures for 1992)	Ottawa, ON	1984	9 FT, 3 PT	5–10
Mackenzie Institute	Toronto, ON	1987	3 FT	under 1
Public Policy Forum	Ottawa, ON	1987	15 FT	1–2
Institute on Governance	Ottawa, ON	1990	12 FT	1–2

Table 1.2 (continued)

Institution	Location	Date Founded	Staff	Budget Category 1999–2000 ($ millions)
Caledon Institute of Social Policy	Ottawa, ON	1992	3 FT, 1 PT	1–2
Pearson-Shoyama Institute	Ottawa, ON	1993	2	under 1
Canadian Policy Research Networks, Inc.	Ottawa, ON	1994	24 FT, 5 PT	2–3
Atlantic Institute for Market Studies	Halifax, NS	1994	5 FT	under 1
Canadian Council for International Peace and Security (defunct, figures for 1999)	Ottawa, ON	1995	2 FT, 1 PT	under 1
Canadian Centre for Foreign Policy Development	Ottawa, ON	1996	4 FT, 2 PT	2–5

Source: This data has been extracted from the following sources: *Associations Canada*; Campbell, "Wonks"; various institute websites; personal correspondence.
Note: FT = full-time staff; PT = part-time staff. Data on personnel did not differentiate between researchers and support staff. When no distinction is supplied, the staff was not specified in the available information.

influential Canadians interested in the study of international affairs and Canada's role in it,[16] than as a policy research institution composed of scholars preparing detailed analyses of world events.[17] There were some organizations committed to the study of domestic policy as well. The National Council on Child and Family Welfare, which eventually led to the creation of the Canadian Council on Social Development (CCSD), was formed in 1920.[18] These organizations, as associations of interested individuals and groups, may not have looked like "policy" think tanks when compared to those south of the border. Nevertheless, they undertook important networking functions, and they did commission some research outside the government. Still, with few exceptions the think tank landscape in Canada remained relatively barren until the early 1960s (for selected profiles see table 1.2).

The Second Wave, 1946–70

By the end of World War II, a new wave of think tanks was emerging in the United States, largely in response to growing international and domestic pressures confronting American policymakers. Acknowledging the invaluable contribution that defence scientists had made during the war, the Truman administration considered the enormous benefits that could be derived by continuing to fund private and university-based research and development centres. By tapping into the expertise of engineers, physicists, biologists, statisticians, and social scientists, policymakers hoped to meet the many new challenges they inherited as the United States assumed its role as a hegemonic power in the atomic age. It was in this environment that the idea for creating the most prominent government contractor, the RAND Corporation (RAND is an acronym for research and development) was born (1948).[19] In addition to making many important contributions to American defence policy, RAND was a prototype for other government contractors, including the Hudson Institute, founded by Herman Kahn, and the domestic-policy-oriented Urban Institute, whose creation was strongly endorsed by President Lyndon Johnson.[20]

In the post–World War II era, policymakers in Washington, like several philanthropists during the early part of the twentieth century, recognized the important role think tanks could play in several crucial policy areas. They also recognized the potential benefits of drawing on the expertise of independent research institutes that had the luxury of engaging in medium- and long-term strategic research, instead of relying on government officials who were often drowned in daily paper work. Particularly in the area of defence policy, it was crucial for the government to be able to rely on think tanks that had assembled some of the best defence scientists in the country and that, unlike policy-makers and bureaucrats in Washington, were unlikely to be influenced by partisan interests.

The United States had entered an era in which its defence and foreign policy would have a profound impact on shaping world affairs. What it required was sound, informative, policy advice, and for much of it, it turned to RAND and the Hudson Institute. But just as the federal government relied on these and other think tanks for advice on defence and security issues, President Johnson looked to the Urban Institute to suggest ways to alleviate the many economic, social, and political problems contributing to urban unrest throughout the turbulent decade of the 1960s. For Johnson the war waging inside the United States deserved as much, if not more, attention at times as conflicts taking place beyond America's borders. The onset of the Cold War and the war on poverty placed new demands on the United States government and provided new opportunities for think tanks to make their presence felt. Like the generation of think tanks before them, government contractors began to fill a void in the policy-research community.

The postwar period in the United States also witnessed the emergence of several other think tanks, including the Center for Strategic and International Studies (CSIS) and the Institute for Policy Studies (IPS), which were not established as government contractors but, nonetheless, quickly became immersed in Washington's policy-making community. Founded in 1962 and home to such luminaries as Zbigniew Brzezinski, national security adviser to President Carter, Admiral William Crowe, former chairman of the Joint Chiefs of Staff, and James Schlesinger, former secretary of defense, CSIS often works closely with incoming administrations to outline foreign and defence policy issues. In many respects CSIS functions both as a research institution and as an advocacy think tank.[21] It has established an impressive research program but has also undertaken considerable efforts to market its ideas. The Institute for Policy Studies (IPS), created in 1963 by Marcus Raskin and Richard Barnett, is another Washington-based think tank known for its interest in American foreign policy. However, unlike the more mainstream CSIS, the IPS has developed a reputation as Washington's think tank of the left for its Marxist/radical approach to U.S. foreign policy. Few would dispute its status as an ideologically driven advocacy think tank.[22]

Several think tanks also emerged in Canada in the postwar period. The Toronto-based Canadian Tax Foundation (CTF) was founded in 1946 by representatives of the national law and accounting societies to conduct and sponsor research on taxation. Eight years later, a branch office of the New York–based Conference Board was established in

Montreal to serve its Canadian members. The Conference Board of
Canada has since evolved into Canada's largest policy institute, with
close to two hundred staff and a budget exceeding $20 million.[23] In
1954 the Atlantic Provinces Economic Council (APEC) was formed to
promote economic development in the Atlantic region. And in 1958
the Private Planning Association of Canada (PPAC) was founded as a
counterpart to the National Planning Association (NPA) in the United
States. PPAC was created by "business and labour leaders to undertake
research and educational activities on economic policy issues."[24] It was
also intended to support the Canadian-American Committee and two
other committees of the NPA, in an effort to help foster dialogue among
business, labour, and government representatives.[25]

The growth of think tanks in postwar Canada did not end there.
The Vanier Institute of the Family was established in 1965 by Governor-
General Georges Vanier and Madame Pauline Vanier to study "the
demographic, economic, social and health influences on contemporary
family life."[26] In 1968 the Parliamentary Centre for Foreign Affairs
was created to provide research support to parliamentary committees
and government departments examining various foreign policy issues.

By the early 1960s the Canadian government had also begun to
demonstrate interest in creating research institutes. Although the federal government had traditionally relied either on bureaucratic departments or on royal commissions and task forces to advise it on key
policy matters, it began to consider other ways to enhance its policy
capacity.[27] But unlike the American government, which relied heavily
on several private think tanks for research and analysis, the Canadian
government decided to establish its own network of policy research
institutes. It created several government councils, including the Economic Council of Canada (1963),[28] the Science Council of Canada
(1966), the National Council of Welfare (1968), and the Law Reform
Commission of Canada (1970) to advise it on a host of policy issues.[29]
As Abelson and Lindquist point out,

These organizations received government funding in amounts that most nongovernmental think tanks could only dream about, but operated at an arm's
length relationship inside the government (full-time staff were public sector
employees). Research activities, including work undertaken on contract by
academics and other researchers outside government, were overseen by councils consisting of representatives from the private and nonprofit sectors
reflecting different constituencies and elements of society. The councils identified new research initiatives, oversaw a rolling portfolio of projects, and
produced consensus reports informed by commissioned research studies.
Although the councils were independent, members were appointed for fixed

terms by the Prime Minister and governments could request that new research initiatives be undertaken by the councils.[30]

Although they operated at arm's length from their employers, tensions between the councils and various governments eventually began to surface. The system of parliamentary and responsible government was simply not conducive to allowing organs of the state, no matter how independent, to express views on public policy that were at variance with government priorities and policies.[31] In its budget of February 1992 the government took drastic measures to sever its institutional ties with the various councils: in that year's budget, the Mulroney government disbanded close to two dozen policy institutes, including the Economic Council of Canada, the Science Council of Canada, the Law Reform Commission, and the Canadian Institute for International Peace and Security. The Chrétien government has taken steps to remedy some of the damage caused by the 1992 budget, including supporting the Privy Council Office's Policy Research Initiative (PRI).[32] The PRI is intended to rectify the diminished policy capacity of government by strengthening the ties between several federal departments and agencies and the external research community. As part of this initiative, a number of think tanks are being called upon to help the government think more strategically about the long-term impact of various economic and social policies, a subject that we will return to later.

The Third Wave, 1971–89

The second wave of think tank development – the emergence of government contractors and government councils – hit the United States and Canada at approximately the same time. However, by the time the third wave was making its presence felt in the United States, multiple waves were simultaneously hitting Canada. In the United States in the mid-1970s and 1980s, a new breed of policy institute – the so-called advocacy think tank, was beginning to attract considerable exposure. What distinguished advocacy think tanks from the earlier types of think tanks already established in the United States was not their desire to study public policy issues but their profound determination to market their ideas to various target audiences. Rather than reflecting on important policy issues from the comfort of their book-lined offices, founders of advocacy think tanks understood the importance of immersing themselves in the political arena. Ideas in hand, they began to think strategically about how to most effectively influence policymakers, the public, and the media. Borrowing from some of the strategies adopted by the American Enterprise Institute (1943), the Heritage Foundation, founded in 1973, was at the forefront of this new wave, elevating political advocacy to new heights.[33] Specializing in quick-response policy research, Heritage emphasized the need to provide members of Congress and the executive with hand-delivered one-to-two-page briefing notes on key domestic and foreign policy issues. It also stressed the importance of marketing its ideas to the media.[34] Encouraged by the critical role Heritage played during the Reagan transition of 1980,[35] dozens of think tanks combining elements of scholarship with aggressive marketing techniques began to take root throughout this period.[36] These included the Rockford Institute (1976), which has enjoyed close ties to Reform presidential candidate Pat Buchanan, the libertarian Cato Institute (1977), and the Economic Policy Institute (1986).

As this new wave of think tanks was hitting the United States, three distinct waves of think tank development were emerging in Canada. First, by the late 1960s the federal government came to realize the potential benefits of having a large independent research institute in Canada similar to ones created in the United States during the early 1900s. Particularly familiar with the work of the Brookings Institution and painfully aware of the absence of such an institution in the country, in 1968 Prime Minister Trudeau commissioned Ronald Ritchie to consider the feasibility of creating an independent interdisciplinary policy institute. The resulting report, submitted the following year, led to the creation of the nonprofit Institute for Research on Public Policy in 1972, with endowment funding from the federal government and plans to receive additional support from the private sector and provincial governments.[37]

Second, four established organizations underwent significant tranformations into modern think tanks during this period, and several new ones were created: the Canadian Welfare Council, established in 1920, was transformed into a social policy institute called the Canadian Council on Social Development (CCSD); the small Montreal office of the New York – based Conference Board relocated to Ottawa, which contributed to its growing expertise in developing economic forecasting models for both the public and private sectors; and the C.D. Howe Research Institute was formed in 1973 (following a merger of the Private Planning Association of Canada (PPAC) and the C.D. Howe Memorial Foundation) to become a centre for short-term economic policy analysis.[38] Finally, the profile of the Canadian Tax Foundation increased significantly during the early 1970s, due to a national debate stimulated by the Royal Commission on Taxation.

Several new think tanks in Canada were created as well. In the area of foreign policy, two new think tanks were established in 1976: the Ottawa-based North-South Institute, which currently receives the bulk of its funding from the Canadian International Development Agency (CIDA) to examine development issues, and the Canadian Institute of Strategic Studies in Toronto. Moreover, the Canadian Centre for Philanthropy was formed in 1981 to advance "the role and interests of the charitable sector for the benefit of Canadian communities."[39] And following Prime Minister Trudeau's North-South initiative, the federal government agreed to establish and fund the Canadian Institute for International Peace and Security (CIIPS) in 1984. (CIIPS was neither a government council, nor, as it discovered after being dismantled in 1992, was it as independent as the Institute for Research on Public Policy.) In addition, in 1986 the Mackenzie Institute opened its doors in Toronto. Notwithstanding its modest resources, the Mackenzie Institute has generated some exposure for its research interests in terrorism and radical ideologies. In 1987 the Public Policy Forum was established to improve public-policy making by providing a forum for representatives from the public, private, and non-profit sectors to consider a wide range of policy initiatives. And in 1990 the Institute on Governance was formed to promote effective governance. Among other things, it advises the Canadian government and governments of developing nations on how to better manage public services and train executives, and it often serves as a broker for Canadian agencies seeking to assist developing governments.

Third, several institutions devoted to the advocacy of particular points of view, reflecting the latest wave of U.S. think tank growth, were also created in this period. The Canada West Foundation, established in Calgary in 1971, was committed to injecting Western perspectives on national policy debates. The Fraser Institute was created in 1974 to promote the virtues of free-market economics. And finally, the Canadian Institute for Economic Policy was formed in 1979 by Walter Gordon, a former liberal finance minister, to sponsor a five-year research program working around the themes of economic nationalism. In 1980 the Canadian Centre for Policy Alternatives (CCPA) was established by supporters of social democratic principles to counter the influence of the Fraser Institute.[40] Not surprisingly, the CCPA has worked closely with the leadership of the New Democratic Party and several public advocacy coalitions, including the Council of Canadians, to convey its concerns on issues ranging from the North American Free Trade Agreement to the latest round of the World Trade Organization (WTO) negotiations. The trend toward more advocacy-driven think tanks also appealed to the Progressive Conservative party. Following their defeat in 1980, several party members supported the creation of a think tank on economic, social, and international issues, but the initiative foundered when the party chose a new leader.

The think tank population in the United States and Canada grew considerably during the 1970s and 1980s as both policymakers and policy entrepreneurs began not only to identify the need for independent policy advice but to discover how effective think tanks could be in influencing public opinion and public policy. The growth of conservative advocacy institutions, in particular, was largely driven by generous benefactors who believed that with sufficient funding think tanks could have a significant impact in shaping the political dialogue, a subject that will be explored further in chapter 3. Think tanks continued to spring up in both countries in the 1990s, although at a much slower pace than in the previous decades. While many recent think tanks share much in common with earlier generations of policy institutes, there are, as the final wave of think tank development reveals, some notable differences.

The Fourth Wave? 1990–98

Vanity or legacy-based, think tanks represent the latest type of think tank to emerge in the United States.[41] Although they may not constitute a new wave, they nonetheless represent a new and interesting development. While legacy-based think tanks such as the (Jimmy) Carter Center (1982) and the (Richard) Nixon Center for Peace and Freedom (1994) have developed a wide range of research programs to help advance the legacies of their founders, some vanity think tanks appear more concerned with engaging in political advocacy.[42] Vanity think tanks are particularly interested in generating, or at the very least repackaging, ideas that will help lend intellectual credibility to the political platforms of politicians, a function no longer performed adequately by mainstream political parties.[43]

Vanity think tanks are also established, some have claimed, to circumvent spending limits imposed on presidential candidates by federal campaign finance laws.[44] Examples of these types of think tanks include Senator Bob Dole's short-lived institute, Better America;[45] the Progress and Freedom Foundation (1993), an organization with close links to former Speaker of the House Newt Gingrich;[46] United We Stand, established by Ross Perot; and Empower America, founded in 1993 by an impressive band of neoconservatives, including Jeane Kirkpatrick, William Bennett, and former republican vice-presidential candidate Jack Kemp.

In theory, there are few barriers to creating legacy-based think tanks in Canada. However, with the possible exceptions of the C.D. Howe Institute, named after its founder, a former liberal cabinet minister, and the Pearson-Shoyama Institute (created in Ottawa in 1993 to examine issues related to citizenship and multiculturalism and named after former prime minister Lester Pearson and former federal deputy finance minister Thomas Shoyama), such institutes have not yet emerged in significant numbers. In an odd sort of way the closest examples of legacy think tanks were the Canadian Institute for Economic Policy, formed, as noted, by a former finance minister to further his ideas on economic nationalism, and the Canadian Institute for International Peace and Security, whose creation was, as mentioned, largely inspired by Prime Minister Trudeau's North-South initiative of 1984. Nevertheless, none of these think tanks can be construed as being committed to promoting the legacy of their namesakes.

A more significant trend in Canada at the end of the twentieth century was the privatization of existing government research. In 1992 the Caledon Institute of Social Policy was created in Ottawa, with support from the Maytree Foundation, to enable Ken Battle, a former executive director of the National Council of Welfare, to develop a research agenda without the constraints of serving a government council. In 1994, CPRN, Inc., was created by Judith Maxwell, former head of the Economic Council of Canada, to sponsor longer-term, interdisciplinary policy-research programs on social and economic policy issues and to lever research capabilities from across Canada. In addition to these think tanks, four other institutes were created: the Atlantic Institute for Market Studies (1994); the Canadian Council for International Peace and Security (1995), which evolved from the Canadian Centre for Arms Control and Disarmament and the Canadian Centre for Global Security; the Centre for the Study of Living Standards (1995); and the Canadian Centre for Foreign Policy Development (1996), currently housed in the Department of Foreign Affairs and International Trade (DFAIT).[47]

The emergence of some of the aforementioned think tanks was influenced by important and telling developments in public sector think tanks. As noted, the federal government, as part of the first wave of serious budget cutting in 1992, eliminated the Economic Council of Canada, the Science Council of Canada, the Law Reform Commission of Canada, and the Canadian Institute for International Peace and Security – only the tiny National Council of Welfare was left untouched. The creation of the Caledon Institute and the Canadian Policy Research Networks were direct reactions to these eliminations. The irony was that the government justified its decision not simply in terms of savings but also because of the great number of nonprofit think tanks that had emerged in Canada since the 1960s. Among other things, Prime Minister Mulroney and his colleagues argued that in the 1990s there was sufficient policy capacity located outside government to supplement the research needs of federal departments and agencies, a claim widely disputed in the media and in some academic circles.[48]

In reviewing these waves, or periods, of think tank growth, it is important to keep in mind that each new wave has not supplanted the institutions that preceded it but rather has added new patches to an already complex and colourful tapestry. Moreover, think tanks of the older types have continued to be created in recent years in both countries. For example, the Institute for International Economics, established in Washington, DC, in 1981, is just one of many think tanks conceived of as a "university without students," or an academic think tank similar to those of the first wave. At the same time, however, a more crowded marketplace of ideas has increased competition for funding and modified the practices of the older institutions, creating a greater awareness of the need to make findings accessible to and easily digested by policymakers.[49] In short, the institutes that comprise the think tank community in the United States and Canada may have been created at different times and with different goals in mind, but they recognize the importance of adopting the most effective strategies to convey their ideas.

To provide additional insights into how some of the more visible think tanks evolved in the United States and Canada and into what resources they have at their disposal to market their ideas, the following section will profile four prominent think tanks that were established in the United States and Canada during each of the four waves of development discussed above. The profiles are intended not to provide a detailed examination of the origins and activities of a select group of think tanks but simply to help further illustrate the considerable diversity of think tanks in the two countries. Among other things, these profiles will demonstrate that while think tanks may have much in common, each seeks to establish its own niche in the policymaking community, a subject that will be further explored in assessing the impact of think tanks.

A PROFILE OF SELECTED THINK TANKS IN THE UNITED STATES AND CANADA

The Brookings Institution

The Brookings Institution is one of the oldest and most prominent think tanks in the United States. Located on Washington's Massachusetts

Avenue, a popular location for several DC-based think tanks, the Brookings Institution was formed, as mentioned, when three separate institutions merged in 1927: the Institute for Government Research (1916), the Institute of Economics (1922), and the Robert Brookings Graduate School of Economics and Government (1924).[50] Recognizing the achievements of the founding institutes, while contemplating an even more significant role for his new institute, Robert Somers Brookings (1850–1932), a St Louis businessman, philanthropist, and social philosopher, was convinced that a nonpartisan interdisciplinary research institute could serve both the needs of policymakers and the greater public interest.[51] His determination to see the institute accomplish these goals was reflected in the organization's charter. It states that the Brookings Institution was established "to promote, carry on, conduct and foster scientific research, education, training and publication in the broad fields of economics, government administration and the political and social sciences generally, involving the study, determination, interpretation and publication of economic, political and social facts and principles relating to questions of local, national or international significance, to promote and carry out these objects, purposes and principles without regard to and independently of the special interests of any group in the body politic, either political, social, or economic."[52]

With approximately two hundred resident and visiting scholars and support staff and an annual budget exceeding $20 million, the Brookings Institution is one of the largest think tanks in the United States. The majority of its revenues come from philanthropic foundations, corporate and private donations, and its $200 million endowment. Only 4 percent of its revenues come from government sources.[53] Brookings, like most universities, maintains separate research departments: its three main departments, economic studies, foreign policy studies, and governmental studies, are headed by a director who is responsible both for overseeing the department's research activities and for generating sufficient funds to cover much of the department's direct costs.[54] In addition, Brookings maintains eight policy centers that focus on specific policy areas or themes. These include the Center for Urban and Metropolitan Policy, the Center for Northeast Asian Policy Studies and the Center on the U.S. and France, which is intended to bring French and American experts together to study relations between the two countries.[55]

Few think tanks in the United States have established a more impressive research record than Brookings. The institute publishes approximately two dozen books each year, a quarterly magazine entitled *The Brookings Review,* and several scholarly journals, including *The Brookings Papers on Economic Activity, The Brookings Papers on Education Policy,* and *The Brookings Wharton Papers on Financial*

Services. Acknowledging the importance of providing policymakers with concise reports and recommendations on key policy issues, Brookings also publishes a series of short papers entitled *Policy Briefs*, which covers a wide range of topical subjects. Brookings, like many advocacy-driven think tanks, does not rely solely on its research products to capture the attention of policymakers and the public. Its scholars also take advantage of various media outlets and opportunities to testify before congressional committees and subcommittees to convey their ideas on a wide range of issues. Its impressive roster of scholars, which includes or has included several former high-level policy advisors among its ranks, such as Alice Rivlin, former director of the White House Office of Management and Budget (1994–96), Charles Schultze, former chair of the President's Council of Economic Advisors (1977–80), and Brookings president Michael Armacost, who served in the U.S. Department of State (1984–89), also helps to enhance Brookings reputation as a prestigious policy research institution.

RAND

Unlike the Brookings Institution, RAND does not owe its existence to a philanthropist who believed in the power of ideas but to a small group of engineers and military leaders who understood how the development of intercontinental missiles could both threaten and enhance America's national security. In late 1945, General H.H. Arnold, commanding general of the Army Air Forces (the Department of the Air Force was established in September 1947), acting on the initiative of two engineers from the Douglas Aircraft Company, Arthur Raymond and Frank Collbohm, proposed a $10 million contract with Douglas to fund Project Rand, "for the study of v-1 and v-2 rocket techniques and other intercontinental air techniques of the future."[56] However, despite the government's initial enthusiasm for the project, relations between the air force and Douglas soured over the next two years. Concerned that Douglas was more preoccupied with making profits than advancing U.S. security interests, the air force removed Project Rand from the aircraft company and proposed that an independent, nonprofit organization be created to undertake the initiative.[57]

With an initial capital investment of $1 million and close to $5 million in remaining funds from Project Rand, the Rand Corporation was chartered in May 1948, "To further and promote scientific, educational, and charitable purposes, all for the public welfare and security of the U.S. of America."[58] Under the leadership of Collbohm, who left Douglas to become Rand's first president, a talented group of scientists, including

Bernard Brodie and Herman Kahn, gathered at the Santa Monica think tank to consider how to protect and promote U.S. security interests during the nuclear age. Using systems analysis, game theory, and various simulation exercises, RAND scientists devoted themselves in the immediate postwar years to serving the needs of the air force.[59]

RAND continues to receive the bulk of its $113.5 million budget from the U.S. Air Force, the U.S. Army, and the Office of the Secretary of Defense, but its research interests are not confined to defense and national security issues.[60] As members of the largest think tank in the United States, RAND's six hundred researchers and four hundred staff carry out research in a dozen major areas, including health care, civil and criminal justice, science and technology, and environment and infrastructure. The majority of RAND's staff work at its Santa Monica headquarters or its office in Washington, DC. Others are based at RAND's Council for Aid to Education in New York City, RAND Europe in the Netherlands, or at one of its smaller sites.

In addition to overseeing an extensive research program that has resulted in the publication of hundreds of books, policy briefs, reports, and academic journals, RAND established its own graduate school in 1970 to help train future policy analysts. The RAND Graduate School stresses the importance of educating students to examine complex policy issues from a multidisciplinary perspective.

The Heritage Foundation

Just as RAND served as a prototype for other government contractors, the Heritage Foundation has become the type of policy institute other advocacy-oriented think tanks have sought to emulate. Heritage was established in 1973 by two congressional aides, Paul Weyrich and Edwin Feulner, with $250,000 in seed money from Colorado brewer Joseph Coors. The idea of creating a think tank that could provide policymakers with timely and policy-relevant information came to Weyrich and Feulner when the two sat down for lunch one day in the Senate Office building. As Feulner recalls,

Weyrich and I were having lunch together and he showed me a study that had the pros and cons on the SST (Supersonic Transport). It was a good analysis, but it arrived on his desk the day after the vote took place. We both kicked that around and said, "Wouldn't it be great if there were an institution that delivered the kind of timely, usable policy analysis so that those of us working on the Hill could really make use of it?" I immediately called up the President of the organization to praise him for this thorough piece of research and asked why we did not receive it until after the debate and the vote. His answer: they did not want to influence the vote. That was when the idea for the Heritage Foundation was born.[61]

Operating from a small office space over a grocery store in one of the less desirable neighbourhoods of Washington, DC, Heritage rocketed from relative obscurity in the early 1970s to become America's most visible think tank during the Reagan years.[62] Now located in an impressive office building only blocks from the Capitol Building, Heritage's profile in Washington's policy-making circles has continued to rise. "Committed to rolling back the liberal welfare state and building an America where freedom, opportunity, prosperity, and civil society flourish," Heritage's main goal is to persuade policymakers, the public, and the media to embrace "the principles of free enterprise, limited government, individual freedom, traditional American values, and a strong national defense."[63]

Like most advocacy-oriented think tanks, Heritage does not try to conceal its mission. As Heritage president Edwin Feulner readily admits, "Our role is trying to influence the Washington public policy community ... most specifically the Hill, secondly the executive branch, thirdly the national news media."[64] Although Heritage publishes several books each year, its main focus is not on long-term studies but on what Feulner refers to as quick-response policy research. Aware that policymakers rarely have the time or inclination to sift through a several-hundred-page report, Heritage has built its research program around providing members of Congress and the executive with concise and timely reports on important domestic and foreign policy issues. At Heritage, marketing ideas is considered as important as, if not more important than, generating them. According to Heritage's executive vice president, Phillip Truluck "We certainly spend as much money on marketing our ideas as we do on research. We keep these two functions in balance because we believe that the process doesn't end when a paper is published ... Our aim is to change public policy – not merely to comment on it – so we have to give marketing a key role in our total mission. We cannot just put out a study and hope that it gets in the right people's hands."[65]

Heritage's formula for balancing policy research with political advocacy has clearly paid off. Its budget has more than doubled in the past ten years, rising from $17.9 million in 1989 to $43.8 million in 1998. Heritage has been particularly successful in marketing its message to large numbers of conservative supporters throughout the United States. Close to two-thirds of its income is generated by more than 240,000 individuals who make annual contributions to the organization.[66] Heritage has also received several generous donations from philanthropists and foundations who look to the organization to promote their conservative beliefs. Its largest contributor has been Pittsburgh billionaire Richard Mellon Scaife, who has donated over $20 million to the organization since its inception. In 1976, three years after Heritage opened its doors, Scaife donated $420,000, or 42 percent of the organization's income. Comparing the generosity of Joseph Coors to Scaife, officials at Heritage have said jokingly, "Coors gives six-packs; Scaife gives cases."[67]

With close to three-dozen visiting and resident research fellows and over 130 staff who conduct research in both domestic and foreign policy, Heritage maintains a visible presence inside the Beltway. Often contacted by journalists to comment on policy issues confronting Congress, Heritage scholars rarely pass up an opportunity to convey their views. But as chapter 4 will examine in more detail, relying on the media is just one strategy Heritage and other think tanks employ to influence public opinion and public policy.

Empower America

Empower America, like the Heritage Foundation, enjoys considerable support among conservatives in the United States. The organization was founded in 1993 by four leading conservatives: William J. Bennett, secretary of education and chairman of the National Endowment for the Humanities under President Reagan and director of the Office of National Drug Control under President Bush; Jeane Kirkpatrick, former U.S. representative to the United Nations; Jack Kemp, secretary of housing and urban development under President Bush and Republican vice-presidential nominee in 1996; and Vin Weber, member of the U.S. House of Representatives (R-MN, 1980–92). Empower America's purpose is to "encourage public policy solutions that maximize free markets and individual responsibility."[68] Its current president is Josette Shiner, former managing editor of the *Washington Times*. Approximately ten full-time and twenty-five part-time staff are employed at the institute.

Unlike dozens of think tanks that simply comment on public policy, Empower America sees itself as a "delivery system" that helps to enact free-market and entrepreneurial principles into law. According to its mission statement, "[We] bridge the gap between the array of think tanks that produce white papers on the public policy debate and the actual enactment of policy."[69] Empower America relies on various strategies to influence how policies are employed, ranging from discussing its ideas with journalists and political leaders to sponsoring consensus-building forums. It also stresses the importance of working with grassroots movements to help promote its concerns.

To date, the organization, which draws on an annual budget of $5 to $10 million generated from individual and corporate donations and grants from philanthropic foundations, has focused on five main policy areas: internet and technology policy, education reform, tax reform, social security reform, and national security. The results of its research are highlighted in three types of publications: *Reality Check, Issue Briefings*, and various *Special Reports*. In addition to distributing these publications, staff from Empower America frequently testify before congressional committees and appear as policy experts on several network newscasts and current affairs programs.

A VIEW FROM CANADA

The Canadian Institute of International Affairs (CIIA)

The Canadian Institute of International Affairs is one of the oldest policy institutes in Canada. Established in 1928 to encourage Canadians to think more critically about international affairs, the institute's origins have been traced to the Royal Institute of International Affairs (RIIA), whose creation was inspired by the Paris Peace Conference of 1919, and to the founding of the Institute of Pacific Relations in Honolulu in 1925. The experience of a handful of Canadians with both organizations convinced them that an institute was required in Canada that would encourage informed discussion and debate on international affairs and Canada's role in the era after World War I.[70]

On 30 June 1928 representatives from the CIIA's five branches (in Montreal, Ottawa, Toronto, Winnipeg, and Vancouver) met in Ottawa to formally draft the organization's constitution. In attendance were several influential Canadians, including Sir Robert Borden, Canada's eighth prime minister (1911–20). As Canada's chief delegate to the Paris Peace Conference and the country's representative at the meetings of the Imperial War Cabinet and the Imperial War Conference in 1817 and 1918, Borden was a logical choice to become the CIIA's first president. Several prominent media figures were also in attendance, including Frederick N. Southam, head of six Canadian newspapers, and John W. Dafoe, editor of the *Winnipeg Free Press*. Dafoe would later serve as vice-president and president of the institute. At the meeting the founding members of the CIIA agreed to two fundamental by-laws: first, that while the purpose of the CIIA was "to promote a broader and deeper understanding of international affairs ... by providing interested Canadians with a nonpartisan, nation-wide forum for informed discussion, debate, and analysis," the institute should not offer any opinion on the conduct of public policy, a principle that it continues to adhere to; second, that membership in the institute should be confined to British subjects, a restriction no longer imposed.[71]

In 1928, 144 members belonged to the CIIA's five branches. Seventy years later, the CIIA had grown to 18 branches with a membership of 1,500. With less than a dozen staff, the CIIA operates on a budget of $1 to $2 million. Barbara McDougall, who held several senior federal cabinet positions, including secretary of state for external affairs, became the CIIA's president and CEO in February 1999. Although the CIIA is Canada's most recognized international affairs institute, it functions in Evert Lindquist's words more as a policy club than as a policy research institution.[72] The institute publishes a quarterly refereed journal, *International Journal*, and an essay series entitled *Behind the Headlines*, and it has recently launched a series of monographs on timely Canadian defence and security-related issues. But unlike several U.S. think tanks specializing in foreign and defence policy, the CIIA has produced little academic research. The institute is perhaps best known for its annual foreign policy conference, which brings together academics, policymakers, and representatives from various nongovernmental organizations and the business community to address current policy issues. From its headquarters at York University's Glendon College, the CIIA maintains the John Holmes Library, an extensive collection on international affairs, and helps to coordinate the work of its individual branches.[73] However, the CIIA is not a research institution in the tradition of the Brookings Institution or other U.S. think tanks created during the Progressive Era. It regards itself as an institution that helps to facilitate discussion, not as an organization that relies on academic research to influence public opinion and public policy.

The Conference Board of Canada

In many respects the Conference Board of Canada is unique among Canadian think tanks. With a staff of over two hundred and an annual budget in excess of $20 million, it is by far the largest research institution in the country. But despite its visible presence in Canada, the Conference Board originated in the United States. In 1916 the Conference Board was established in New York to "facilitate a cross-fertilization of facts and ideas in industry as a way of identifying and solving its problems and enhancing the public's understanding of these problems."[74] Like many other think tanks created during the Progressive Era, the founder of the Conference Board insisted that the organization engage in "unbiased fact finding" and "refrain from all political activity."[75]

During the decades following its founding, the Conference Board established itself as a highly credible and competent research organization that proved capable of addressing the needs of both American and Canadian companies. Indeed, as Lindquist points out, "With 40 large Canadian companies alone participating in the u.s.-based organization, the creation of a Canadian office seemed a natural step."[76] In 1954 the Conference Board opened a small office in Montreal to respond to an expanding number of Canadian companies, Canadian-based u.s. subsidiaries, and u.s. companies interested in obtaining more information about Canada.[77]

The Conference Board of Canada has created a well-defined niche in the policy-making community. Unlike many smaller think tanks that attempt to influence public debates through their various publications and exchanges with policymakers and journalists, the Conference Board specializes in providing knowledge in key areas to its members in the public and private sectors. In exchange for a membership fee the Conference Board "[helps its] members anticipate and respond to the increasingly changing global economy ... through the exchange of knowledge about organizational strategies and practices, emerging economic and social trends and key public policy issues."[78] Its primary goal is to help its members become better prepared to adapt to changes in the marketplace.

As well as providing members with access to its publications and conferences, the Conference Board undertakes contract research. Known for its expertise in economic forecasting and analysis, the board also specializes in several other areas, including corporate social responsibility, human resource management, public sector management and information, and innovation and technology.[79]

Given its size and the breadth of its research expertise, it is not surprising that the Conference Board attracts more media attention than any other policy institute in Canada, a finding that will be explored further in chapter 5. Its commitment to producing independent and unbiased research may also help explain why it has developed a reputation as one of the most credible institutes in Canada.

The Fraser Institute

Well before Prime Minister Trudeau announced in his Christmas message in 1974 that "the marketplace was not a reliable economic institution and would increasingly have to be replaced by government action in order to sustain the economic well-being of Canadians," the seeds for creating the Vancouver-based Fraser Institute had already been planted.[80] Increasingly concerned by the federal government's Keynesian economic policies and the election of the first NDP government in British Columbia in 1972, T. Patrick Boyle, a senior industrial executive and then vice-president of planning at MacMillan Bloedel, began considering how best to inform Canadians about the crucial role that markets play in economic development. After meetings with several business leaders and economists, including Csaba Hajdu and Michael Walker, Boyle "conceived the establishment of an economic and social research institution which he felt had to be unlike any other in existence in Canada."[81]

In early 1974 Boyle enlisted the support of the Honourable J.V. Clyne to raise seed money for the institute and managed to generate $75,000. Boyle also began working closely with Walker, Hajdu, and several other individuals, including John Raybould and Sally Pipes, to draft the institute's mission statement and operating plan. On 21 October 1974 the charter of the Fraser Institute, "so named for the mighty Fraser River, thereby giving this new institute a geographical, rather than ideological reference point," was granted by the Canadian government.[82]

The Fraser Institute experienced little difficulty locating its geographical or its ideological reference point during its first year, but like most think tanks in Canada and the United States it became preoccupied with staying afloat. With meagre resources during its first year of operation, fundraising became the greatest challenge confronting the newly created organization. Sir Antony Fisher, Fraser's acting director and founder of several other policy institutes, including the Institute of Economic Affairs in London, coordinated Fraser's fundraising efforts in 1975. A year later Fisher left the staff of the Fraser Institute, and Sally Pipes, who had worked in the British Columbia government's statistical agency and for the Council of Forest Industries in the province, assumed fundraising and membership responsibilities. Michael Walker, who before joining Fraser had worked in the Department of Finance and at the Bank of Canada, became the Institute's research and editorial director.[83]

The Fraser Institute's operating revenue and media profile steadily increased in the last quarter of the twentieth century. With a full-time staff of thirty-five and a budget exceeding $3 million, Fraser has become one of Canada's most talked about and written about think tanks.[84] Particularly conscious of how much media attention Fraser generates, Michael Walker and his staff often equate media visibility with policy influence.[85] Not surprisingly, as one of Canada's most visible think tanks, Fraser also claims to be among the country's most influential policy institutes. The Fraser Institute is also interested in other organizations and in issues that attract media coverage; its National Media Archive maintains the only live data base of current and historic news and public affairs programming on CTV and the CBC.

Fraser also oversees an active research program that has resulted in the publication of a monthly opinion journal, *The Fraser Forum*, and dozens of books, conference reports, and bulletins. Because it also recognizes the importance of encouraging and training future generations of conservative thinkers, the institute sponsors a university student internship program and an annual student essay competition.

The Fraser Institute, like the Heritage Foundation, has cultivated a reputation, and deservedly so, as a conservative advocacy-oriented think tank that places considerable emphasis on shaping public opinion and public policy. Indeed, its obvious bias toward relying on market solutions to economic problems has often made it an easy target for critics. Still, it is important to keep in mind that think tanks from the entire political spectrum engage in some form of political advocacy. As the final think tank profile illustrates, even more liberal think tanks with far more modest resources than the Fraser Institute recognize the importance of conveying their ideas to policymakers and the public.

The Caledon Institute of Social Policy

It is difficult to discuss the Ottawa-based Caledon Institute without immediately invoking the name of its director Ken Battle. In fact, few other think tank directors in Canada, perhaps with the exception of Michael Walker, have become so closely identified with a policy institute. Battle's reputation as one of the country's most astute thinkers on social policy is well known in Ottawa's key policy-making circles. Often invited to advise senior policymakers on a range of social and tax policies, including old age security and child welfare benefits, Battle served as director of the National Council of Welfare, a citizen's advisory body to the minister of national health and welfare, before founding Caledon in 1992.

After spending close to fifteen years at the National Council of Welfare, Battle became increasingly sensitive to how critical a publicly funded policy institute could be of government policies. As one of the Mulroney government's most vociferous critics, Battle was convinced that both his position and the future of the National Council of Welfare could be in jeopardy as long as he remained in charge. "At the time, I began looking around for other positions," Battle stated. "I thought for a while that I would try to become director of the

Canadian Council on Social Development [ccsd], but then something else came up."[86]

What came up was a meeting with Toronto businessman and philanthropist Alan Broadbent, who wanted to fund a public policy organization that would have an impact. Although Battle initially approached Broadbent for funds to help rebuild the ccsd, Broadbent was more interested in creating a new organization that would study social and welfare policies than in revitalizing an existing institution: "Alan is one of those capitalists with a social conscience who clearly wanted to fund an organization that would make a difference ... When he made me an offer to head up a new institute, I accepted."[87]

Following a handful of meetings with Broadbent, Battle developed the Caledon Institute's mission statement, which reads: "The Caledon Institute of Social Policy is a leading private, non profit social policy think tank that conducts social policy research and analysis. As an independent and critical voice that does not depend on government funding, Caledon seeks to inform and influence public and expert opinion and to foster public discussion on poverty and social policy. Caledon develops and promotes concrete, practicable proposals for the reform of social programs at all levels of government and of social benefits provided by employers and the voluntary sector."[88]

With roughly $300,000 from Broadbent's Maytree Foundation, Caledon opened its doors in February 1992. It currently receives about $700,000 from the foundation and an additional $300,000 to $400,000 in project-specific funding. From its inception, Caledon has purposely maintained a lean operation; its board of directors, which meets once a year, barely satisfies the minimum legal requirement of three people. In addition to Battle, the board consists of Broadbent, a lawyer, and a financial analyst. "The advantage of having a lean operation is that we can change direction fast if we have to," Battle notes. "This allows us to move ahead of the government and influence substantive policies and the political agenda."[89] Caledon maintains a tiny research staff. Assisting Battle are Sherri Torjman, vice-president of Caledon, who has written extensively on several issues including social spending, health care, and fiscal arrangements, and senior scholar Michael Mendelson, a former deputy secretary of the cabinet in Ontario, who has several publications on social and fiscal policy to his credit.

With a small research staff, Caledon has managed to establish an impressive publication program. Its commentaries on various social policy issues, "Caledon's most useful product," according to Battle, are widely circulated to policymakers, social advocacy organizations, and the media. Caledon's media profile is modest compared to several other think tanks such as the Fraser Institute and the C.D. Howe Institute, but, as chapter 5 will demonstrate, its contribution to policy formulation is well recognized by directors of party research offices and senior policymakers.[90]

This chapter has explored in some detail, the evolution and growing diversity of the think tank community in Canada and the United States. In the process, it has helped confirm why it is so difficult to define what a think tank is. The think tank landscape does not consist of organizations with similar profiles. Rather, it resembles an ever-expanding patchwork that consists of institutes of all shapes and sizes. Although think tanks are far more numerous in the United States than in Canada, it is clear that the same types of policy institutes have taken root in both countries.

CHAPTER TWO

Thinking about Think Tanks: A Conceptual Framework

As think tanks have come to occupy a more visible presence in both advanced and developing countries, scholars have employed various theoretical approaches to explain their role and significance in the policy-making community. In this chapter we explore what these approaches are and what steps can be taken to provide more informed insights about their impact in shaping public policy. As we will discover, it is important to move beyond the existing literature in the field to develop a more useful conceptual framework to evaluate their involvement in policy-making.

Scholars who study think tanks tend to do so from three different perspectives. First, a number of political scientists regard think tanks as elite organizations that rely on their expertise and close ties to policymakers to advance the political agendas of their corporate and philanthropic sponsors. Second, other scholars regard think tanks not as elite organizations but rather as one of many groups in an increasingly crowded marketplace of ideas that seek to influence public attitudes and policy decisions. And finally there is a handful of scholars who focus less on the elite or pluralist nature of think tanks and the policy environment they inhabit and more on the institutional structure and orientation of the organizations themselves. It is to these particular approaches that we now turn.

THINK TANKS AS POLICY ELITES

For several scholars, including Joseph Peschek, Thomas Dye, William Domhoff, and John Saloma, to name a few, think tanks not only regularly interact with policy elites; they help comprise part of the nation's power structure.[1] Particularly in the United States, where think

tanks frequently serve as talent pools for incoming presidential administrations to draw on and where high-level policymakers often take up
residence after leaving office, think tanks are portrayed as elite organizations well positioned to influence public policy. The multimillion
dollar budgets enjoyed by a handful of American think tanks and the
many prominent and distinguished business leaders and former policymakers who serve on their boards of directors also help to reinforce
the image of think tanks as policy elites. At the very least, the close
ties that exist between affluent corporate and philanthropic donors and
several think tanks suggest that think tanks often serve as instruments
of the ruling elite. In exchange for large donations, think tanks are
willing, according to some proponents of elite theory, to use their
policy expertise and connections with key policymakers to advance the
political agendas of their generous benefactors.[2]

The Brookings Institution, the Council on Foreign Relations, the
Hoover Institution, and RAND, among others, may indeed warrant the
label "elite." After all, they represent but a handful of think tanks in
the United States that possess both the financial resources and the staff
to secure close and lasting ties to policymakers throughout government. However, as noted in the previous chapter, these types of institutions are not representative of the think tank community in the
United States. The vast majority of think tanks in the United States,
like their Canadian counterparts, have modest institutional resources.

By closely examining the interaction between the largest think tanks
in the United States and key officials in government, scholars may be
justified in concluding, as some have, that think tanks play a critical
role in shaping both the policy-making environment and important
policy decisions. Unfortunately, since very few institutes resemble
Brookings or RAND, we must question the utility of employing an
approach that assumes that think tanks, by their very nature and purpose, are well positioned and equipped to promote the interests of the
ruling elite. We must also question whether think tanks, as nonprofit
organizations engaged in policy analysis, should be treated as elites.

While elite theorists portray the political system as being dominated
by a select group of individuals and organizations committed to
advancing common political, economic, and social interests, it would
be naive to assume that all think tanks have the desire or the resources
to help advance an elite agenda, however that may be defined. Think
tanks are in the business of shaping public opinion and public policy,
but as noted, they have very different ideas of how various domestic
and foreign policies should be formulated and implemented. Several
think tanks, for instance, may embrace the views of some elites that
free market solutions to economic problems should be pursued. The

C.D. Howe Institute, the Fraser Institute, the Heritage Foundation, and the American Enterprise Institute, among others, would certainly favour such an approach. But there are many other think tanks, including the left – leaning, Washington-based Institute for Policy Studies and the Ottawa-based Caledon Institute that have profoundly different views of how governments should resolve economic and social problems. Should these think tanks, which often oppose the interests of the ruling elite, be considered part of the elite?

Despite some limitations that will be explored in more detail below, adopting an elite approach to the study of think tanks has some advantages. As Domhoff and others have discovered, examining the close and interlocking ties between members of think tanks and leaders in business and government can provide interesting and useful insights into why some policy institutes may enjoy far more visibility and notoriety than others.[3] Moreover, by keeping track of who sits on the boards of directors of think tanks, we may be able to explain why some institutes generate more funding than their competitors. Nonetheless, it is important to keep in mind that while members of think tanks frequently interact with high-level business leaders and policy-makers, their ties to key figures do not necessarily allow them to exercise policy influence. Such ties may facilitate access to important officials in the executive, Congress, and the bureaucracy, but their ability to influence public policy depends on a wide range of factors.

It is tempting for scholars to treat think tanks as policy elites, because it enables them to make sweeping assertions about who controls public policy. The story line of most scholars employing this approach proceeds as follows. Large corporations and philanthropic foundations looking to influence public attitudes and public policy turn to like-minded think tanks that are capable of producing timely and policy-relevant research. Think tanks, which find themselves in an increasingly competitive marketplace of ideas, are more than willing to sacrifice their independence and credibility if they can secure access to sizeable funds. And in order to preserve large budgets, think tanks employ a wide range of strategies to influence public policy in a manner consistent not only with their own goals but with those of their generous donors.

As appealing as this approach might be, it is also problematic for several reasons. Although it allows scholars to identify the close ties between those who fund think tanks and the individuals who operate them, it tells us little about the ability or inability of think tanks to exercise influence at different stages of the policy cycle. It tells us even less about how to assess or evaluate the impact of think tanks in policy-making. In short, an elite approach assumes that with the right connections think tanks can and will be able to influence public policy. Unfortunately, it offers little insight into how this will be achieved.

THE PLURALIST TRADITION:
ONE VOICE AMONG MANY

Members of think tanks may occasionally travel in elite policy circles, but according to some political scientists, including David Newsom, they represent but one of many types of organizations that populate the policy-making community.[4] According to this perspective, which is deeply rooted in the American pluralist tradition, think tanks, like interest groups, trade unions, environmental organizations, and a host of other nongovernmental organizations, compete among themselves for the attention of policymakers.[5] Since the government is perceived simply as a moderator or referee overseeing the competition between these groups, pluralists devote little attention to assessing government priorities. They view public policy not as a reflection of a specific government mandate but rather as an outcome of group competition.

Studying think tanks within a pluralist framework has its advantages. For one thing, it compels scholars to acknowledge that despite the perception that think tanks have assumed increased importance in the policy-making community, they remain one of many organizations competing for power and influence. This approach also serves as a reminder that think tanks, like interest groups and other nongovernmental organizations, rely on similar strategies to shape public policy, a subject that will be explored further in chapter 4. The pluralist approach, however, has serious weaknesses. To begin with, although pluralists assume that public policy is an outcome of group competition, they provide little insight into why some organizations may be better positioned to influence policy decisions than others. Is it simply a matter of which groups have the most members, largest budgets, and staff and resources that determines who does and does not have influence? Or do other factors, such as the amount of money groups donate to political campaigns, offer better insight into which organizations are destined to succeed in the political arena?

The major deficiency of the pluralist approach is not that it assumes that all groups can influence public policy. Rather, it is that it cannot adequately explain why some do. Moreover, by treating think tanks as simply one of many voices in the policy-making community, pluralists overlook why policy institutes are often better positioned to shape government priorities than interest groups and other nongovernmental organizations. Think tanks may indeed be part of the chorus, but they possess unique attributes that allow them to stand out. Indeed, by acknowledging the differences between think tanks and other types of NGOs, pluralists might be more reluctant to suggest that all groups compete in the same political arena. Think tanks, by virtue of their expertise and close ties to policymakers, may compete among themselves for prestige and status, but they do not necessarily compete with the hundreds of other participants in the policy-making community. In fact, in some policy areas think tanks may face little competition at all.

Pluralists must also acknowledge that policymakers often have a vested interest in influencing the outcome of group competition. Rather than behaving as referees, they can and do select organizations that may help to advance their own agendas. That is why, as I will examine in chapters 6 and 7, presidential candidates often turn to a select group of think tanks for advice during their campaigns and why the federal government engaged the services of a handful of think tanks in 1992 to keep the constitutional negotiations afloat. Morever, as will be discussed, members of congress and members of parliament also play an important role in determining which organizations contribute to public policy at critical stages of the policymaking process. Among other things, they decide who will testify before congressional and parliamentary committees.

Recognizing the limitations of both approaches, some scholars have elected to study think tanks from a different perspective. Focusing more on think tanks as a diverse set of organizations that possess different institutional structures and priorities than as a members of the policy elite or the broader policy-making community, this approach appears more promising. As we will discover below, a better understanding of how think tanks function in the policy-making community can allow scholars to make more informed insights about their role and impact.

THINK TANKS: AN INSTITUTIONAL APPROACH

Three distinct institutional approaches to the study of think tanks have surfaced in the literature in recent years. The first approach, or stream, which represents the vast majority of the literature on think tanks, focuses either on the history of specific think tanks or on the evolution and changing role of think tanks in particular countries. Several scholars have written institutional histories of the Brookings Institution, the Council on Foreign Relations, the Heritage Foundation, and RAND, among others.[6] A number of studies have also detailed the rise of think tanks in the United States, Canada, and other advanced and developing countries.[7] The obvious advantage of providing detailed histories of think tanks is that one can acquire a wealth of information on the nature and mandate of organizations, the research projects they have conducted over time, and the various institutional changes they have undergone.[8] The main disadvantage, however, is that many of these studies are simply histories and offer little concrete data to support or deny claims that particular think tanks have played a major role in shaping specific public policies.

The second and more systematic institutional approach has concentrated on the involvement of think tanks in what students of public policy commonly refer to as epistemic or policy communities.[9] These communities consist of individuals and organizations that, by virtue of their policy expertise, are invited to participate in policy discussions with government decision makers. The formation of policy or epistemic communities is often seen as a critical stage in policy formulation and regime formation. This approach has been undertaken by a handful of political scientists, including Hugh Heclo, Evert Lindquist, Diane Stone, and others, who regard think tanks as important participants in these communities.[10]

By examining think tanks within a policy or epistemic community framework, scholars can make several important observations. To begin with, by focusing on specific policy issues, such as child welfare benefits or the creation of a National Missile Defense (NMD) system, they can better identify the key organizations and individuals who have been invited to share their thoughts with policymakers. In addition to determining which groups and individuals participate in the "subgovernment," a term used to describe the various nongovernmental and governmental policy experts that coalesce around particular policy issues, this approach offers better insight into the nature of the policy-making process itself. Among other things, a policy or epistemic community framework compels scholars to delve far deeper into the mechanics of policy-making. Rather than treating policy decisions as an outcome of interest group competition or as a reflection of elite interests, this approach requires scholars to think seriously about how policy decisions can be influenced through discussions between nongovernmental and governmental policy experts.

There are other advantages to adopting this approach as well. Once the actors participating in the subgovernment have been identified, it is possible to compare the recommendations made by participants to the actual policy decisions that were made. Access to minutes of meetings, personal correspondence, testimony before legislative committees, published recommendations, and other information may not enable scholars to make definitive conclusions about which participants in a policy community were the most influential. Nonetheless, these and other materials can offer useful insights into whose views generated the most support.

Given the involvement of policy experts from think tanks in different policy communities, it is not surprising that this framework is being used more often. It is important to keep in mind, however, that while this approach may be better suited to the study of think tanks than either an elite or a pluralist framework, it too has its shortcomings. Examining think tanks within a policy community is useful in identifying which institutes are called upon to offer their expertise at an important stage in policy formulation. Unfortunately, it does not tell us what, if any, impact think tanks inside policy communities or those operating outside the subgovernment have in shaping public attitudes and the policy preferences and choices of policymakers. This approach may tell us who is sitting at the table when key issues are being discussed, but it does not profess to tell us whose voices have struck a responsive chord with those in a position to influence policy decisions. Since we cannot assume that all, or any, important policy decisions are made inside specific policy communities – after all, politicians, not policy experts, cast votes in the legislature – a third group of scholars have begun to consider using a more inclusive approach in studying the involvement of nongovernmental organizations in policy-making.

Recognizing that nongovernmental organizations vary enormously in terms of their mandate, resources, and priorities, John Kingdon and Denis Stairs, among others, suggest that rather than trying to make general observations about how much or how little impact societal groups have on shaping policy-making and the policy-making environment, scholars should examine how groups committed to influencing public policy focus their efforts at different stages of the policy cycle.[11] Although Kingdon and Stairs do not write specifically about think tanks, their approach to studying how groups seek to place issues on the political agenda and how they try to convey their ideas to policymakers throughout the policy-making process is well suited to the study of think tanks.

POLICY CYCLES AND POLICY INFLUENCE: A NEW CONCEPTUAL FRAMEWORK

For several political scientists, including Kingdon and Stairs, trying to determine which domestic and external forces shape public policy constitutes an enormous and, at times, overwhelming undertaking. In fact, as the policy-making community in the United States and in Canada has become increasingly crowded with nongovernmental organizations seeking to influence public policy, it has become difficult, if not impossible, to identify those groups that have had a direct impact on specific policy issues. As a result, instead of making generalizations about which groups influence public policy, Kingdon and Stairs, among others, recognize that not all organizations have the desire or the necessary resources to participate at each stage of the policy cycle: issue articulation, policy formulation, and policy implementation. Put simply, while some organizations may have an interest in placing issues on the political agenda by articulating their concerns through a number of channels (issue articulation), others may be more inclined to enter the policy-making process at a later stage (policy formulation or policy implementation). In other words, some organizations may be more interested in sharing their ideas with the public than in working closely with policy-makers to formulate or implement a specific policy.

By drawing on Kingdon and Stairs' observations about the nature of the policy-making process, it is possible to construct a conceptual framework that allows scholars to make more insightful observations about the role and impact of think tanks in policy-making. At the very least, a framework that recognizes the diversity of think tanks and their distinct missions will discourage scholars from making sweeping and often unfounded observations about their impact.

The conceptual framework employed in this book is based on a simple premise: think tanks in Canada and the United States are a diverse set of organizations that share a common desire to influence public policy but seek to do so in very different ways. In other words, not only do think tanks vary enormously in terms of the resources they have at their disposal, but they assign different priorities to participating at various stages of the policy cycle. This becomes particularly clear in comparing how think tanks function in different political systems. It also becomes important in interpreting data such as media citations and testimony before legislative committees that can be used to evaluate think tank performance.

While acknowledging that not all think tanks seek to become actively engaged at each stage of the policy cycle, we must still consider what indicators can be used to evaluate the influence or relevance of think tanks. To obtain a more comprehensive understanding of which think tanks in the United States and Canada appear to be having the greatest impact at different stages of the policy cycle, my framework considers both tangible and intangible performance indicators. While considerable attention is devoted to measuring media exposure and testimony, it is also important to consider intangible indicators, such as presentations before cabinet ministers, participation in presidential campaigns, and conferences with high-level policy-makers, that are difficult to quantify but may nonetheless be critical in allowing think tanks to influence public opinion and public policy.

Unlike scholars who assume that think tanks are elite organizations well suited and positioned to influence public policy, I am more cautious in making such pronouncements. I am also reluctant to fully embrace the views of pluralists who suggest that think tanks should be treated like any other type of nongovernmental organization competing in the political arena. As noted, think tanks possess certain attributes that distinguish them from other NGOs. Elite and pluralist approaches to the study of think tanks provide some insight into their behaviour, but an institutional framework that focuses on the involvement of think tanks at different stages of the policy cycle can offer scholars considerably more. An understanding of where in the policy cycle think tanks in the United States and Canada seek the greatest access and of how we can best measure their impact at each stage will provide much-needed insight into a field of growing interest.

CHAPTER THREE

In the Arena:
Opportunities, Constraints,
and Incentives for Think Tanks
in the United States and Canada

In an ideal world, think tanks would have few, if any, financial concerns, conduct research on a wide range of timely and policy-relevant issues, and from the comfort of their book-lined offices observe their ideas translated into concrete policy decisions. The world of think tanks and the reality of the policy-making process, however, is far from ideal. The vast majority of think tanks in the United States, like those in Canada, lack the resources they require to examine the many complex policy questions confronting government. Many also lack the resources to convey their ideas effectively to decision makers. Moreover, since policymakers are usually compelled to juggle competing political interests, think tanks often have to struggle to capture their attention.

Aware of the complexity of the policy-making process, as well as the demands placed on their limited resources, think tanks must make a number of strategic decisions, not the least of which is where in the policy cycle they will seek to have the greatest impact. As I will discuss in this chapter, although think tanks in both countries make similar choices, those in the United States have far more opportunities to become involved in policy-making than their Canadian counterparts. But why is this the case? Does the highly fragmented and decentralized nature of the u.s. government, combined with a weak party system, provide think tanks and other nongovernmental organizations with more opportunities to influence policy-making?[1] Conversely, do the principles of strong party unity, cabinet solidarity, and the presence of a permanent civil service entrusted with advising senior officials limit opportunities for think tanks in Canada to participate in policy-making and hence reduce their effectiveness?

Comparing the institutional environments in which think tanks in the two countries function offers some insight into why u.s. policy institutes have established a more visible presence than those in Canada. Several features of the U.S. political system have indeed facilitated the access of think tanks to various stages of the policy-making process. However, differences in political structures cannot account entirely for American think tanks appearing to play a more significant role in policy-making than those in Canada, nor can they explain why some institutes in both countries are more influential than others. In fact, as some directors of Canadian think tanks, including David Zussman of the Public Policy Forum, have argued, the structure of the Canadian government may have very little to do with whether think tanks are effective or ineffective at conveying their ideas. The political structure of a country may influence the types of strategies nongovernmental organizations use to reach policymakers, but according to Zussman the modest resources available to most policy institutes have limited their impact far more than the political system they work in. Gaining access to policymakers in Canada is not a problem, Zussman claims, but obtaining sufficient funds to conduct long-term research and analysis is.[2]

If Zussman is correct, then it is important to draw a distinction, as this chapter does, between opportunities for think tanks to participate in policy-making and the constraints that may undermine their effectiveness. In doing so, it can be demonstrated, as Diane Stone has done in a study comparing think tanks in Great Britain to those in the United States, that parliamentary democracies and their structures may not pose as much of a barrier to think tank access as previously thought.[3]

This chapter examines the opportunities for think tanks in both countries to participate in policy-making, as well as some of the internal and external constraints that might undermine their efforts to influence policy formulation and the policy-making environment. It also looks more closely at the incentives decision makers in both countries may have to turn to think tanks for policy expertise. The central argument here is that while think tanks in the United States and Canada function in very different political systems, their ability or inability to market their ideas effectively may have as much to do with how they define their missions, the directors who lead them, the resources they have, and the strategies they employ to achieve their stated goals as with the political environment. In other words, the structure of the political system may frustrate or facilitate the efforts of think tanks to influence public policy, as has been argued, but this factor alone cannot account for their success or failure.[4] The amount of funding they have and the quality of their staff may be more important in determining how influential they become.

OPPORTUNITIES FOR THINK TANKS
IN THE UNITED STATES AND CANADA

It is difficult to isolate parts of the policy-making process or a branch or department of the u.s. government where think tanks have not made their presence felt.[5] In Congress, the executive, the bureaucracy, and, more recently, the judiciary, think tanks specializing in a wide range of domestic and foreign policy areas have conveyed their ideas to key policymakers.[6] There are also think tanks at the state level, including the New York – based Manhattan Institute, which has established strong ties to local government leaders.[7] As will be discussed later in this section, dozens of staff from think tanks have become policymakers themselves.

Among the many factors that have contributed to the proliferation of think tanks in the United States is the structure of the political system. As several scholars have observed, few other countries provide an environment more conducive to the development of think tanks.[8] With a government based on separate branches sharing power, a party system in which members of Congress are free to vote as they wish, and a growing number of presidential candidates trying to develop new ideas, think tanks have multiple opportunities to shape public opinion and public policy. In Congress alone there are 535 elected officials, not to mention dozens of staff and committee aides, whom think tanks can approach to consider their policy ideas.[9] Recognizing this, think tanks have employed several strategies to attract attention, ranging from testifying before congressional committees and delivering by hand concise summaries of key policy issues to members of Congress to inviting representatives and senators, as well as their staff, to participate in seminars and workshops.[10] A select group of policy experts from some of America's leading think tanks can now rely on another channel to share their expertise regularly with members of Congress: in March 1998 the newly formed Congressional Policy Advisory Board (which meets quarterly) met for the first time to discuss several policy issues with the House leadership. Of the twenty-eight policy experts who comprise the board, twenty-one are currently affiliated with u.s. think tanks, including the board's chair, Martin Anderson, a senior fellow at the Hoover Institution.[11] A more detailed assessment of these and other channels think tanks rely on to influence policy-making will be discussed in the next chapter.

Since members of Congress are not bound by party unity, they need not be concerned that their association with particular think tanks or their endorsement of some of their policy ideas would undermine party cohesion. Rather than evaluating ideas from think tanks in terms of their compatibility with party interests and policies, they can evaluate them on their own merits. Moreover, as Weaver and others have argued, the weak party system in the United States not only provides opportunities for think tanks to influence policy-making but has in some ways increased the demand for them.[12] In Germany political parties have created their own think tanks or foundations to conduct research and analysis; political parties in the United States have not.[13] There are a handful of Congressional research institutes or public think tanks, including the Congressional Research Service and the General Accounting Office, from which members of Congress can request information.[14] However, these bodies cannot be expected to provide timely and policy-relevant research, as do many independent think tanks.

A number of think tanks, including the advocacy-oriented Heritage Foundation, assign the highest priority to influencing Congress. Nonetheless, they also recognize the importance of solidifying ties to the bureaucracy, the executive, and the many agencies that advise the president. The Executive Office of the President (EOP), which comprises several important agencies, including the National Security Council and the Office of Management and Budget, provides think tanks with further opportunities to influence government. During several recent administrations, for instance, presidents have appointed senior staff from think tanks to serve in cabinet- and subcabinet-level positions and on advisory boards and executive agencies.[15] Many of these appointees have previously served on policy task forces and on transition teams in presidential elections, a subject that will be discussed in more detail below.[16]

It is not uncommon for presidential candidates to establish task forces during the primaries and the general election to investigate policy concerns. These groups are particularly important for challengers who lack the resources available to an incumbent president or who lack experience in federal politics. For instance, during the presidential election campaign of 2000, Governor George W. Bush enlisted the support of scholars and policy analysts from a handful of think tanks, including the Hoover Institution and the American Enterprise Institute.[17] Moreover, twenty years earlier, during the 1980 election, Martin Anderson and Richard Allen of the Hoover Institution were responsible for organizing close to fifty task forces on domestic and foreign policy to advise Governor Reagan on a host of issues.[18]

It is rare, however, for Canadian federal party leaders to organize task forces during campaigns. Part of the problem is logistical: the election period is far shorter in Canada – it typically lasts thirty-six days, from the time the prime minister advises the governor-general of his or her intention to call an election to the day Canadians vote – compared to the lengthy primary season and general election in the United States.[19] The electoral cycle in Canada is also more unpredictable, since the government can call an election at any time during its mandate, up to a maximum of five years after taking office. This element of uncertainty poses additional problems for think tanks contemplating a more active role during elections. In addition, most Canadian party leaders do not turn to the broader policy community for advice but rely on their own staff, party research caucus, and party members instead.[20] The prime minister may have even less need for policy task forces during campaigns, for in addition to his or her own staff, the prime minister enjoys the support of the Prime Minister's Office (PMO), which serves as a "practical policy think-tank charged with an advisory capacity on the political fortunes of the prime minister and his cabinet."[21] With a staff of over one hundred, including approximately a dozen researchers, the prime minister has little incentive to seek the advice of think tanks during campaigns. Staff from think tanks are more likely to be called on when the prime minister establishes a royal commission or commission of inquiry to study a particular policy issue, such as free trade or the creation of a security intelligence agency.[22]

While there is little to prevent think tanks in Canada from releasing studies before or during elections or discussing ideas with party members, they do not, for the reasons given above, engage as actively in electoral politics as some of their U.S. counterparts. Yet it is important to point out that while institutional and logistical constraints may limit the involvement of think tanks during elections, so too does the desire of some think tanks, primarily for legal and political reasons, to maintain an arm's-length relationship with political parties.[23] The Vancouver-based Fraser Institute is a case in point. Although Fraser has rarely concealed its conservative leanings or support for many of the policies advanced by the Canadian Alliance, it has been reluctant to become too closely associated with the party itself. According to Paul Wilson, former director of research for the Canadian Alliance, while there has been some interaction between members of his party and the Fraser Institute, "Fraser is concerned about being too close to us. They do not want to be seen as a Reform [or an Alliance] mouthpiece. We, on the other hand, are less choosey about the [think tanks] we talk to. Parties are like intellectual prostitutes. We will take good ideas from any source."[24] Other think tanks, however, appear less concerned about their ties to political parties; the Ottawa-based Canadian Centre for Policy Alternatives (CCPA), for instance, maintains very close links to the New Democratic Party (NDP). As Judy Randall, senior researcher with the NDP Caucus Research Office acknowledged, "our strongest link to a think tank is the CCPA, although we also use a lot of the work done by the Canadian Council on Social Development, the National Council of Welfare, the National Anti-Poverty Organization and other organizations ... Several of our members have served on [the CCPA's] Board of Directors and their executive director Bruce Campbell worked for us."[25]

There appear to be both external and internal limits to how much direct access think tanks have to party leaders during campaigns. There also appear to be limits to how much impact think tanks have during government transition periods. As previously mentioned, a handful of think tanks, including the Heritage Foundation and CSIS, have played key roles in assisting incoming presidential administrations make the transition to power. In addition to serving on the transition staff, several think tank scholars have helped by identifying topical issues and have advised on placing appropriate people in the hundreds of vacant positions that become available when governments change. These functions provide think tanks that are close to transitions with further opportunities to influence policy.

By contrast, think tanks in Canada rarely offer or are called upon to assist in transition planning, although some, including the Ottawa-based Public Policy Forum (PPF) have undertaken major projects on managing transitions.[26] Again, there are several reasons for this. First, unlike in the United States, the transition period before a new government assumes power in Canada does not take three months but is completed in less than two weeks. This short time-frame makes it extremely difficult for think tanks to communicate their ideas to transition leaders. Second, few Canadian think tanks have the resources or expertise to arrange the types of transition planning seminars organized by the Heritage Foundation and CSIS.[27] Third, and perhaps more importantly, the federal transition process is overseen and orchestrated by the Privy Council Office (PCO), which is "staffed by career civil servants [and serves as] a major policy-advising agency of the federal government." [28] Furthermore, unlike U.S. think tanks, which take advantage of transition periods to fill vacant positions in the bureaucracy, either with their own staff or like-minded colleagues, Canadian think tanks have little incentive to closely monitor job vacancies after an election. An incoming U.S. president must find hundreds of people to fill vacant positions in a new administration, but a Canadian prime minister has the power to fill only a limited number of senior bureaucratic positions after an election, usually at the level of deputy minister. The majority of individuals who obtain these positions are career civil servants, not think tank staffers.

If think tanks in Canada do not make their presence felt during elections and transitions, where do they have an impact? Canadian think tanks, like many in the United States, do not always select the same target audiences or stages in the policy cycle to become most actively involved. Where and how they exercise policy influence ultimately depends on their mandate and resources, which, as the previous chapter demonstrated, vary enormously.

The priority for some think tanks in Canada, including the Fraser Institute and the C.D. Howe Institute, is to influence both the policy-making environment and the policy-making process. As a result, both institutions welcome opportunities to enhance their visibility by submitting articles to newspapers or by giving interviews on radio and television. Moreover, these and other think tanks acknowledge how critical it is to secure access to the cabinet and senior levels of the bureaucracy, where political power in Canada is concentrated. Although think tanks frequently testify before parliamentary committees and provide party research offices, middle and senior-level policy analysts in government departments, and MPs with their publications, they devote less attention to influencing the fate of bills being considered by Parliament.[29] They are reluctant to devote resources to influencing debates in the House of Commons, particularly after a bill has passed first reading, largely because of the presence of a strong party system. The time to influence the content and direction of a proposed bill is before it reaches the floor of the House. Once the government (assuming it has a majority of seats) has endorsed a bill, there is little opposition parties can do to prevent its passage.

Publishing op-ed articles in newspapers and testifying before parliament might be useful ways to reach policymakers, but to have a real impact, think tanks must get further inside the policy-making process. Ken Battle, president of the Caledon Institute, realized this shortly after he published an article in the *Globe and Mail* in late 1993 on the ill-fated seniors' benefits. As a result of his article, Battle was approached by several provincial premiers for advice, and, later, by some senior cabinet ministers interested in drawing on his expertise in these and related areas.[30] According to Battle, "I recall getting a call at home one afternoon from Paul Martin [the Liberal finance minister], who proceeded to grill me for the better part of an hour on a piece I wrote on the social security review. It was worse than the grilling I took during oral exams at Oxford."[31]

Judith Maxwell, president of the CPRN, Inc., acknowledges that to have an impact in policy-making, think tanks must rely on diverse and, at times, less visible forms of policy influence. Although Maxwell does not downplay the importance of media exposure, she maintains, like Battle and Zussman, that think tanks exercise the most influence working with key stakeholders behind the scenes, not by discussing policy issues with reporters. [32] Maxwell believes that part of the CPRN's role is to bring together senior bureaucrats, academics, and representatives from the private and nonprofit sector in closed door meetings to discuss social and economic policy issues: "We are interested in creating new mental maps for policy makers. Our research [and workshops] are not intended to simply summarize issues, but to generate new thinking. We want to help start conversations between people that would have never taken place before."[33]

Canadian think tanks may not have as many channels to influence policy making as those in the United States, but the political structure in Canada does not hinder their access to policymakers as much as some have suggested. What may restrict their influence more than the political environment they function in are the limited resources most Canadian and, indeed, American think tanks have at their disposal.

CONSTRAINING IDEAS: DO CANADIAN AND AMERICAN THINK TANKS FACE SIMILAR CONSTRAINTS?

Different types of political systems impose different types of constraints on nongovernmental organizations seeking access to power. Clearly, the political system in the United States is more permeable than the system in Canada and in some other parliamentary systems. Nonetheless, to better understand why U.S. think tanks appear to be more firmly entrenched in the policy-making community than those in Canada, several factors unrelated to the institutional structure of the Canadian and American government must be considered.

In Canada, as in the United States, most think tanks have modest financial and human resources. The Brookings Institution, with its sizeable endowment, multimillion dollar operating budget, and over two hundred staff and researchers is sometimes mistakenly regarded as a typical U.S. think tank. However, as noted, Brookings and the handful of other institutes with comparable resources are anything but typical. The typical think tank in Canada and the United States has approximately a dozen staff and a budget between $1 and $2 million, fewer resources in fact than several trade associations: the Ontario Federation of Labour, for example, has thirty-five full-time staff and a budget of $3 to $5 million; in 1999 the Alliance of Manufacturers' and Exporters' Canada had seventy-five full-time staff and a budget exceeding $5 million.[34]

The major difference between think tanks in the two countries is that while the United States has such prominent repositories of policy expertise as Brookings, the Hoover Institution, the Heritage Foundation, and RAND, think tanks that generate considerable attention in the media and in some scholarly circles, Canada has few if any of comparable size and stature. Even its largest institute, the Conference Board of Canada, functions more as a business-oriented planning organization than as a traditional interdisciplinary policy research institute like Brookings.[35]

The absence of a think tank of this scale in Canada cannot be attributed to the lack of qualified individuals to staff it; for decades Canada has had a surplus of PHDs in the social sciences – the degree most policy research institutes require of applicants. The pool of graduating PHDs in the social sciences in the United States and in Canada has remained constant over the past several years. In 1994, for instance, 3,627 people received doctorates in the social sciences in the United States and 614 in Canada.[36] Thus Canada, with a population one-tenth that of the United States, produces almost twice as many doctorates in the social sciences per capita.

While finding qualified people to staff a large think tank in Canada is not a problem, although it could become one if the demand for faculty to teach at Canadian universities begins to far exceed the supply, locating sufficient sources of revenue is.[37] As in the United States, the majority of think tanks in Canada do not have sizeable endowments to ensure financial security and independence. The Institute for Research on Public Policy (IRPP) and the Caledon Institute are among the few in Canada whose core funding is secured through endowments. The current market value of the IRPP's endowment, provided primarily through government funds, is $40 million. In the 1998–99 fiscal year, the endowment generated two-thirds of the IRPP's $3 million budget.[38] The Caledon Institute's endowment from the Maytree Foundation pales in comparison: it has grown from approximately $300,000 in 1992 to over $700,000 in 1999.[39]

Without endowments to draw on, think tanks in Canada have no alternative but to consider how to secure adequate revenue. For some, including the North-South Institute and the various defence and foreign policy institutes at over a dozen Canadian universities, this has meant relying heavily on government funds, often in the form of specific contracts, and on support from private foundations. This dependence places think tanks in a vulnerable position; Roy Culpeper, president of the North-South Institute, agrees that receiving large sums of money from only a few sources can be "both a blessing and a curse."[40] Since government agencies and philanthropic foundations often have vested interests in ensuring that their recipients express views consistent with theirs, think tanks might be reluctant to be overly critical of policies supported by their donors. As several government-funded institutes experienced first-hand following the 1992 Canadian federal budget, so long as governments have the power to change their priorities, there is little they can do to ensure their survival.

The financial security of think tanks that receive little or no government funding is also precarious. These organizations must turn to the private sector, to the public and to foundations, for support. In the United States, the Ford, Rockefeller, and Carnegie Foundations, among others, have long supported social science research, much of which has been at think tanks.[41] This generous tradition of philanthropic support in the United States, however, has not taken root to the same extent in Canada, where the majority of think tanks struggle to keep afloat.

Relying too heavily on philanthropic foundations and corporations can also be risky, of course. As mentioned, like governments that require foreign aid recipients to make certain concessions, philanthropic foundations and large corporate donors must be satisfied that the organizations they are making grants to act in a manner consistent with their institutional missions. Failing to appease the political agenda of philanthropic and corporate donors can, as the American Enterprise Institute discovered in the mid-1980s, have serious repercussions. When the AEI president, William Baroody Jr, was unable to satisfy several right-wing foundations, including the Olin Foundation and the Reader's Digest Foundation, that the AEI was committed to pursuing a truly conservative agenda, these and other like-minded donors withdrew their significant financial support, with the result that the AEI was brought to the verge of bankruptcy.[42] Conversely, acting in the interests of affluent donors can pay handsome dividends for some think tanks, as the Washington-based conservative think tank Citizens for a Sound Economy (CSE) discovered after it began its campaign to derail a multibillion-dollar federal plan to restore the Florida Everglades in 1998. For its efforts, CSE received $700,000 in contributions from Florida's three largest sugar enterprises, "which stand to lose thousands of acres of cane-growing land to reclamation if the Army Corps of Engineers plan goes into effect."[43]

For most think tanks in Canada, and in the United States for that matter, achieving financial independence is the most significant obstacle they must overcome to ensure a strong presence in the policy-making community. Without a sizeable budget, think tanks will not able to mount the extensive research and media relations program necessary to attract the attention of policymakers. More importantly, without ample resources think tanks will not be able to recruit the type of people most qualified to produce policy-relevant research, as will be discussed in more detail shortly.

Some consideration should also be given to important cultural differences between Canada and the United States, which could also affect the prominence of think tanks in the policy-making process. One significant cultural factor that may account for their playing a less visible role in Canada is the relative absence of a strong, vocal entrepreneurial class in the private sector. As Abelson and Carberry point out, "In the U.S., independent policy entrepreneurs have provided important leadership in the formation of think tanks dedicated to providing information and advice to government. In Canada, on the other hand, such leadership is likely to come from the government itself or from senior public servants. This difference reflects both the incentives created by the institutional structure of each form of government as well as cultural understandings of the appropriate repositories of policy expertise."[44]

John Kingdon's work on policy entrepreneurs, defined as "advocates for proposals or for the prominence of an idea," demonstrates how these individuals can have an important impact on policy issues: "their defining characteristic, much as in the case of a business entrepreneur, is their willingness to invest their resources – time, energy, reputation, and sometimes money – in the hope of a future return."[45] Why do policy entrepreneurs undertake these investments? They do so, according to Kingdon, "to promote their values, or affect the shape of public policy."[46]

Without effective and meaningful government initiatives to establish policy institutes like the IRPP and the Canadian Centre for Foreign Policy Development, leadership must come from one or more policy entrepreneurs. According to the limited research conducted in this area, there is some evidence to suggest that, at least with respect to the private sector, these entrepreneurs are likely to be more prominent in the United States than in Canada. In their study of the environmental agenda in the two countries, Harrison and Hoberg observed a difference in policy entrepreneurship.[47] Among other things, they discovered that policy entrepreneurs in the United States played an important role in the promotion of certain environmental issues, particularly the effects of radon, and were able to facilitate their discussion on the political agenda. They also noticed that there was an absence of similar activity in Canada. Harrison and Hoberg note how the presence of policy entrepreneurship is, in a certain sense, tied to the institutional arrangements of each political system.[48] The highly fragmented American political system, combined with an absence of strong party unity, provides incentives to private policy entrepreneurs to shape the political agenda. By contrast, the relatively closed and party-driven system in Canada offers few allurements to such entrepreneurs.

As discussed in chapter 1, several think tanks in the United States owe their existence and, indeed, their success to the efforts of policy entrepreneurs committed to injecting their political and ideological views into the policy-making process. Robert Brookings, Andrew Carnegie, and the Heritage Foundation's Edwin Feulner represent but a handful of such entrepreneurs who have created think tanks as institutional vehicles to promote their beliefs. This entrepreneurial spirit is also evident in the vanity and legacy-based think tanks in the United States.

By way of comparison, there are few examples of think tanks in Canada that are the direct creation of *private* sector policy entrepreneurship.[49] The Fraser Institute, under the initial guidance of Sir Antony Fisher, Patrick Boyle, and economists Sally Pipes and Michael Walker, and the defunct CIIPS, which was inspired by Prime Minister Trudeau's global peace initiative, are notable exceptions.[50] On the other hand, the *public* sector has been a viable source of leadership. Senior public servants, including Michael Pitfield and Michael Kirby,[51] played important roles in creating the IRPP, the Economic Council of Canada, the Science Council of Canada, and other governmental advisory bodies.[52]

The fact that major initiatives for creating Canadian centres of policy expertise come from inside the government and not from the private sector, as in the United States, is not surprising. In part it reflects the cultural understandings of the relationship between government and the provision of policy expertise in both countries. This role for governmental leadership in Canada is not unexpected, given the importance granted to bureaucratic and party policy advice in the parliamentary process.[53] Colin Gray, former chairman of the Virginia-based National Institute for Public Policy, has suggested that the culture of "officialdom" in the Canadian and British bureaucracies discriminates against those groups seeking to provide external advice to government. This ethos of officialdom is contrasted with the relatively open access of the U.S. system, in which the role of the bureaucracy in providing policy advice is often overshadowed by the presence of "independent" advisors operating in the private sector.[54]

The difference in think tank development in the two countries, particularly in the source of their creation and growth, may reflect broader societal trends: sociological analyses of Canadian and American societies provide an interesting comparison. Canada has long been viewed as more "conservative, traditional ... statist, and elitist" than the United States.[55] By contrast, American attitudes about individualism and the limited role of the state have supported a culture encouraging private entrepreneurship. As Lipset argues, "If one society leans toward communitarianism – the public mobilization of resources to fulfill group objectives – the other sees individualism – private endeavor – as the way an 'unseen hand' produces optimum, socially beneficial results."[56]

In sum, think tank development in the United States is supported by cultural influences: a value system stressing individual effort, a tradition of philanthropy, and the presence of independent advisors operating alongside the bureaucracy. This has promoted policy entrepreneurship from the private sector, with think tanks originating from society. The Canadian cultural context provides a different environment for think tanks, particularly its bureaucratic ethos, which, at times, discourages external advice. Governments in Canada have taken, and continue to take, an active role in their formation and maintenance, as evidenced by the recent creation of a handful of institutes, including the Saskatchewan Institute of Public Policy in June 1998.[57] This does not mean that private entrepreneurship is unwelcome, but it means that it may face substantial challenges to overcome both the cultural climate and institutional arrangements in order to secure a meaningful role in policy debates.[58]

The opportunities for think tanks to convey their ideas to policymakers and the constraints that may undermine their efforts help to shed light on some of the differences between them in Canada and the United States. Still, it is also important to consider another issue – the incentives for government officials to turn to think tanks for advice. A closer look at this factor may help to better explain why think tanks in the United States appear to be more relevant in policy making than the majority in Canada.

EXPLORING INCENTIVES:
WHY POLICYMAKERS TURN TO THINK TANKS

There are several reasons why policymakers in the United States would turn to think tanks for information and advice. To begin with, a number of U.S. think tanks have established impressive research programs in domestic and foreign policy by recruiting not only first-rate academics but many former high-level policymakers to their institutions. The presence of former cabinet secretaries and other seasoned policymakers also provides an incentive for members of Congress, the executive, and presidential candidates to solicit their advice. Access to think tank luminaries, including Zbigniew Brzezinski, Harold Brown, Jeane Kirkpatrick, Robert Bork, and George Shultz, may help to open other doors for officeholders or for those aspiring to become policymakers. In short, members of Congress, the executive, and the bureaucracy can benefit from the wealth of expertise and the extensive network of contacts available at several u.s. think tanks. Moreover, unlike most university professors, who have little incentive to produce timely and policy-relevant research, scholars at think tanks are more sensitive to the policy needs of officeholders. Put simply, they can provide decision makers with what they need – clear and concise summaries of the costs and benefits associated with particular policy proposals.

There are other incentives to turn to. As previously mentioned, several think tanks have been able to assemble talent pools of scholars for incoming administrations to draw on to fill important positions in government. For instance, during the Carter and Reagan administrations, many think tanks, including the Brookings Institution, the Hoover Institution, and the American Enterprise Institute, contributed key personnel.[59] A handful of scholars have been recruited from some of these think tanks to serve in President George W. Bush's administration as well. Politicians and aspiring officeholders can also turn to think tanks for ideological support: advocacy-oriented think tanks like the Heritage Foundation often help to validate or reinforce the ideological views of incumbents and challengers.[60]

It is less clear why policymakers in Canada would turn to think tanks for advice. To begin with, some preliminary data reveals that the majority of researchers at most private think tanks in Canada, unlike their colleagues at equivalent institutions in the United States, do not possess doctorates, despite the availability of individuals with PHDs in Canada. Most have an undergraduate or a masters' degree in the social sciences.[61] Furthermore, with few exceptions the majority of think tank analysts have little or no government experience. For example, of the eight researchers currently working at the North-South Institute, less than half have any government experience. Indeed, with the exception of the NSI's president, Roy Culpepper, none of the institute's researchers have held a senior level position in the Canadian government. The Canada West Foundation has a similar institutional profile; only two members of its nine-member research team have government experience at the provincial or federal level.[62] This is not to suggest that prior government experience is necessary to provide informed observations about government or the issues confronting elected officials, but it is to suggest that policymakers may be more inclined to rely on think tank personnel who have worked in government in some capacity and who have some direct experience working with stakeholders. Their extensive government experience may in fact explain why Judith Maxwell and Ken Battle are often approached by cabinet ministers and senior officials for advice. It may also explain why, compared to several other think tanks, CPRN, Inc. and the Caledon Institute have become so firmly entrenched in the policy-making process. Second, unlike in the United States, where there appears to be a revolving door between think tanks and government, it is rare for think tank scholars in Canada to be recruited into senior positions in the bureaucracy or for former cabinet ministers, bureaucrats, and experienced parliamentarians to go to think tanks after leaving public office.[63]

Some directors of Canadian think tanks have, as noted, held important government positions. However, few think tanks have been able to hire leading policy experts, in large part because of limited financial resources. Others, like the Public Policy Forum, elect not to actively recruit high-profile policy analysts, preferring instead to hire individuals with an array of talents.[64] Regardless of the importance think tank directors place on hiring prominent academics or policymakers, the absence of high-profile experts may discourage some government officials from using think tanks – but so too will the uneven quality of research being produced at some institutes. As Lindquist has noted, to be relevant think tanks must produce work that contributes to a better understanding of the intricacies of important policy issues. But as he discovered in his detailed examination of Canadian policy institutes, it is questionable how much some think tanks have added to major policy debates, a subject that will be addressed below.[65] Finally, while many think tanks in the United States may lend intellectual credibility to the ideological agenda of policymakers or aspiring officeholders, this function is less critical for policymakers in Canada. Members of parliament may benefit from and, indeed, welcome ideological support from think tanks, but it is the party caucus, not independent think tanks, that determine the party line.

Policymakers in Canada appear to have fewer incentives to rely on think tanks for expertise, but this could be changing. As the internal policy capacity of government diminishes, a subject that will be examined in the concluding chapter, public servants are beginning to strengthen their ties to the external policy-research community. In this environment Canadian think tanks may be able to overcome some important obstacles and constraints and play a more decisive role in the policy-making community.

Comparing think tanks across nations and understanding how political structures can promote or impede their access to policymakers is invaluable in explaining why, for instance, think tanks in the United States and in other democracies enjoy more opportunity to shape public opinion and public policy than independent institutes operating in countries with totalitarian and authoritarian regimes. Yet, as this chapter has illustrated by comparing two countries, it is important not to exaggerate the extent to which institutional differences are responsible for elevating or diminishing the profile of think tanks. In other words, the significant differences in the governmental systems of the United States and, say, China helps explain why, compared to u.s. think tanks, those in China enjoy modest visibility. On the other hand, the differences in the political systems of the United States and Canada cannot account entirely for think tanks in Canada not gaining as much prominence as their u.s. counterparts. Several features of Canada's parliamentary system have indeed limited their opportunities to influence policymaking, but the country's political structure does not dictate how much or how little impact think tanks actually have. How effective think tanks are at employing often modest resources to advance their institutional goals and the willingness of policy entrepreneurs and philanthropists to support their mandate may be far more decisive in determining their success or failure than the political environment they inhabit.

Gray has noted that "American-style think-tanks could not function in Canada or Great Britain ... because of the differences in political culture and government structure."[66] But, as this chapter and chapter 1 have demonstrated, the same types of think tanks that exist in the United States have not only emerged in Canada but have contributed in some instances both to policy making and to shaping the policy-making environment. They have accomplished this in many ways, including by advising cabinet ministers, as Ken Battle and others have done, and by helping to increase public awareness about the costs and benefits of introducing different pieces of legislation by sharing their ideas with the media, as the Fraser Institute, the C.D. Howe Institute, and others frequently do. Moreover, as the next chapter reveals, contrary to Gray's assertions, not only have American-style think tanks taken root in Canada, but they have adopted many of the strategies employed by u.s. think tanks to influence policymakers and the public.

CHAPTER FOUR

Competing in the Marketplace of Ideas: The Strategies of Think Tanks

Think tanks are in the business of developing and promoting ideas and like corporations in the private sector, they devote considerable attention to marketing their product. Unlike corporations, however, think tanks measure success not by profit margins but by how much influence they have in shaping public opinion and the policy preferences and choices of leaders. Unfortunately, for think tank directors and those who study these institutions, it is far simpler to read their annual reports than to measure their performance. In this chapter, I lay the foundation for assessing the impact of think tanks by exploring the many channels policy research institutes use to market their ideas. It is important to keep in mind that while think tanks in Canada and the United States have very different missions, resources, and priorities, they tend to rely on similar strategies to influence policy. Where they differ is in the emphasis they place on pursuing each strategy. In other words, while generating media exposure is a preferred tactic for more advocacy-oriented think tanks, including the Heritage Foundation and the Fraser Institute, to name a few, it is not considered a priority for some institutes, like the Public Policy Forum and CPRN, Inc., which pay little attention to the media exposure they generate, preferring instead to commit their resources to strengthening ties to key policymakers.

The chapter begins by highlighting the strategies think tanks generally employ to generate attention in the public arena and in important policy circles. Particular emphasis is placed on what has become the most visible method think tanks pursue to attract exposure – gaining access to the media. Finally, some of the many methodological problems that arise in assessing think tank influence and what steps can be taken to provide more informed judgments about the impact of think tanks will be discussed.

PUBLIC INFLUENCE

Though often portrayed as elite organizations composed of scholars pursuing research in relative isolation, think tanks have become increasingly visible. As more think tanks have entered the marketplace of ideas, there has been a growing awareness among both newer and older generations of policy institutes that they must compete for the attention of policymakers and the public, not to mention the financial support of government agencies, individuals, and corporate and philanthropic donors.[1] While some of the strategies think tanks rely on to exercise influence are concealed from the public, many can be easily identified. In fact, to varying degrees, think tanks in the United States and Canada employ some or all of the following strategies to influence policymakers and the public:

- holding public forums and conferences to discuss various domestic and foreign policy issues,
- encouraging scholars to give public lectures and addresses,
- testifying before committees and subcommittees of Congress and Parliament,
- publishing books, opinion magazines, newsletters, policy briefs, and journals that have wide distribution,
- selling audio tapes to the public that summarize key policy issues,
- creating web pages on the internet,
- targeting the public during annual fund-raising campaigns, and
- enhancing their media exposure.

Holding public forums or conferences is among the most common strategies think tanks employ to increase awareness about a particular domestic or foreign policy issue. Policymakers, journalists, academics, and representatives from the private and nonprofit sectors are regularly invited to discuss timely and often controversial issues before public audiences. At times conferences are also arranged to generate exposure for a newly released study. A well-publicized and well-attended conference on an important topic such as free trade, several of which have been organized by Canadian policy institutes including the CCPA, the IRPP, the Fraser Institute, and the C.D. Howe Institute, or a conference on a topic such as the potential impact of technology on future U.S. presidential elections, which Brookings recently sponsored, can benefit think tanks in many ways. In addition to taking credit for encouraging opinion makers to discuss issues they have helped identify, think tanks use conferences to educate those in attendance about the role of their institute and the work they engage in.

To reach even more individuals who might be interested in the type of research they conduct, think tanks in both countries encourage their resident scholars to give lectures at universities, Rotary associations, and other organizations interested in contemporary political affairs. Once again, high-profile speakers from think tanks can serve as ambassadors for their institutes as they travel across the country, sharing their thoughts on a host of policy issues. Michael Walker of the Fraser Institute regularly performs this role and, in the process, reminds his audience of the efforts his organization is undertaking to convince policymakers to follow the right path.

Several think tanks also recognize the importance of conveying ideas to policymakers and the public in a more formal manner. Some policy institutes in Canada and the United States accomplish this by testifying before legislative committees – although some, including the Brookings Institution, the Heritage Foundation, the Canadian Council on Social Development, and the Conference Board of Canada, clearly assign a higher priority to performing this function than others. Providing testimony, particularly to a prominent committee, can attract considerable attention. The oral presentations and written briefs policy experts provide are included as part of the official record and are often cited by journalists and academics. Agreeing to appear before legislative committees can also promote the credibility of think tanks in the eyes of some policymakers and help think tank directors to convince potential donors of the widespread influence of their institutes. This may explain why several think tanks in the United States and Canada prominently display the testimonies given by staff on their web site.

There are several other strategies think tanks employ to market their message. Many, particularly those with well-established research programs, such as the Brookings Institution, the Heritage Foundation, the AEI, and the IRPP, rely on opinion magazines, journals, newsletters, and books to reach their various target audiences. For example, the Heritage Foundation publishes *Policy Review*, an opinion magazine that contains brief articles by many leading conservatives on current policy issues. The *Brookings Review*, published by the Brookings Institution, *The American Enterprise*, produced by the AEI, and *American Outlook*, published by the Hudson Institute, are other examples of opinion magazines distributed by U.S. think tanks. Several think tanks in Canada also publish opinion magazines, including *Policy Options* and *The Fraser Forum*, published by the Institute for Research on Public Policy and the Fraser Institute respectively. For many think tanks, these types of publications are their most effective product, because unlike books, which are often outdated by the time they are released, opinion magazines provide policymakers with insights into current policy problems. Often on a particular theme, these publications help to frame the parameters of important and relevant policy debates, and more importantly for policymakers, who have hectic schedules, they can be read in a matter of minutes, not hours or days.

Think tanks produce publications for other consumers as well. Several, for example, publish refereed scholarly journals that are intended to be read by university students and academics. Among these are *Foreign Affairs*, the flagship journal of the New York – based Council on Foreign Relations, *Foreign Policy*, produced by the Carnegie Endowment for International Peace, *The Washington Quarterly*, a publication of the Center for Strategic and International Studies, and *International Journal,* published by the Canadian Institute of International Affairs. In addition to scholarly journals and opinion magazines, dozens of think tanks produce books and monthly newsletters that are intended to keep readers informed about the most important developments at their institutes.

A number of think tanks also reach potential consumers through other forms of communication. The Heritage Foundation, for instance, produces *Monthly Briefing Tapes*, which include interviews with some of their policy experts, as well as speeches given by prominent (mostly conservative) opinion makers. To market this product, Heritage often seeks the endorsement of high-profile policymakers. Among those who have helped sell the monthly briefing tapes is former speaker of the house Newt Gingrich. In his endorsement, which appeared in various Heritage publications, Gingrich referred to the tapes as "A monthly dose of conservative common sense. You'll wonder how you ever got along without it."

Those who can get along without listening to audio tapes but still want to be kept apprised of what certain think tanks are doing can access their web sites. To date, hundreds of think tanks in the United States and Canada have created home pages on the internet to publicize their work. They provide a wealth of information, ranging from an institute's most current publications and staff directory to upcoming conferences and seminars. Some sites also provide links to important data bases. The Urban Institute, for instance, provides a link to the National Center for Charitable Statistics, a repository of data on the nonprofit sector in the United States that includes information on the budgets of thousands of non-profit organizations throughout the US. Others – such as the one maintained by the Heritage Foundation, one of the more sophisticated web sites constructed by u.s. think tanks – go so far as to advise young conservatives on how to find policy jobs in Washington.

Fundraising is yet another way think tanks in both countries can market themselves to the public and to policymakers. Again, some think tanks, particularly in the United States, have enlisted the support of high-profile policymakers to convince the American public to make donations. For instance, in 1982, at the request of Heritage Foundation president Edwin Feulner, Edwin Meese III, a special adviser to President Reagan and later U.S. attorney-general, wrote a letter to potential Heritage donors telling them that in exchange for a tax-deductible donation of one thousand dollars, they would be allowed to join the *President's Club*. The club, according to Meese, would entitle them to "a series of meetings with the most senior members of the administration and Congress." In an accompanying fundraising letter, Feulner added, "you will be provided with an access to Washington policymakers which cannot be had at any price. I have no doubt that you will find your membership fee returned to you many times over."[2] Dismissing claims that he was directly asking people to give money to the Heritage Foundation, Meese remarked, "I am enthusiastic about the establishment of the Heritage Foundation President's Club ... [It is] a vital communications link [between the White House and those who support President Reagan and] this administration will fully cooperate with your efforts."[3]

Of all the public uses of think tank influence, none is more visible than the efforts of think tanks to secure access to the media. As will be discussed in more detail later in this chapter, since several directors of think tanks often equate media exposure with policy influence, many devote considerable resources to enhancing their public profile. By ensuring that they are regularly quoted in the print and broadcast media, think tanks seek to create the perception that they play a critical role in shaping public policy. However, as we will discover, while it is important for think tanks to communicate their views to the public on television broadcasts or on the op-ed pages (opposite the editorial page) of Canadian and American newspapers, media exposure does not necessarily translate into policy influence. Generating media attention may enable some think tanks to influence public opinion, but it does not necessarily guarantee access to other critical stages of the policy-making process.

PRIVATE INFLUENCE

The many channels think tanks rely on to exercise public influence are relatively easy to observe and document. However, it is often difficult to monitor how think tanks seek to influence policy-makers privately. The following list provides examples of how think tanks and the scholars affiliated with them have attempted to exercise private influence. As will become apparent, most of these strategies are unique to u.s. think tanks. Among the many private uses of influence are

- accepting cabinet, subcabinet, or bureaucratic positions in administrations,
- serving on policy task forces and transition teams during presidential elections and on presidential advisory boards,
- maintaining liaison offices with the House of Representatives and the Senate,
- inviting selected policymakers to participate in conferences, seminars, and workshops,
- allowing bureaucrats to work at think tanks on a limited-term basis,
- offering former policymakers positions at think tanks, and
- preparing studies and policy briefs for policymakers.

There are few ways experts from think tanks can get closer to the policy-making process than by becoming policymakers themselves. As previously noted, in several presidential administrations dozens of personnel from think tanks have been recruited into senior-level positions in the government. Many, including Jeanne Kirkpatrick (AEI) and Zbigniew Brzezinski (CSIS) have served in cabinet and subcabinet positions, while others have been appointed to important positions in the bureaucracy. More recently, as will be discussed in chapter 6, a handful of prominent policy experts, including Lawrence Lindsey and Robert Zoellick, have left their positions at think tanks to join the administration of President George W. Bush. For think tanks there are several potential benefits of having staff members appointed to an incoming administration, not the least of which is the publicity surrounding the appointment itself. By assembling a talent pool of scholars for administrations to draw on, not only do think tanks enhance their prestige, but they can foster even stronger ties to those making critical policy decisions. This may explain why some think tanks, like the Heritage Foundation, closely monitor vacancies in the bureaucracy in the hope of placing like-minded colleagues in important positions.

Think tanks can establish and strengthen ties to key decision makers through other channels as well. Presidential elections, for example, provide think tanks, particularly those that are ideologically in tune with certain candidates, with a tremendous opportunity to help shape the political platform and agenda of aspiring officeholders. As chapter 6 will illustrate, several presidential candidates have turned to experts from think tanks for information and advice on how to address a wide range of domestic and foreign policy issues. In the process, a number of experts have been invited to serve on policy task forces or on the transition team to assist presidential candidates and the president-elect in assuming power. Furthermore, during some administrations several think tank scholars have been appointed to important presidential advisory boards, including the President's Foreign Intelligence Advisory Board (PFIAB), the President's Intelligence Oversight Board (PIOB), and the President's Economic Policy Advisory Board (PEPAB).[4]

Since political power in the United States, unlike in Canada, is not concentrated in the executive but is largely shared with the legislative branch, U.S. think tanks also develop strategies to strengthen their ties to members of Congress. Several, including Heritage, do this by establishing liaison offices with the House of Representatives and the Senate. Maintaining close contact with the legislature enables think tanks to meet with members regularly to discuss their concerns and policy needs. It also allows them to monitor and track the most important issues on the floor of the House and Senate, which, in turn, helps them prepare the type of research policymakers require to make critical choices. By contrast, think tanks in Canada, as noted, do not devote considerable resources to establishing strong ties to the legislature. Unlike in the U.S. Congress, parliament is not composed of hundreds of elected officials who can freely embrace the ideas of outside policy experts even if they are at variance with the wishes of their party. While think tanks routinely distribute their publications to members of parliament, there is less incentive for think tanks in Canada to try to persuade individual MPs to endorse their studies; more can be gained by working closely with cabinet members and senior officials in the bureaucracy who are in a position to implement policy changes.

To discuss certain policy issues in more detail, some think tanks regularly invite members of Congress to attend private seminars, conferences, and workshops. Once again, this strategy enables policy experts at think tanks to share their insights with policymakers who are in a position to influence the content of legislation. Think tanks like the Hoover Institution also realize that many newly elected members of Congress, as well as some seasoned policymakers, could benefit from acquiring more knowledge of particular policy issues. They also realize the importance of establishing good communications with congressional staff and legislative assistants who regularly advise members of Congress.

Established in 1980, the Hoover Institution's two-day Washington Seminars at their institute in Palo Alto have played an important role in facilitating the exchange of ideas between Hoover scholars and policymakers. Limited to twelve to fifteen participants, the seminars have been attended by Democratic and Republican members of Congress and congressional staff members from the House and Senate Committees on International Relations/Foreign Relations, Appropriations, the Budget, Armed Services, Finance, Ways and Means, and Intelligence and by the offices of the senate majority leader and the house speaker, the minority leader, and the majority whip. The seminars are usually followed by meetings in Washington to bring together individuals who have participated in the program, Hoover scholars, and other government officials. According to the Hoover Institution, "these meetings and seminars are now playing a critical role in the ongoing dialogue between scholars and policymakers, which is so important to the effective development and implementation of legislative and executive department policies and programs."[5]

Some think tanks maintain close contact with bureaucratic departments and agencies, as well. For instance, through the State Department's Diplomat in Residence Program, diplomats can, between assignments, take up residence at think tanks to write, conduct research, and deliver lectures. Diplomats have been sent to several think tanks, including the American Enterprise Institute, the Hoover Institution, RAND, the Council on Foreign Relations, the Carnegie Endowment for International Peace, and the Heritage Foundation.

Some policymakers, particularly in the United States, are so impressed with think tanks that they decide to make them their permanent home after completing their public service. However, it is important to point out that many former high-profile policymakers are not recruited to think tanks because of their potential as researchers but because of their ability to attract funds, which is likely why think tanks have often approached former presidents and cabinet secretaries to join their ranks.

Finally, think tanks in both countries often hold informal meetings with key policymakers to discuss studies that their institutes have produced or simply to outline a range of policy options elected officials have at their disposal. Most of these meetings are rarely publicized or talked about, but they nonetheless can help shape public policy. Indeed, for many think tanks working quietly behind closed doors might be the most effective channel they have to influence policy-making.

The strategies think tanks use and the emphasis they place on each is influenced not only by the political environment they inhabit but by their mandate and resources. In other words, for advocacy-oriented think tanks such as the Heritage Foundation and the Fraser Institute, which are committed to influencing the public dialogue and which have the resources to market their ideas effectively, producing opinion magazines, securing access to the media, and holding public forums will be a top priority. On the other hand, as previously noted, for institutes like the Public Policy Forum, the Caledon Institute, and CPRN, Inc., which prefer to exchange ideas with policymakers in meeting rooms instead of with journalists on the air, less consideration and fewer resources will be devoted to marketing their message to the public. Put simply, think tanks develop strategies that allow them to reach their specific target audience most effectively.

MARKETING THE MESSAGE: THINK TANKS AND THE MEDIA

Testifying before a high-profile congressional or parliamentary committee or publishing a study on a controversial domestic or foreign policy issue may attract attention in some policy-making circles. However, it is unlikely to generate the exposure that an appearance on the CBS or CBC evening news or an op-ed article in the *New York Times* or the *Globe and Mail* would generate. This may explain why some think tanks devote considerable time and resources to gaining access to the print and broadcast media. It might also explain why the competition between think tanks for media exposure is so intense. As Patricia Linden explains, for think tanks to compete, "their ideas must be communicated; otherwise the oracles of tankdom wind up talking to themselves. The upshot is an endless forest of communiques, reports, journals, newsletters, op-ed articles, press releases, books, and educational materials. The rivalry for attention is fierce; so much so that the analysts have come out of their think tanks to express opinions on lecture and TV circuits, at seminars and conferences, press briefings and Congressional hearings."[6]

Securing access to the media on a regular basis provides think tanks with a valuable opportunity to shape public opinion and public policy. At the very least, media exposure allows think tanks to plant seeds in the mind of the electorate that may develop into a full-scale public policy debate. For instance, by discussing her institute's recent study on the problems confronting day care centres in Canada on the CBC and CTV evening news, Judith Maxwell reminded policymakers and the public of the need to provide better funding for and more spaces in daycare facilities.[7] Although Maxwell's institute, the CPRN, Inc., is not the first organization to raise this issue, its well-publicized study could generate further policy discussion. In doing so, it will have accomplished some of its goals.

In addition to contributing to the public dialogue, think tanks understand that media exposure helps foster the illusion of policy influence, a currency they have a vested interest in accumulating. The

more exposure think tanks generate, the more influential their directors claim they are. The Fraser Institute is just one of many think tanks that equates media exposure with policy influence. Although Fraser Institute chairman Alan F. Campney acknowledged in the Institute's 1976 annual report that it "is almost as difficult to measure the effects of the Institute's work as it is to ascertain what Canada's economic problems are," Fraser has consistently relied on media coverage to assess its impact. According to its twenty-five-year retrospective, "One of the indicators the Institute has used from its inception [to measure performance] is media coverage. How many mentions does an Institute book receive in daily newspapers? How many minutes of airtime do Institute authors and researchers receive during interviews?"[8] Such data, as the next chapter will reveal, may tell us which think tanks attract the most attention, but it provides little insight into how much impact institutes have in the policy-making process.

Few think tanks have devoted more time and resources to securing access to the media than the Heritage Foundation. In 1998 Heritage spent close to $8 million, or 18 percent of its budget, on media and government relations.[9] Fraser, by contrast, allocated approximately $60,000 of its $3 million budget (2.1 percent) to marketing its research to journalists.[10] Heritage's public relations program is based on a simple premise: "provide journalists, opinion leaders and the general public with the positive message of responsible conservatism and conservatism will remain competitive, and even triumph, in the marketplace of ideas." Its goal is even simpler: "Make sure journalists never have a reason for not quoting at least one conservative expert – or for not giving the conservative 'spin' in their stories."[11] The Heritage Foundation has clearly accomplished its goal: the mainstream media in the United States relies disproportionately on Heritage and a handful of other conservative think tanks inside the Beltway for their expertise and political commentary.[12] In Canada, the media appears to rely heavily on a handful of conservative think tanks as well.[13]

To make sure journalists do not overlook the views of their scholars, the Heritage Foundation and several other think tanks, including the Hoover Institution and the AEI, have developed programs designed to flood the mainstream print media with hundreds of op-ed articles each year. For example, in 1998 alone more than 150 articles written by Heritage scholars appeared in some of America's leading newspapers, including the *Chicago Tribune*, the *Christian Science Monitor*, the *Los Angeles Times*, the *New York Times*, *USA Today*, the *Wall Street Journal*, the *Washington Times*, and the *Washington Post*.[14] Several think tanks have also given considerable thought to how to increase their exposure on the air. While some American institutes have created

their own television programs or have had documentaries or conferences broadcast on cable TV, most viewers recognize think tank scholars from their regular appearances on network newscasts (CBS, ABC,
NBC, and CNN), *The Newshour with Jim Lehrer*, or a host of political
talk shows including *Meet the Press* and *This Week* (with Sam Donaldson and Cokie Roberts, and formerly with David Brinkley). Scholars
from Canadian think tanks regularly appear on the CBC and CTV
evening news.

    Establishing personal relationships with journalists is also critical for
think tanks trying to enhance their media profile. As Brian Lee Crowley, president of the Halifax-based Atlantic Institute for Market Studies
observed, to secure access to the media, think tanks should ensure that
their institutional interests coincide with those of journalists. According to Crowley, "having sound ideas and doing the research to back
them up are only one-half of your job. The other half is putting a lot
of energy into strategic communications, and putting that strategy into
effect. The place to start is not with ideas, but with personal relationships. Journalists are moved much more by personal contact than by
the best ideas in the world. One way that they economize on scarce
time is by having a stable of people, experts in their field, in whom
they can have confidence, knowing that if they are told something by
these people, they can put a great deal of weight on it without running
the risk of looking stupid and foolish."[15]

    The potential benefits of being a guest commentator on a national
newscast or radio program or of publishing op-ed articles on a regular
basis are great. Not only do these activities bode well for think tank
scholars looking for a broader audience to which to convey their ideas,
but they can also promote the goals of the institutions they represent.
As William J. Taylor Jr, of the Center for Strategic and International
Studies (CSIS), freely admits, he takes advantage of every opportunity
to appear on television, not so much for personal reasons "but for the
glory of CSIS and its mission of informing the public. When we're on
television, we're up there as individuals, but it says CSIS under our
name."[16] Yet, as Howard Kurtz, a reporter with the *Washington Post*
and a regular guest on various CNN talk shows points out, what the
viewer fails to learn from the title flashing under Taylor's name – "CSIS
Military Analyst" – is that "CSIS is a markedly conservative organization that forms a sort of interlocking directorate with the Washington
establishment ... That it has received $50,000 to $250,000 from such
defense contractors as Boeing, General Dynamics, Rockwell, Honey-
well and Westinghouse. [And that its annual report boasts: 'we network in Washington with the Congress, the executive branch, the
scholarly community, the corporate and labor communities and the
media.'"[17]

It is not difficult to understand why think tanks covet media attention. After all, as the Heritage Foundation, the AEI, the Brookings Institution, the Fraser Institute, the C.D. Howe Institute, and others have discovered, media coverage can and does play a critical role in allowing institutes to effectively market their message. But what makes some think tanks more media friendly than others? Although this topic will be examined more fully in the next chapter, a few factors are worth noting. First, think tanks that have large and diverse research programs supported by dozens of staff are likely better positioned to attract more media exposure than institutes offering only a narrow range of expertise. Think tanks such as many of those mentioned above appeal to journalists because they can comment on a range of domestic and foreign policy issues. In a sense, the AEI, the Heritage Foundation, and the Brookings Institution function as one-stop policy shops. They also appeal to journalists who are consciously looking for a particular political perspective on an issue. When reporters call the Heritage Foundation or the Fraser Institute, which are well known for their commitment to free market principles, they can be assured that any proposal by the president or Congress or by the prime minister to increase taxes will be criticized. Knowing what positions think tanks will generally take may also account for the media's reliance on the same group of think tank scholars. The reliability of policy experts is also a consideration, as Crowley noted, particularly when journalists are under tight deadlines. Sam Donaldson of ABC news agrees:

Clearly there are problems with going to the same people ... [But] to sit down while you're facing a deadline and say, "Gee, there must be some other experts we haven't thought of. Let's beat the bushes and launch a search of the city or the country for them." Well, that takes a lot of time and energy because for TV it involves a lot more than flipping a card on the Rolodex. A second reason is that we know [some guys] provide a succinct response. You can't come to me and say, "Sam, I know you're on a deadline, you need to comment on such and such, go out and take a chance on Mr X. No, I'm sorry folks, I don't have the time to take a chance with Mr X ... I know Mr Y ... is going to deliver the goods.[18]

As Donaldson implies, how effective pundits are at communicating their ideas to the public in a straightforward and meaningful way is also important. Tammy Haddad of *Larry King Live* agrees, observing that "there are so many people out there who know so much, but they're lousy guests. They have to be able to explain [issues] in such a way that my mother in Pittsburgh understands what they're talking about."[19] During newscasts it becomes even more crucial for guests to be succinct – they do not have the time to offer long exposés on the state of the world. Those scholars who realize what the broadcast media require will continue to find their names on newsroom rolodexes.

STUDYING THINK TANK INFLUENCE

Think tanks frequently boast about their influence in the policy-making community. For example, a few months after Ronald Reagan entered the oval office, Heritage Foundation president Edwin Feulner claimed that over 60 percent of the policy recommendations included in his institute's mammoth study, *Mandate for Leadership*, had been or were in the process of being implemented by the Reagan administration. Feulner's remarks, to his delight, appeared in several newspapers throughout the United States. What most journalists failed to point out, however, was that many of the recommendations Feulner was taking credit for had been proposed by other individuals and institutes years before. The illusion of the Heritage Foudation's newly acquired policy influence, fostered in part by the media, had become reality.[20] Similarly, when asked to consider what federal government programs or policies his institute had helped shape in the previous ten years, Michael Walker of the Fraser Institute remarked, in part, "the Fraser Institute has played a central role in most policy developments during the last decade and it is simply too onerous a task to specify."[21]

Equally onerous is determining the extent to which think tanks have influenced public opinion and public policy. Although the Fraser Institute would like potential donors to believe Milton Friedman, the Nobel prize winning economist who stated that "the Fraser Institute has become a remarkably influential think tank: one of the most influential in the world," or former British prime minister Margaret Thatcher, who acknowledged that "the great work [Fraser has done] has had a tremendous influence," it is notoriously difficult to assess the influence of think tanks.[22]

To a large extent, evaluating think tank influence is inherently difficult because directors of policy institutes, not to mention those who study them, have different perceptions of what constitutes influence and how it can best be obtained. For some think tank directors, the amount of media exposure their institute generates or the number of publications they produce is indicative of how much influence they wield. Conversely, some think tank directors rely on other performance indicators, such as how many staff have been appointed to senior government positions or the size of their budget, to assess their impact. What makes evaluating their influence even more difficult is that the policymakers, academics, and journalists who subscribe to think tank publications or attend conferences they sponsor invariably have different impressions of how useful or relevant their work is. In short, scholars cannot assume that think tanks measure influence in the same way, nor can they assume that policymakers and other consumers of their products use similar criteria to evaluate their work.

Even if think tanks used the same performance indicators and assigned the same priority to becoming involved at each stage of the policy-making process, numerous methodological obstacles would still have to be overcome to accurately measure their influence on public policy. Since dozens of individuals and organizations seek to influence policy debates through various channels, tracing the origin of a policy idea becomes problematic. In an increasingly crowded political arena, it is often difficult to isolate the voice or voices that made a difference. Moreover, it can take months, if not years, before an idea proposed by a think tank or any other nongovernmental organization for that matter, has any discernible impact. Indeed, by the time a policy initiative is introduced, it may not resemble a think tank's initial proposal at all.

Directors of think tanks can, and often do, provide anecdotal evidence to flaunt how much influence their institutes wield, but such pronouncements offer little insight into the relevance of think tanks in the policy-making process; claiming to have influence is far simpler than documenting how it was achieved. In the following chapter we will examine one approach that can be used to make more informed judgements about the relevance of think tanks at different stages. Rather than assuming that think tanks in general have influence or that some think tanks have more influence than others, we will evaluate which think tanks in Canada and the United States appear to be most actively involved at key stages of the policy-making process. Drawing on extensive empirical data for a handful of performance indicators, including media citations, parliamentary and congressional testimony, and consultations with bureaucratic departments, it is possible to demonstrate, particularly in Canada, that policymakers do not always rely on the most visible think tanks for information and advice. Several think tanks that generate little media attention are also invited to participate in various stages of policy-making.

CHAPTER FIVE

Public Visibility and Policy Relevance: Assessing the Influence of Think Tanks

Much has been written in recent years about the growing influence of the Heritage Foundation, the Fraser Institute, and several other think tanks in the United States and Canada. Those who study the burgeoning think tank population in these countries point to their ever-expanding output of publications, their appearances before congressional and parliamentary committees, and their considerable media exposure as evidence of their heightened importance in the policy-making community. This perception, as noted, is reinforced by directors of think tanks who often credit their institutes with influencing major policy debates and government legislation. While it is not surprising that think tanks exaggerate their impact in policy making, it is surprising that few journalists, or scholars for that matter, have considered whether the increased media visibility of policy institutes is indicative of how relevant or active they are. Indeed, rather than acknowledging that think tanks exercise different types of influence at different stages of the policy-making cycle, it is assumed that the most talked-about and written-about think tanks are those best suited and equipped to influence public policy.

As funding agencies begin to place more pressure on think tanks to provide some indication of how much of an impact they have had in shaping public policy and as scholars struggle to assess the nature of policy influence, it is important to consider ways in which we can provide more informed observations about the involvement of think tanks in the policy-making process. One approach is to undertake a quantitative assessment of think tank performance by measuring, for instance, how much media exposure they have generated and how often staff from various think tanks have testified before legislative committees. Keeping track of other performance indicators, such as the number of publications think tanks produce and how many conferences and seminars they hold, might also be worth considering.[1]

Although there are potential pitfalls in relying too heavily on a quantitative assessment of think tank performance, as will become clear, there are also some important benefits. At the very least, by tracking how much media exposure think tanks generate and how often they appear before legislative committees, we can more easily determine how active or inactive think tanks are.

The purpose of this chapter, in undertaking a quantitative assessment of think tank influence, is to challenge the widely held perception that the most visible think tanks must also, by implication, be the most influential. To do so, I will address one important and frequently ignored question: Do policy institutes that generate high media exposure (hereafter referred to as public visibility) also engage actively in other important phases of the federal government's policy formulation process – consultation with government departments and testimony before congressional and parliamentary committees (two indicators of policy relevance)? In other words, can we expect think tanks that are effective at capturing media attention to be as effective at or interested in participating in other stages of policy-making? Interestingly enough, in comparing the media visibility and policy relevance of think tanks in Canada and the United States, two very different patterns emerge.

As Kent Weaver and Andrew Rich discovered in examining the visibility of fifty-one U.S. think tanks, institutes that attract considerable media exposure are more likely to be called upon to testify before congressional committees than are those with modest media profiles.[2] Moreover, as Rich observed in a separate study, there appears to be a relationship between think tanks that enjoy high media exposure and those that policy-makers and other opinion leaders consider the most influential.[3]

By contrast, when the public visibility and policy relevance of a select group of Canadian policy institutes is measured, a different set of observations come to light.[4] As in Weaver and Rich's study, the data on the public visibility of Canadian think tanks reveal that with few exceptions the print and broadcast media in Canada rely disproportionately on the same group of policy institutes: the Conference Board of Canada, the Fraser Institute, the C.D. Howe Institute, and the now-defunct Economic Council of Canada rank among the think tanks most often cited by the media. Several factors that will be discussed could account for the media's reliance on these institutes. However, in Canada high media exposure does not appear to be a precondition for advising senior public servants and policy-makers. In fact, two institutes that advise several government departments, the Canadian Policy Research Networks, Inc., and the Caledon Institute of Social Policy, have, relative to other institutes in Canada, limited public visibility. A simple ranking test confirms that there is no correlation between public visibility and the number of departments institutes consult with. Furthermore, no correlation is found between the number of departments Canadian think tanks consult with and the number of appearances they make before parliamentary committees. Nonetheless, a strong relationship appears to exist between public visibility and parliamentary testimony.

This chapter begins by evaluating Weaver and Rich's work on the visibility and impact of American think tanks and the many lessons that can be drawn from their analyses. Then the public visibility of a cross-section of Canadian think tanks will be discussed. Several reasons will be offered to explain why some think tanks in Canada have generated considerably more media exposure than others. Following this, the relevance of Canadian policy institutes during the phases of policy formulation mentioned above will be examined. Think tanks will be ranked according to the number of departments that list them as consultants and the number of appearances they have made before parliamentary committees. A Spearman's rho, a statistical test to measure the correlation between two sets of ranked variables, will be used to assess the relationship between media visibility and policy relevance. The final section will briefly discuss what additional steps scholars can take to assess the influence of think tanks.

THINK TANKS AND THE AMERICAN MEDIA

As the previous chapter discussed, gaining access to the media has become one of the most common and important methods think tanks employ to convey their ideas to policy-makers and to the public. And for think tanks committed to advocating a particular point of view, achieving widespread media exposure is critical: "Without a mass constituency backing their efforts, the influence of expertise-providing organizations often depends on the visibility their research obtains. Moreover, media visibility is often assessed as a measure of the organizational viability and success of research organizations by those who might fund their activities."[5]

To determine which think tanks in the United States generate the most media exposure, Weaver and Rich analyzed references to fifty-one national and regionally focused think tanks in six national newspapers (the *Washington Post*, the *New York Times*, the *Christian Science Monitor*, USA *Today*, the *Wall Street Journal* and the *Washington Times*) between 1991 and 1996.[6] A sample of their findings is given in table 5.1.

In analyzing these data, Weaver and Rich discovered that among the many factors that could explain why some think tanks generated considerably more media exposure than others, two important variables

Table 5.1
Newspaper Citations for Selected American Think Tanks, 1991–97

Institute	Washington Post DC	New York Times	Christian Science Monitor	USA Today	Wall Street Journal	Washington Times DC	Total
Brookings Institution	1,205	881	416	493	526	699	4,220
American Enterprise Institute	602	487	239	171	487	737	2,723
Carnegie Endowment for International Peace	647	317	153	335	384	236	2072
Cato Institute	320	165	57	132	332	831	1,837
Center for Strategic and International Studies	240	123	150	139	146	780	1,578
Heritage Foundation	105	142	39	46	255	731	1,318
Institute for Policy Studies	306	339	101	74	227	151	1,198
Progressive Policy Institute	315	261	155	62	127	236	1,156
Urban Institute	418	246	76	94	155	119	1,108
Worldwatch Institute	114	81	41	40	176	271	723
Hoover Institution	208	68	44	36	114	167	637
Hudson Institute	69	192	21	24	141	95	542
Manhattan Institute	67	49	74	24	21	38	273
RAND	74	35	11	9	6	53	188
Rockford Institute	3	7	2	0	8	50	70

Source: Data set compiled by R. Kent Weaver and Andrew Rich.

stood out – funding and location. First, as the authors observe, "Money is critical for a think tank to gain visibility and get its message out ... Our analysis suggests that this funding translates into media visibility, which, in turn, may encourage additional financing for visible organizations." With some notable exceptions, including RAND, which boasts the largest budget of all U.S. think tanks, and the well-heeled Urban Institute and Hoover Institution, think tanks with significant financial resources generated the most media attention.[7] Of the top five institutes ranked by media visibility, none had budgets of less than $10 million. By contrast, think tanks with budgets below $1 million generated very little exposure.

Second, being located in Washington clearly provides think tanks with an advantage over institutes not based there in establishing contacts with the media. Weaver and Rich's data confirm that think tanks headquartered in Washington attract considerably more media attention: "Washington-based think tanks remain the overwhelmingly dominant players relative to think tanks based outside the beltway, not just as a function of size, but also of proximity, which promotes the development of personal relationships and networks among social scientists, journalists, and policymakers' staffs."[8] In short, think tanks with a Washington address have the added benefit of cultivating ties to journalists who cover national politics. As the previous chapter demonstrated, once journalists have assembled a list of local experts to contact, there may be little need to expand their rolodex.

Weaver and Rich did not examine the amount of exposure think tanks generated in the broadcast media during the same period, but it appears from table 5.2 that they would likely have arrived at similar conclusions. All those that ranked high in print media exposure also attracted the attention of television journalists. Ranked first in the number of citations it received in the print media, the Brookings Institution topped the list of institutes that received the most attention on America's four major televison networks (ABC, NBC, CBS, and CNN). Between 1991 and 1997, staff from Brookings appeared on evening news broadcasts 171 times, more than twice as often as staff from the Carnegie Endowment for International Peace (69 times) and the American Enterprise Institute (61 times) and more than three times as often as spokespersons from the Heritage Foundation (47 times). With the exception of RAND, think tanks located outside the Beltway received little, if any, television exposure.

But Are They Relevant?

Think tanks that attract considerable media exposure in the United States are also effective at relying on other channels to shape public

Table 5.2
ABC, NBC, CBS, and CNN Evening News Citations
for Selected American Think Tanks, 1991–97

Institute	1991	1992	1993	1994	1995	1996	1997	Total
Brookings Institution	47	40	26	12	15	13	18	171
Carnegie Endowment for International Peace	15	8	12	19	7	7	1	69
American Enterprise Institute	10	9	14	9	8	6	5	61
Heritage Foundation	8	11	7	1	8	4	8	47
Center for Strategic and International Studies	7	5	8	15	2	1	4	42
RAND	2	4	3	3	1	5	6	24
Progressive Policy Institute	1	5	0	1	5	0	1	13
Worldwatch Institute	2	3	2	2	0	0	3	12
Urban Institute	0	0	0	0	0	1	1	2
Cato Institute	0	0	0	0	0	1	0	1
Hoover Institution	0	0	0	1	0	0	0	1
Rockford Institute	0	0	0	0	0	0	0	0
Manhattan Institute	0	0	0	0	0	0	0	0
Institute for Policy Studies	0	0	0	0	0	0	0	0
Hudson Institute	0	0	0	0	0	0	0	0

Source: Vanderbilt University Television News Archive.

policy. Indeed, many of the think tanks that dominate the airwaves and the op-ed pages of newspapers also make regular appearances before congressional committees. And just as bias in certain news organizations may account for why some think tanks are quoted more often than others, the ideological preferences of committee members appear to influence which institutes appear before Congress.[9] As Weaver and Rich note in a separate study, "data on congressional testimony demonstrate the powerful effects of 'gatekeeping' by the majority parties in Congress." They state that "Prior to the Republican takeover of Congress in 1994, staff members from the Brookings Institution were the most frequent think tank testifiers at Congressional hearings in most years, often followed by witnesses from the more conservative American Enterprise Institute. In 1995, with Republican legislators and staff controlling the bulk of witness slots, the Heritage Foundation became the most frequently represented think tank, followed by the AEI, the libertarian Cato Institute, and Brookings, in that order. Testimony by liberal think tanks lagged far behind."[10]

Many of the conservative think tanks that frequently testify before Congress are perceived to have the most influence in the political process. In a 1997 survey conducted for the global consulting firm Burson-Marstellar, Rich noted that of the 110 congressional staff and

Washington-based journalists surveyed, "68 percent of respondents identified conservative think tanks as having a greater impact on policy-making than liberal think tanks: only five percent named liberal think tanks as being most influential."[11] The Heritage Foundation was considered by 42 percent of respondents as the single most influential think tank; Brookings was ranked second by 28 percent of respondents. However, when asked to rank institutes according to their credibility, think tanks with no identifiable ideology ranked considerably higher than either the liberal or the conservative think tanks.

Weaver and Rich's findings on the media visibility and policy relevance of U.S. think tanks provide an interesting contrast when making a similar study of those in Canada. While the size and funding of institutes are important in attracting media exposure, being located in Ottawa does not offer policy institutes a decisive advantage. An Ottawa address may explain why some think tanks appear before parliamentary committees and consult with federal government departments more often than those located outside the nation's capital. Yet, with few exceptions institutes that receive the most media attention are based elsewhere. In short, the amount of media exposure think tanks in Canada generate may have more to do with the type of expertise they offer than with their proximity to policy-makers.

In addition, unlike the situation in the U.S. Congress, the frequency with which think tanks testify before parliamentary committees does not appear to be heavily influenced by the party in power. The gatekeeping phenomenon identified by Weaver and Rich is clearly not as important a factor in Canada as it appears to be in the United States. Finally, while there is a moderately strong correlation between think tanks that generate high media exposure in Canada and those that are invited to testify before legislative committees, the most visible think tanks are not necessarily those that policymakers always consider the most relevant. If consultations with federal government departments can be considered an indicator of policy relevance, some of the least visible think tanks in Canada may be having the greatest impact at the most critical stages of the policy cycle.

THINK TANKS AND THE CANADIAN MEDIA

Although references to think tanks in newspapers and on radio and television tell us little about their impact in shaping public opinion or about the quality of their commentaries, data on media exposure can offer some insight into which institutes are actively attempting to influence specific policy debates. It can also reveal in which parts of the country think tanks generate the most attention and whether the age, size, and financial resources of institutes influence the amount of exposure they receive

Together, four think tanks, the Conference Board of Canada, the C.D. Howe Institute, the Fraser Institute, and the now defunct Economic Council of Canada, generated 60 percent of all media citations between 1985 and 1999. The Conference Board alone, which ranks first in public visibility, received close to 25 percent of all media coverage. Indeed, it is only on CBC Radio that the Conference Board does not rank first in citations – it shares a sixth-place ranking with the Mackenzie Institute (table 5.3), which places nineteenth in overall visibility. The Canadian Tax Foundation (CTF), well known for its

Table 5.3
References to Selected Canadian Think Tanks on CBC Radio, 1988–96

Institute	Total
C.D. Howe Institute	110
Fraser Institute	58
Economic Council of Canada	43
Canadian Institute of Strategic Studies	27
Caledon Institute of Social Policy	21
Canadian Centre for Policy Alternatives	21
Conference Board of Canada	18
Mackenzie Institute	18
Canada West Foundation	14
Science Council of Canada	14
National Council of Welfare	13
North-South Institute	12
Canadian Council on Social Development	10
Institute for Research on Public Policy	10
Pearson-Shoyama Institute	10
Canadian Tax Foundation	8
Canadian Institute for International Peace and Security	7
Canadian Council for International Peace and Security[1]	7
Canadian Institute of International Affairs	2
Parliamentary Centre	2
Public Policy Forum	2
Canadian Policy Research Network[2]	–

Source: These data were obtained from the CBC Radio Archives, Toronto. In 1994, the CBC introduced a new computer system (Prolog) for logging citations on newscasts and radio talk shows. Though more comprehensive in scope than the previous database, the majority of institutes in this table could not be accessed by Prolog. As a result, this table underestimates citations. The trends that are observed, however, provide an indication of think-tank visibility on radio programs.

[1] Includes data for its two predecessors, Canadian Centre for Arms Control and Disarmament and Centre for Global Security.

[2] Data not included.

commentary on tax reform and budgetary matters, rounds off the top five institutes in the media visibility category, despite securing a fifth-place ranking in only one category, newspaper citations (including the *Globe and Mail*). Beyond the top four think tanks there is tremendous fluctuation in media rankings. The former Science Council of Canada received more citations than the Canadian Tax Foundation in the *Globe and Mail*. On CBC Radio the Canadian Tax Foundation was out-ranked by eleven institutes, including the Science Council, the National Council of Welfare, the Canadian Council on Social Development, and the Canadian Centre for Policy Alternatives. Moreover, on the CBC and CTV national evening news, the Toronto–based Canadian Institute of Strategic Studies generated more coverage than the Canadian Tax Foundation. On CTV three other institutes, the National Council of Welfare, the Mackenzie Institute, and the Canada West Foundation had slightly more on–screen appearances or text references than the Cana-dian Tax Foundation. Of the twenty-two policy institutes for which data on media citations were collected, only half generated more than 1,000 references. The eleventh-ranked institute, the Canadian Institute of Strategic Studies, received 1,007 citations, 915 more than the lowest-ranked institute, the Parliamentary Centre (92) (table 5.4).

What factors could account for these rankings? Why do the media rely disproportionately on four to five policy institutes? A number of possible explanations are worth exploring. A useful point of departure is to consider when the institutes generating the most media attention were created, since one might expect the more established think tanks to attract more exposure. Of the five institutes registering the highest media ranking, the oldest is the Canadian Tax Foundation, established in 1945, followed by the Conference Board (1954), the Economic Council (1963), the C.D. Howe Institute (1973), and the Fraser Institute (1974).

The longevity of an institute may go some way to establish its legitimacy in the policy- making community, but it does not appear to be a crucial factor in attracting media attention, a finding consistent with Weaver and Rich's study of U.S. think tanks. Several policy institutes including the Canadian Council on Social Development (CCSD, 1920) and the Canadian Institute of International Affairs (CIIA, 1928), with considerably lower media rankings, predate C.D. Howe, Fraser, and the Conference Board by decades.

The size of an institute's budget, which in turn influences how many staff it employs and the range of expertise it offers, may provide a more compelling explanation. The Conference Board, the largest policy institute in Canada, ranks first, with an annual budget in excess of $20 million, close to ten times that of the majority of Canadian think tanks. Only five other institutes, three of which were created and funded by the government (the Economic Council, the Science Council and the Canadian Institute for International Peace and Security), had budgets in excess of $2 million. Of the remaining two, the Canadian Policy Research Networks, Inc., receives 70 percent of its close to $3 million budget from the federal government, while the Fraser Institute does not accept any of its approximately $3 million budget from government sources.[12] There appears to be a strong relationship between high media visibility and the amount of funding think tanks draw on; however, there are notable anomalies as well. The C.D. Howe Institute, which ranks third overall in visibility, has a budget of between $1.5 and $3 million, comparable to that of several less visible institutes, including the Parliamentary Centre, the North-South Institute, and the Canadian Institute of International Affairs.

Closely related to the budgets of institutes is the number of staff they employ. Again, the Conference Board ranks first. It employs over 200 people who provide research and analysis on economic and social issues.[13] Its ability to construct economic forecasting models is particularly attractive to government and to a large number of corporations who form part of its extensive client list. The Conference Board's size may help to explain why it attracts almost twice the amount of media exposure as the Fraser Institute. The next largest institute, the Economic Council of Canada, employed 118 people prior to being disbanded; the Fraser Institute, also considered large by Canadian standards, employs 35 full–time and 13 part–time people; the C.D. Howe Institute follows with a staff of 13. However, there are a handful of others that are comparable in size to or larger than the C.D. Howe Institute, including the Canadian Council on Social Development (24), the North–South Institute (18), and the Institute for Research on Public Policy (14), but that have much less visibility. In short, with the exception of some anomalies, the size of an institute's budget and the number of staff it employs may explain why some generate more exposure than others.[14]

Not surprisingly, think tanks with limited funding and few staff will not be able to undertake long-range research projects or organize regular conferences and seminars that could generate media attention. Moreover, it is unlikely that they would employ staff for the sole purpose of marketing their institute's outputs; with limited funds, this function is normally shared among the staff. Think tanks with large budgets can, should they elect to, hire public relations specialists to enhance their institute's profile. The Heritage Foundation, the Brookings Institution, the Hoover Institution, and the American Enterprise Institute, to name a few, have well-established public relations departments.

Table 5.4
Media Citations for Selected Canadian Think Tanks

	Newspaper Total[1]	Globe and Mail[2]	CBC Radio[3]	CBC TV News[4]	CTV News[4]	Total	Rank
Conference Board of Canada	6,289	2,204	18	57	59	8,627	1
Fraser Institute	3,790	761	58	47	27	4,683	2
C.D. Howe Institute	3,053	1,290	110	55	45	4,553	3
Economic Council of Canada	2,033	1,318	43	40	17	3,451	4
Canadian Tax Foundation	999	473	8	22	4	1,506	5
Science Council of Canada	714	618	14	12	4	1,362	6
National Council of Welfare	952	286	13	13	9	1,273	7
Canadian Council on Social Development	885	354	10	19	4	1,272	8
Institute for Research on Public Policy	747	347	10	3	2	1,109	9
Canada West Foundation	824	210	14	16	5	1,069	10
Canadian Institute of Strategic Studies	770	162	27	33	15	1,007	11
North South Institute	497	279	12	3	0	791	12
Canadian Centre for Policy Alternatives	629	118	21	13	4	785	13
Canadian Institute for International Peace and Security	558	119	7	10	3	697	14
Canadian Council for International Peace and Security[5]	479	173	7	0	0	659	15
Public Policy Forum	490	91	2	1	0	584	16
Caledon Institute of Social Policy	381	124	21	5	0	531	17
Canadian Institute of International Affairs	360	159	2	5	3	529	18
Mackenzie Institute	291	42	18	7	8	366	19
Canadian Policy Research Networks	136	60	0	2	1	199	20
Pearson-Shoyama Institute	154	21	10	0	0	185	21
Parliamentary Centre	60	30	2	0	0	92	22

[1] Source: Infomart, includes citations from January 1985 to December 1999 for papers as described in appendix 1.

[2] Source: Info Globe, includes citations from January 1985 to December 1999.

[3] Source: CBC Radio Archives; includes citations from January 1988 to December 1996.

[4] Source: National Media Archive, Fraser Institute; includes citations and appearances from January 1988 to December 1999.

[5] Includes references to its two predecessors, Canadian Centre for Arms Control and Disarmament and Canadian Centre for Global Security, for all media citations, with the exception of CBC and CTV National News

Table 5.5
Newspaper Citations for Selected Canadian Think Tanks, 1985–99

	Ottawa Citizen	Toronto Star	Montreal Gazette	Vancouver Sun	Edmonton Journal	Calgary Herald	Halifax Daily News	Toronto Sun	TOTAL
Conference Board of Canada	1,261	984	961	780	787	801	436	279	6,289
Fraser Institute	549	455	366	1,007	480	482	187	264	3,790
C.D. Howe Institute	619	652	581	346	332	275	155	93	3,053
Economic Council of Canada	473	534	341	216	177	162	76	54	2,033
Canadian Tax Foundation	219	165	164	115	115	128	50	43	999
National Council on Welfare	177	214	129	118	133	119	31	31	952
Canadian Council on Social Development	208	193	138	92	94	115	31	14	885
Canada West Foundation	70	51	67	76	225	309	17	9	824
Canadian Institute of Strategic Studies	161	150	70	104	90	99	60	36	770
Institute for Research on Public Policy	216	116	170	90	69	54	24	8	747
Science Council of Canada	234	184	94	85	60	38	16	3	714
Canadian Centre for Policy Alternatives	136	97	65	153	64	58	46	10	629
Canadian Institute for International Peace and Security	183	123	59	65	59	55	11	3	558
North-South Institute	173	123	98	37	32	24	7	3	497
Public Policy Forum	228	34	56	20	73	56	9	14	490
Canadian Council for International Peace and Security[1]	127	170	48	55	38	26	11	4	479
Caledon Institute of Social Policy	105	74	37	38	42	44	29	12	381

Table 5.5 (continued)

	Ottawa Citizen	Toronto Star	Montreal Gazette	Vancouver Sun	Edmonton Journal	Calgary Herald	Halifax Daily News	Toronto Sun	TOTAL
Canadian Institute of International Affairs	93	71	103	28	30	19	10	6	360
Mackenzie Institute	41	58	19	67	35	21	10	40	291
Pearson-Shoyama Institute	20	56	2	6	3	66	1	0	154
Canadian Policy Research Networks	29	28	10	12	37	12	6	2	136
Parliamentary Centre	24	9	3	6	9	6	2	1	60
Total	5,346	4,541	3,581	3,516	2,984	2,969	1,225	929	25,091

Source: Infomart.

[1] Includes references to its two predecessors, Canadian Centre for Arms Control and Disarmament and Canadian Centre for Global Security.

With few exceptions, however, this does not appear to be the pattern in Canadian think tanks; even policy institutes with reasonably high budgets by Canadian standards rarely assign more than a fraction of it for marketing purposes.[15]

A related and perhaps more important consideration in discussing media exposure is the diversity of an institute's research; think tanks that offer expertise in a wide range of policy areas are likely to attract more media exposure than those that focus on only one or two. For example, the North–South Institute and the Canadian Institute of Strategic Studies may be asked to comment on foreign policy developments, but they are unlikely to write about or provide commentary on tax and constitutional issues, subjects that generate considerable press coverage. How think tanks use their expertise in novel ways to engage the public is also a consideration in explaining their success in attracting media attention. For instance, the Fraser Institute's annual pronouncement of Tax Freedom Day, the day when Canadians, not the Canada Customs and Revenue Agency, begin to keep the money they have earned generates dozens of media citations for the free market-oriented institute each year.

The mandate of institutes may also explain why some organizations receive more exposure than others and why some institutes generate more media attention in specific regions of the country. The Calgary-based Canada West Foundation is a case in point. Established to study the social and economic characteristics of the western and northern regions of Canada and to assess the West's economic and social contributions, the Canada West Foundation , not surprisingly, receives the majority of its media exposure in Western newspapers, such as the *Calgary Herald* (309) and the *Edmonton Journal* (225) (table 5.5). Combined, these two papers account for close to 65 percent of its media exposure in Canadian newspapers (*Globe and Mail* excluded). In the *Globe and Mail* table 5.6, which, until recently, was regarded as Canada's only national newspaper, the Canada West Foundation received just over 2 percent of references to think tanks. The Canada West Foundation's emphasis on regional issues may also explain its limited exposure relative to other think tanks on the CTV (2.4 percent) and CBC (4.4 percent) national evening news (tables 5.7 and 5.8).

Despite these findings, being located outside the nation's capital need not be a disadvantage for think tanks seeking media visibility. In Canada a very different pattern emerges from that in the U.S.; ranked second in overall visibility, Vancouver's Fraser Institute is close to three thousand miles from Ottawa; the C.D. Howe Institute, the third ranked institute, is in downtown Toronto. Meanwhile, several think tanks based in Ottawa, including the Parliamentary Centre, the Caledon

Table 5.6
Globe and Mail Citations for Selected Canadian Think Tanks, 1985–99

Institute	Total
Conference Board of Canada	2,204
Economic Council of Canada	1,318
C.D. Howe Institute	1,290
Fraser Institute	761
Science Council of Canada	618
Canadian Tax Foundation	473
Canadian Council on Social Development	354
Institute for Research on Public Policy	347
National Council of Welfare	286
North-South Institute	279
Canada West Foundation	210
Canadian Council for International Peace and Security[1]	173
Canadian Institute of Strategic Studies	162
Canadian Institute of International Affairs	159
Caledon Institute of Social Policy	124
Canadian Institute for International Peace and Security	119
Canadian Centre for Policy Alternatives	118
Public Policy Forum	91
Canadian Policy Research Networks	60
Mackenzie Institute	42
Parliamentary Centre	30
Pearson-Shoyama Institute	21

Source: Info Globe.

[1] Includes references to its two predecessors, CCACD and CGS.

Institute, the Canadian Centre for Policy Alternatives, the Pearson-Shoyama Institute, and the Canadian Council for International Peace and Security, have limited public visibility. Thus, it may be that a determining factor in generating media exposure for Canadian think tanks is not location but their mandate and resources

Think tank resources are important when considering their media visibility, but so too are other less tangible factors. Simply put, the priorities they assign to attracting media attention may help explain why some think tanks receive more exposure than others. For instance, for institutes committed to shaping the parameters of national public debates, gaining access to the media will undoubtedly be a high priority. It would, after all, be difficult for think tanks to influence public opinion without publicizing their ideas in print or on the air. As a result, individuals from some think tanks, including the Fraser Institute and the Canadian Institute of Strategic Studies, like their counterparts in the Heritage Foundation and CSIS, welcome opportunities to appear on network newscasts. These and other think tanks

Table 5-7
CTV National Evening News Citations for Selected Canadian Think Tanks, 1988–99

Institute	1988	1989	1990	1991	1992	1993	1994	1995	1996	1997	1998	1999	Total
Conference Board of Canada	1	5	7	9	7	7	5	4	5	3	3	3	59
C.D. Howe Institute	1	0	2	6	2	3	3	0	1	15	11	1	45
Fraser Institute	0	1	0	2	4	2	6	5	2	1	2	2	27
Economic Council of Canada	3	2	4	2	4	0	0	1	1	0	0	0	17
Canadian Institute of Strategic Studies	0	2	5	3	3	0	2	0	0	0	0	0	15
National Council of Welfare	0	0	2	1	0	1	0	1	1	0	2	1	9
Mackenzie Institute	0	0	0	1	0	0	0	2	0	3	2	0	8
Canada West Foundation	0	0	0	3	2	0	0	0	0	0	0	0	5
Canadian Tax Foundation	0	0	1	0	0	1	0	2	0	0	0	0	4
Science Council of Canada	0	0	0	0	2	0	0	0	0	0	2	0	4
Canadian Centre for Policy Alternatives	0	0	0	0	0	1	0	2	0	0	0	1	4
Canadian Council of Social Development	0	1	0	1	0	2	0	0	0	0	0	1	4
Canadian Institute for International Peace and Security	0	0	2	1	0	0	0	0	0	0	0	0	3
Institute for Research on Public Policy	0	0	2	0	0	0	0	0	1	0	0	2	3
Canadian Institute of International Affairs	0	0	0	0	0	0	0	0	0	0	1	0	1
Canadian Policy Research Network	0	0	0	0	0	0	0	0	0	0	0	0	0
Canadian Council for International Peace and Security[1]	0	0	0	0	0	0	0	0	0	0	0	0	0
Caledon Institute of Social Policy	0	0	0	0	0	0	0	0	0	0	0	0	0
North-South Institute	0	0	0	0	0	0	0	0	0	0	0	0	0
Parliamentary Centre	0	0	0	0	0	0	0	0	0	0	0	0	0
Pearson-Shoyama Institute	0	0	0	0	0	0	0	0	0	0	0	0	0
Public Policy Forum[2]	0	0	0	0	0	0	0	0	0	0	0	0	0
Total	5	11	25	28	24	17	16	17	11	22	23	11	210

Source: The national Media Archive, Fraser Institute
1 Data do not include information on its two predecessors, Canadian Centre for Arms Control and Disarmament and Canadian Centre for Global Security.
2 Data not included.

Table 5.8
CBC TV National Evening News Citations for Selected Canadian Think Tanks, 1988–99

Institute	1988	1989	1990	1991	1992	1993	1994	1995	1996	1997	1998	1999	Total
Conference Board of Canada	5	7	7	7	9	6	1	3	3	4	3	2	57
C.D. Howe Institute	2	3	4	5	2	4	7	4	4	11	7	2	55
Fraser Institute	0	2	0	5	3	8	4	9	6	2	4	4	47
Economic Council of Canada	9	1	4	12	7	2	1	2	1	0	0	1	40
Canadian Institute of Strategic Studies	1	1	5	12	5	4	2	1	1	0	0	1	33
Canadian Tax Foundation	0	2	0	1	0	5	3	4	1	3	1	2	22
Canada West Foundation	0	0	2	5	5	1	0	0	2	0	1	0	16
Canadian Council on Social Development	1	1	0	1	5	3	2	0	2	0	1	3	19
Canadian Centre for Policy Alternatives	0	2	0	4	1	1	0	2	2	0	1	0	13
National Council of Welfare	2	2	1	1	1	1	0	0	1	1	3	0	13
Science Council of Canada	1	0	0	4	2	0	0	0	0	2	3	0	12
Canadian Institute for International Peace and Security	0	2	4	3	1	0	1	1	1	1	0	0	10
Mackenzie Institute	0	0	0	0	1	0	0	1	1	1	1	1	7
Canadian Institute of International Affairs	1	0	0	0	0	0	0	0	2	1	0	1	5
Caledon Institute of Social Policy	0	0	0	0	0	0	2	0	1	0	1	1	5
Institute for Research on Public Policy	1	0	2	0	0	0	0	0	1	0	0	0	3
North-South Institute	0	0	0	0	0	1	0	1	1	0	0	0	3
Canadian Council for International Peace and Security[1]	0	0	0	0	0	0	0	0	0	0	0	0	0
Canadian Policy Research Network, Inc.	0	0	0	0	0	0	0	0	0	0	0	2	2
Parliamentary Centre	0	0	0	0	0	0	0	0	0	0	2	0	2
Pearson-Shoyama Institute	0	0	0	0	0	0	0	0	0	0	0	0	0
Public Policy Forum[2]	0	0	0	0	0	0	0	0	0	0	0	1	1
Total	23	23	29	60	43	36	23	27	28	25	26	20	363

Source: The National Media Archive, Fraser Institute.
[1] Data for CCACD and Centre for Global Security, the two predecessors of CCIPS, not included.
[2] Data not included.

also submit op-ed articles to newspapers on a regular basis, in the hope of stimulating public debate.

A less tangible factor, but one that nevertheless deserves consideration, is how the political environment in Canada can enhance or diminish the profile of some think tanks. For instance, as Prime Minister Mulroney moved closer to adopting the type of neo-conservative agenda that his close friends and allies Ronald Reagan and George Bush were adopting south of the border, the policy recommendations of the free-market-oriented Fraser Institute also began to receive more public attention. In other words, the amount of coverage an institute receives can be influenced by the political climate of the day.

Numerous other factors can influence the media ranking of policy institutes. Although only passing reference has been made to media bias (whether regional, ideological, or both), it may also be an important consideration when interpreting the data on public visibility. While many factors, such as the size and research diversity of an institute, may also explain why some are called upon to advise government departments or to testify before parliamentary committees, other factors, which will be explored below, might account for why think tanks with limited media visibility appear nonetheless to be actively engaged in critical stages of the policy-making process.

Assessing Policy Relevance

The policy-making process consists of several stages, or cycles, including agenda setting, policy formulation, and policy implementation.[16] This section focuses on the involvement of think tanks during two stages of policy formulation – consultations with government departments and parliamentary testimony. Although it is difficult to weigh the relative importance of different stages of policy-making, it is, nonetheless, possible to make more informed judgments about the relevance of institutes during particular phases.

Think tanks may become involved in policy formulation in several ways. They may, for instance, distribute copies of their reports on an issue to policy-makers and bureaucrats, in the hope that their findings will have an impact, or they may invite members of parliament and the bureaucracy to participate in conferences and workshops or hold private meetings with officials. Depending on their area and level of expertise, they may be called upon to consult with government departments or to testify before a parliamentary committee. At times the federal government might also enlist the support of think tanks to organize public hearings on policy issues. The data on think tank involvement during these particular stages of policy formulation may tell us little about the quality of their advice, but it does provides some indication of how active institutes have been in using these channels to convey their ideas.

As part of ongoing efforts to assess the policy capacity of the federal government, a task force headed by Ivan Fellegi, chief statistician of Canada, and Ole Ingstrup, then principal of the Canadian Centre for Management and Development, was created in late 1994 to investigate, among other things, the state of the external policy research community.[17] To this end, an umbrella group composed of assistant deputy ministers was formed to make recommendations on how to strengthen policy development and practices. The report, released in July 1997, made several recommendations on how to enhance the policy capacity of government, including improving ties between federal departments and policy institutes. This recommendation was based in part on responses from a survey distributed to government departments that asked senior civil servants to provide the names of research institutes that assist them in policy development. This list, summarized in table 5.9, offers additional insights into which think tanks are called upon to consult with government departments.

Some of the methodological weaknesses in how the data were gathered must be pointed out before discussing the ranking of institutes in government consultations. Many of these weaknesses reflect the tremendous difficulty that policymakers, not to mention scholars, encounter in trying to isolate the influence of think tanks from the influence of the multitude of other organizations that have vested interests in influencing policy-making. Thus, despite some apparent gaps in the questionnaire distributed to government departments, these data should not be considered unreliable but should be regarded as suggestive and preliminary.

While government departments were asked to provide a list of policy research organizations they turn to for advice and guidance (table 5.10), they were not asked several related questions that are critical to arriving at conclusions about their relevance. For instance, they were not asked what criteria they relied on to identify the policy research organizations among the dozens of other nongovernmental organizations committed to influencing public policy. In other words, it is conceivable that senior bureaucratic officials consulted with institutions that they may not have regarded as policy-research organizations but that are in fact policy-research organizations according to many studies. As a result, the lists that departments provided may not be entirely accurate. Furthermore, officials were not asked to comment on the frequency of consultations with institutes or the period over which the consultations took place. We are not told, for example, if

Table 5.9
Ranking Research Institute Consultations

Institute	Number of Department Consulting Think Tanks	Departments
Conference Board of Canada	9	Environment Canada, Department of Foreign Affairs and International Trade, Human Resources Development Canada, Industry Canada, National Defence, Natural Resources Canada, Canada Mortgage and Housing Corporation, Department of Finance, Canadian Heritage
Canadian Policy Research Networks	6	Environment Canda, Human Resources Development Canada, Industry Canada, Citizenship and Immigration Canada, Health Canada, Department of Justice
Canadian Council on Social Development	5	Human Resources Development Canada, Citizenship and Immigration Canada, Indian Affairs and Northern Development, Canada Mortgage and Housing Corporation, Department of Finance
Caledon Institute of Social Policy	3	Human Resources Development Canada, Canada Mortgage and Housing Corporation, Department of Finance
C.D. Howe Institute	3	Environment Canada, Industry Canada, Department of Finance
Public Policy Forum	2	Environment Canada, Natural Resources Canada
Canadian Institute of Strategic Studies	2	Department of Foreign Affairs and International Trade, National Defence
Institute for Research on Public Policy	2	Industry Canada, Department of Finance
Fraser Institute	2	Industry Canada, Department of Finance
CIIA	1	Department of Foreign Affairs and International Trade

Source: Department of Finance, Umbrella Group on Policy Management, Report.

Table 5.10
Federal Government Departments Consulting with Selected Think Tanks

	Number of Departments	Rank
Conference Board of Canada	9	1
Canadian Policy Research Networks	6	2
Canadian Council on Social Development	5	3
C.D. Howe Institute	3	4
Caledon Institute of Social Policy	3	4
Fraser Institute	2	5
Institute for Research on Public Policy	2	5
Canadian Institute of Strategic Studies	2	5
Public Policy Forum	2	5
Canada West Foundation	1	6
Canadian Institute of International Affairs	1	6
Economic Council of Canada	0	7
Canadian Tax Foundation	0	7
Science Council of Canada	0	7
National Council of Welfare	0	7
North-South Institute	0	7
Canadian Institute for International Peace and Security	0	7
Canadian Council for International Peace and Security	0	7
Canadian Centre for Policy Alternatives	0	7
Mackenzie Institute	0	7
Pearson-Shoyama Institute	0	7
Parliamentary Centre	0	7

Source: Department of Finance, Umbrella Group on Policy Management, Report.

Environment Canada consulted with the Caledon Institute once or one hundred times during a particular period. We are not even told what policy issues these institutes were consulting on or what the nature and products generated from these consultations were. Did institutes submit reports? Were they widely circulated? More importantly, were their analyses and recommendations, assuming some were made, found to be very useful, moderately useful, or not useful at all? Responses to the last question would be particularly revealing in relation to the size and prominence of departments. Thus, having moderate influence in high-profile departments such as Finance or Foreign Affairs and International Trade (DFAIT) may be more important for some think tanks than exercising considerable influence in a less visible department. Answers to these and other questions would provide a better sense of the data. In the absence of such information, however, we are left with only one indicator of relevance – the number of government departments that list policy-research organizations as consultants.

On the basis of these data, problematic and preliminary as they are, we can again provide a simple ranking. As in many other categories, the Conference Board ranks first in government consultations (9), a reflection no doubt of its wide-ranging expertise. The Canadian Policy Research Networks, Inc., according to the survey, consulted with at least six departments, one consultation more than the Canadian Council on Social Development.[18] Of the remaining institutes in the study, the Caledon Institute of Social Policy and the C.D. Howe Institute had three consultations, one more than the Canadian Institute of Strategic Studies, the Institute for Research on Public Policy, the Public Policy Forum, and the Fraser Institute.

The number of departments that turn to particular policy institutes for assistance can be attributed to several factors. First and foremost, the think tanks' areas of expertise will determine a department's decision about which one to consult. It is unlikely that the Canada Mortgage and Housing Corporation would seek policy input from CISS, which studies defence and foreign policy issues. A related factor is a department's perception of the quality of expertise offered by institutes. This, in turn, can be influenced by a host of other factors, including the personal and professional contacts personnel of think tanks have established with senior public servants. In other words, directors or personnel of think tanks who previously served in government may be better positioned to foster close ties to the public service than those with limited knowledge or experience with, or in, the bureaucracy.

A more reliable set of data on the relevance of policy institutes could be obtained by tracking the number of appearances think tanks make before parliamentary committees. Providing testimony to a committee as it considers implementing or revising legislation affords think tanks an important opportunity to convey their recommendations directly to policymakers. Extending invitations to members of think tanks to provide testimony can indicate how useful policymakers believe their input might be.

Individuals testifying before parliamentary committees (table 5.11) have either received a formal invitation to appear from the committee or have requested the opportunity to present their views. The decision about who will be invited to appear is made by committee members, often in consultation with staff members and public servants.[19] Between 1980 and 1999 no policy institute appeared before parliamentary committees more than the Economic Council of Canada, which registered 117 appearances (table 5.12), more than twice as many as the second-ranked institute, the Canadian Council on Social Development (57). It was followed by the Conference Board (44), the Fraser Institute (43), the North-South Institute (42), the Science Council

Table 5.11
Parliamentary Committee Reports Consulted for Think Tank Testimony

HOUSE COMMITTEES

Aboriginal Affairs and International Development
Acid Rain (Sub-Committee for Fisheries and Forestry)
Agriculture
Alternative Energy and Oil Substitution
Arms Exports
Bill C-17 (Sub-Committee for Finance Committee)
Bill C-29: Public Sector Compensation Act
Business of Supply (Sub-Committee for Procedure and House Affairs)
Canadian Heritage
Canadian Institute for International Peace and Security
Canadian Security Intelligence Service Act and Security Offenses Act Review
Communication and Culture
Consumer and Corporate Affairs
Electoral Reform
Employment Opportunities for the 1980s
Energy, Mines and Resources
Environment
Equality Rights (Sub-Committee for Justice and Legal Affairs)
Expenditure Priorities (Sub-Committee for Finance Committee)
External Affairs and International Trade
External Affairs and National Defence
Federal-Provincial Fiscal Arrangements
Finance, Trade and Economic Affairs
Government Operations
Health and Welfare
Human Resources and Development
Human Rights (Foreign Affairs and International Trade Committee)
Human Rights and Status of Disabled Persons
Immigration Consultants and Diminishing Returns
(Citizenship and Immigration Committee)
Indian Affairs and Northern Development
Industry, Science and Technology, Regional and Northern Development
International Debt
International Development (Sub-Committee of Committee
on External Affairs and National Defence)
International Financial Institutions (Sub-Committee for Finance Committee)
International Human Rights
International Trade (External Affairs and International Trade Committee)
Justice and Legal Affairs
Labour, Manpower and Immigration
Meech Lake Accord Proposed Companion Resolution
National Resources and Public Works
National Trading Corporation
North-South Relations
Peace Process in Central America

Table 5.11 (continued)

HOUSE COMMITTEES (CONTINUED)

Pension Reform
Procedure and House Affairs
Public Accounts
Reform of the House of Commons
Regional Development
Regulations and Competitiveness (Sub-committee for Finance Committee)
Regulatory Reform
Research, Science and Technology
Review of Employment Equity Act
Transport
Veterans Afairs

SENATE COMMITTEES

Agriculture and Forestry
Banking, Trade and Commerce
Bill C-21
Bill C-22
Canadian Security Intelligence Service
Energy and Natural Resources – Environment and Natural Resources
Fisheries
Foreign Affairs
Health, Welfare and Science
Mass Media
Meech Lake Constitutional Accord (Senate Submissions Group)
National Defence
National Finance
Northern Pipeline
Poverty
Retirement Age Policies
Science Policy
Social Affairs, Science and Technology
Training and Employment (Sub-Committee of Social Affairs,
Science and Technology Committee)
Transport and Communications
Veterans Affairs (Sub-Committee of Social Affairs, Science and Technology
Youth

JOINT COMMITTEES

Canada's Defence Policies
Canada's International Relations
Regulations and Other Statutory Instruments
The 1987 Constitutional Accord

Table 5.12
Appearances by Selected Think Tanks before Parliamentary Committees, 1980–99

	Number of Appearances	Rank
Economic Council of Canada	117	1
Canadian Council on Social Development	57	2
Conference Board of Canada	44	3
Fraser Institute	43	4
North-South Institute	42	5
Science Council of Canada	40	6
C.D. Howe Institute	38	7
Institute for Research on Public Policy	38	7
National Council of Welfare	37	8
Parliamentary Centre	34	9
Canadian Centre for Policy Alternatives	26	10
Caledon Institute of Social Policy	23	11
Canadian Council for International Peace and Security[1]	20	12
Canadian Institute for International Peace and Security	19	13
Canadian Institute of Strategic Studies	15	14
Canada West Foundation	14	15
Canadian Policy Research Networks	10	16
Canadian Institute of International Affairs	9	17
Canadian Tax Foundation	8	18
Mackenzie Institute	6	19
Public Policy Forum	4	20
Pearson-Shoyama Institute	4	20
Total	648	

Source: Parliamentary Committee Reports, Thirty-Second to Thirty-Sixth Parliament, First Session, 1980–99

[1] Includes references to its two predecessors, the Canadian Centre for Arms Control and Disarmament and the Canadian Centre for Global Security.

of Canada (40), the C.D. Howe Institute and the Institute for Research on Public Policy (both had 38), and the National Council of Welfare (37). Eight other institutes registered 10 or more appearances. Unlike the data on government consultants, the figures on parliamentary testimony reveal that far more policy institutes were represented at this stage of policymaking.

What factors influence how often think tanks appear before parliamentary committees? Again, the nature of their expertise, as well as their willingness and ability to invest the time and resources necessary to prepare testimony would have to be considered; proximity to Ottawa may be advantageous. The ideological orientation of committee members and their desire to invite like-minded think tanks to testify may also be worth taking into account. In the United States, as noted, there has been a marked increase in the number of appearances before congressional committees by conservative think tanks since the Republicans assumed control of both houses of Congress.[20] As gatekeepers, they have clearly made an effort to fill congressional hearings with analysts from avowedly conservative think tanks, including the Heritage Foundation, the American Enterprise Institute, and the libertarian Cato Institute. In Canada, however, there does not appear to be any relationship between the party in power and the ideological orientation of think tanks invited to testify. For instance, the Fraser Institute, not known for concealing its conservatism, has appeared before parliamentary committees more often under the Liberal government of Jean Chrétien than under Prime Minister Mulroney's Conservatives (see tables 5.13, 5.14 and 5.15).

While the ideological orientation of political parties and think tanks may not help to determine why some policy institutes are invited to testify more regularly than others, some consideration should be given to the range of committees think tanks are qualified to appear before. For think tanks that have a narrow range of expertise, such as the Canadian Institute of International Affairs and the Mackenzie Institute, the number of committees they could make presentations before are quite limited. Nonetheless, while they might appear before only a few committees, they may do so far more regularly than those institutes sharing their expertise with several committees. Much insight can be gained by focusing on the participation of think tanks before parliamentary committees, particularly high-profile committees; however, we cannot assume that all think tanks assign the same importance to using this channel to reach policymakers: briefing members of parliament may be a priority for some institutes, but it could also be a channel deliberately avoided by others. For instance, concerned about being perceived as a policy advocate, the highly visible Canadian Tax Foundation has made a conscious decision not to give testimony on a regular basis.[21] Since 1980 it has made only eight appearances before committees.

Interpreting the Results:
Comparing Public Visibility to Policy Relevance

To compare the public visibility and policy relevance of think tanks, three Spearman's rank correlation coefficients were used to test the correlation between the following pairs of variables: media ranking and parliamentary testimony, media ranking and government consultations, and government consultations and parliamentary testimony.[22] The results of the tests are shown in table 5.16. According to the tests, there is a strong correlation between media visibility and parliamentary

Table 5.13
Appearances of Institutes for House Committee Testimony, 1980–99, by Parliamentary Session

	Session				
Institute	32 (14/4/80–9/7/84) *Liberal*	33 (5/11/84–1/10/88) *PC*	34 (12/12/88–08/9/93) *PC*	35 (17/1/94–27/4/97) *Liberal*	36 (22/09/97–18/09/99) *Liberal*
C.D. Howe Institute	1	3	8	7	6
Caledon Institute				10	7
Canada West Foundation			1	6	
Canadian Tax Foundation					5
CCIPS	1	3	5	1	
CCPA			3	7	11
CCSD	10	1	6	7	6
CIIA	2				1
CIIPS			12		
CISS	1	1	7		
Conference Board of Canada		3	7	4	3
CPRN			1	1	5
Economic Council of Canada	8	12	16		
Fraser Institute	1	3	8	10	9
IRPP	2	1	7		
Mackenzie Institute			1		
National Council of Welfare		3	6	2	4

Table 5.13 (continued)

Institute	Session				
	32 (14/4/80–9/7/84)	33 (5/11/84–1/10/88)	34 (12/12/88–08/9/93)	35 (17/1/94–27/4/97)	36 (22/09/97–18/09/99)
	Liberal	*PC*	*PC*	*Liberal*	*Liberal*
North-South Institute	3	2	13	6	6
Parliamentary Centre	1			3	
Pearson-Shoyama Institute				2	
Public Policy Forum					1
Science Council of Canada	3	8	7		

Source: Parliamentary Committee Reports, 1980–99

Table 5.14
Appearances of Institutes for Senate Committee Testimony, 1980–99, by Parliamentary Session

Institute	Session				
	32 (144/80– 9/7/84) Liberal	33 (5/11/84– 1/10/88) PC	34 (12/12/88– 8/9/93) PC	35 (17/1/94– 27/4/97) Liberal	36 (22/9/97– 18/9/99) Liberal
C.D. Howe Institute	3	3	4		
Caledon Institute			5	1	1
Canada West Foundation	1				
Canadian Tax Foundation	1		2		
CCIPS		3			1
CCPA			3		
CCSD		8	16		
CIIA			1		
CIIPS		4	2		
CISS	1		1		
Conference Board of Canada	5	4	15	2	
CPRN				2	1
Economic Council of Canada	22	18	37	2	
Fraser Institute	1	1	3	3	3
IRPP	4	3	19		3
Mackenzie Institute		1	1		
National Council of Welfare	2	7	12	1	2

Table 5.14 (continued)

Institute	Session				
	32 (14/4/80–9/7/84)	33 (5/11/84–1/10/88)	34 (12/12/88–8/9/93)	35 (17/1/94–27/4/97)	36 (22/9/97–18/9/99)
	Liberal	*PC*	*PC*	*Liberal*	*Liberal*
North-South Institute		3		3	
Parliamentary Centre	3	4	21		
Pearson-Shoyama Institute				2	
Public Policy Forum			2	1	
Science Council of Canada	9	5	7		

Source: Parliamentary Committee Reports, 1980–99

Table 5.15
Appearances of Institutes for Joint Committee Testimony, 1980–99 by Parliamentary Session

Institute	Session				
	32 (14/4/80–9/7/84)	33 (5/11/84–1/10/88)	34 12/12/88–8/9/93)	35 17/1/94–27/4/97)	36 (22/9/97–18/9/99)
	Liberal	PC	PC	Liberal	Liberal
C.D. Howe Institute		2			
Caledon Institute					
Canada West Foundation	3	2		2	
Canadian Tax Foundation					
CCIPS		3		2	
CCPA		1		1	
CCSD	1	1	1		
CIIA		3		2	
CIIPS		1			
CISS		2		2	
Conference Board of Canada				1	
CPRN					
Economic Council of Canada	1		1		
Fraser Institute				1	
IRPP		2			
Mackenzie Institute					
National Council of Welfare				1	

Table 5.15 (continued)

Institute	Session				
	32 (14/4/80–9/7/84)	33 (5/11/84–1/10/88)	34 (12/12/88–8/9/93)	35 (17/1/94–27/4/97)	36 (22/9/97–18/9/99)
	Liberal	*PC*	*PC*	*Liberal*	*Liberal*
North-South Institute					
Parliamentary Centre	1	2		4	
Pearson-Shoyama Institute		1			
Public Policy Forum					
Science Council of Canada			1		

Source: Parliamentary Committee Reports, 1980–99

Table 5.16
Spearman's Rank Correlation Coefficient Results

Pairs of variables	Correlation coefficient	p
Media citations vs. parliamentary testimony	0.664	<.0010
Media citations vs. government consultations	0.207	<.356
Parliamentary testimony vs. government consultations	0.169	<.451

Significant at p <.01

testimony, but there is no correlation between media visibility and government consultations and between parliamentary testimony and government consultations.

What do the results of the tests tell us about the nature of think tank influence? Perhaps most importantly, they tell us that it should not be assumed that the most visible think tanks are necessarily the most influential and credible institutes in the policy-making process. It is important to recognize, as this chapter has shown, that the relevance or impact of think tanks varies at different stages of the policy cycle. Think tanks like the Cato Institute, the Fraser Institute, and the Canadian Institute of Strategic Studies might be effective in shaping the national agenda or enlarging "the terms of political discourse," as Les Pal observes,[23] but they might be less influential in contributing to policy development at more formal stages, while, on the other hand, think tanks with more modest media profiles, such as RAND, the Caledon Institute of Social Policy, and the Canadian Council on Social Development, might play a more active role in more formal stages of policy formulation.

Monitoring how often think tanks are quoted in the media or provide testimony may not allow scholars to ascertain with any degree of certainty which think tanks are the most or least influential; indeed, such data may tell us very little about their impact. Nonetheless, collecting data on these and other indicators helps to shed light on where in the policy cycle think tanks appear to be most actively engaged, if they are engaged at all. If some think tanks devote little time and energy to conveying their views to the media, one could argue with some degree of confidence that their influence on public opinion is limited. After all, how can think tanks influence the way people think if the public is unaware of their views? Similarly, how can think tanks claim to have policy influence if they do not convey their ideas directly to policymakers? However, by tracking which think tanks rely most heavily on the media to promote their views and which depend on other channels to market their ideas, we can look more closely at their involvement at different stages of the policy-making process.

In the following two chapters, I will take a closer look at how a select group of think tanks in the United States and Canada has sought to influence the policy-making environment and specific policy debates. Beginning with a detailed examination of the involvement of several American think tanks in presidential campaigns in chapter 6, I will explore how they have taken advantage of a critical opportunity to influence the policy direction of incoming presidents. In addition to identifying which think tanks have contributed ideas to presidential candidates, some consideration will also be given to why some candidates actively seek the advice of think tanks. Following this, chapter 7 will focus on how a small group of Canadian think tanks became involved in a major policy debate in Canada – the Renewal of Canada Initiative – which was intended to generate public discussion about the future of constitutional reform. Although one must be careful not to generalize about the impact of think tanks by relying on a handful of case studies, the following chapters will highlight the many different ways think tanks can make their presence felt.

On the Road to the White House: Presidential Candidates and the Think Tanks That Advised Them

In April 1998 Republican presidential candidate George W. Bush interrupted a fundraising trip for a gubernatorial candidate in Northern California to meet with several scholars from the Hoover Institution. The purpose of the meeting, which took place at the home of former secretary of state and Hoover fellow George Shultz, was to allow the governor of Texas to get acquainted with some of the nation's leading policy experts. Although before accepting Shultz's invitation, Bush had little knowledge of the Hoover Institution or the work many of its scholars engaged in, his friendship with Hoover fellow and economist Michael Boskin may explain why Bush gravitated toward the California think tank.[1] As a result of the close to four-hour meeting, Bush "engaged 12 or so Hoover fellows to advise his presidential campaign on issues from taxation to welfare to foreign affairs."[2] In addition to relying heavily on scholars from the Hoover Institution to help educate him on the intricacies of domestic and foreign policy issues, Bush enlisted the support of several other policy experts, including his top economic adviser, Lawrence Lindsey, former Federal Reserve governor and fellow at the American Enterprise Institute, and Robert Zoellick, who stepped down as president of the Center for Strategic and International Studies after only four months to advise Bush.[3]

Bush's decision to turn to some of the nation's most prominent think tanks for policy advice is not surprising. Indeed, it has become common for presidential candidates, particularly those who lack experience in federal politics, to establish close ties to think tanks. Eager to find candidates who can help translate their ideas into concrete policy decisions, it has also become common for think tanks to provide much of the intellectual ammunition presidential contenders require to sell their message to the electorate. As Martin Anderson of the Hoover Institution points out, "it is during this period that presidential candidates solicit the advice of a vast number of intellectuals in order to establish policy positions on a host of domestic and foreign policy issues. Presidential candidates exchange ideas with policy experts and test them out on the campaign trail. It's like a national test marketing strategy."[4]

In this chapter, which is intended to provide a snapshot of how some think tanks in the United States seek to influence public policy, I explore how a select group of think tanks have capitalized on presidential elections to share their ideas with candidates and incoming administrations. By doing so, I demonstrate one way policy institutes in the United States have tried to make a difference. The chapter begins by examining the various factors that motivate presidential candidates to turn to think tanks for policy advice and the general willingness of institutes to assist in their endeavours. As will be discussed, both presidential candidates and the think tanks that advise them recognize the enormous benefits that can be derived from a successful partnership. Following this, the close ties that were established between think tanks and four presidential candidates, Jimmy Carter (1976), Ronald Reagan (1980), Bill Clinton (1992), and George W. Bush (2000), will be examined. These candidates and their elections have been selected for a number of practical and empirical reasons: first, in each election, the close ties established between the leading presidential candidates and a select group of think tanks can be identified. Materials obtained from presidential archives and from other primary sources enable scholars to make some preliminary observations on the participation of think tanks in these elections. Of course, considerable gaps will remain unfilled until the remaining records from the Reagan years and the complete records of the Clinton presidency become available. Second, by focusing on these elections, scholars can demonstrate that the think tanks that became involved mattered in different ways and at different times. For instance, unlike several scholars from the Hoover Institution who provided their expertise to Ronald Reagan during the 1980 campaign, the Heritage Foundation's contribution to the candidate's policy education was modest. Nonetheless, by providing Reagan's closest advisors with a detailed blueprint on how to reform government, Heritage played a decisive role during Reagan's transition to power. Thus, these and other think tanks made their presence felt, but not necessarily in the same way. The final section of the chapter will consider some of the many lessons to be drawn from the participation of think tanks in presidential campaigns: among other things, why think tanks may find it difficult to resist the temptation to enter the political arena in such a highly visible way, and some of the potential repercussions of their involvement.

A PERFECT UNION: THINK TANKS AND PRESIDENTIAL CANDIDATES

To launch a successful presidential bid, candidates require not only a sufficient cash flow but a steady stream of policy ideas that they can share with the American public. Although the former is often in short supply, particularly during the presidential primaries when candidates must raise their own funds, candidates rarely are confronted by a shortage of policy ideas.[5] Surrounded by political strategists, pollsters, media consultants, party loyalists, and lobbyists for various causes, candidates are inundated with policy advice. Yet, despite being bombarded by information and advice from multiple sources, several presidential candidates have turned to think tanks to help develop, reinforce, and market their election platform. Why do candidates try to forge close ties to think tanks? And why are so many think tanks willing to offer their services?

To begin with, candidates, especially those with little or no experience at the federal level, can tap into the wealth of knowledge available at some of America's most distinguished think tanks.[6] Jimmy Carter, Ronald Reagan, and other presidential candidates who spent little time in Washington before assuming the presidency recognized the enormous benefits of relying on think tanks that had many former high-profile policymakers and leading policy experts. By drawing on experts at these organizations, candidates can not only obtain insights about the inner workings of Washington politics but also significantly enhance their understanding of policy issues. Moreover, by attending meetings at think tanks like the Council on Foreign Relations and the Brookings Institution, which include several former policymakers and prominent business leaders among their ranks, candidates can develop additional contacts in the private and public sectors that may prove invaluable as they travel the country soliciting support. However, even more important than the network of contacts think tanks can offer is the credibility they can give to a candidate's ideas. Receiving the endorsement of leading economists like Milton Friedman of the Hoover Institution or, better yet, having academics of such a high calibre providing advice can significantly enhance the intellectual depth of a candidate's platform. Candidates can also benefit from their visible association with think tanks that are in a position to reinforce the ideological underpinnings of their policy ideas.

The support and assistance of think tank staff costs candidates very little. Unless policy experts from think tanks take a leave of absence from their institute to work on a campaign, they generally offer their services free.[7] In sum, for candidates there are few costs and potentially enormous benefits in relying on think tanks that can help them strike a responsive chord with the electorate; for think tanks, there can be considerable benefits from aligning themselves with a winning presidential candidate. Not only does an election victory bring prestige and, at times, job offers, but a higher profile can translate into more funds from affluent donors.

Although some candidates have relied more heavily on think tanks than others, a clear pattern is emerging. When candidates need policy advice from seasoned policy experts, they are turning to these organizations with great regularity, and to the delight of many think tanks candidates appear willing to rely on them as they embark on the long and often difficult road to the White House.

JIMMY CARTER AND THE SEARCH FOR POLICY ADVICE

When President Ford granted Richard Nixon "a full, free and absolute pardon" for "any and all crimes" committed during the Watergate scandal, it seemed even more probable that a Democrat would become the next president. Tainted by widespread corruption and unable to bring about an expeditious conclusion to the Vietnam War, the Republican party failed to convince the American electorate that it could provide effective and responsible leadership. In fact, well before President Nixon resigned in August 1974, several political commentators were convinced that a Democrat would win the 1976 presidential campaign.[8] Yet, while a number of prominent Democrats entered the presidential race, including Henry "Scoop" Jackson and George Wallace, it was Jimmy Carter, a relatively unknown one-term governor of Georgia who was sworn into office in January 1977.

While Jimmy Carter's rapid rise to power continues to baffle some political analysts, his ties to prestigious policy research institutions in New York and Washington, DC, may in part explain his ability to gain national exposure. By analysing Carter's dependence on think tanks for policy advice, it is possible to identify the organizations that played a major role during and after his bid for the presidency. A closer examination of his association with a handful of prominent Northeastern think tanks also reveals how research institutions seek to expand their networks of influence throughout the policy-making community.

Shortly after Jimmy Carter became governor of Georgia in 1970, he began to set his sights on the nation's highest office. However, it soon became apparent to Carter and his political and financial supporters that if he was to launch a successful presidential campaign, he would have to attract the attention of several prominent Democrats. Although Carter enjoyed the backing of many prominent leaders in Atlanta's business and policy-making circles, it was the support of leading academics, financiers, and journalists in the Northeast that he dearly coveted. According to Laurence Shoup, by gaining access to the Eastern Establishment, Carter hoped to become part of the national power structure in the United States.[9]

As early as 1971 Carter became preoccupied with gaining national exposure. And through some of his close personal advisors, such as former secretary of state Dean Rusk, he met a number of individuals who were in a position to broaden his base of political support. Among these most influential contacts were David Rockefeller, chairman of the Chase Manhattan Bank, and Hedley Donovan, editor-in-chief of *Time* magazine. Following a *Time* cover story on Carter and the New South in May 1971, Carter met with Donovan, who in turn introduced him to George S. Franklin, a Rockefeller in-law and executive director of the Council on Foreign Relations.[10] It was through one or more of these connections that Carter became known to David Rockefeller, who invited the governor to lunch with him at the Chase Manhattan Bank in November 1971.

Carter's southern disposition and Kennedy-style approach to state politics must have impressed Rockefeller, for when the latter decided to establish the Trilateral Commission in 1973, Carter was invited to become a member.[11] Zbigniew Brzezinski, who helped Rockefeller select individuals for the Trilateral Commission, maintained that Carter was asked to join because he seemed to share the organization's commitment to improving international economic relations: "we were very impressed that Carter had opened up trade offices for the state of Georgia in Brussels and Tokyo. That seemed to fit perfectly into the concept of the Trilateral."[12]

While Carter's international economic initiatives appeared to coincide with the Trilateral Commission's mandate, the possibility of having one of their members occupy the Oval Office also appears to have influenced Rockefeller and Brzezinski's decision. As Barry Goldwater points out, Carter's invitation to join the Trilateral Commission was motivated by political as well as institutional interests. "David Rockefeller and Zbigniew Brzezinski found Jimmy Carter to be their ideal candidate. They helped him win the nomination and the presidency. To accomplish this purpose, they mobilized the money power of the Wall Street bankers, the intellectual influence of the academic community – which is subservient to the wealth of the great tax-free foundations – and the media controllers represented in the membership of the CFR [Council on Foreign Relations] and the Trilateral."[13]

Goldwater and other conservative spokespersons recognized that a Carter election victory would pay handsome dividends to the Trilateral Commission, but Carter also derived many benefits from participating in this organization. According to Laurence Shoup, "By becoming a member of the Trilateral Commission, Carter met and became friends with powerful upper class individuals who had contacts and influence where it mattered – in business, the mass communications media, in governments at home and abroad, in universities, in the associations and foundations. Jimmy Carter ... whom few people outside Georgia had even heard of in 1973, had become part of a group which could help him become President of the u.s."[14]

Few political commentators identified the close connection between Carter and the Trilateral Commission during the early 1970s, but by 1976 it became increasingly apparent that the Democratic presidential candidate was relying heavily on his trilateral colleagues for policy advice. For instance, in June 1976 the *Los Angeles Times* described a "task force" that helped the candidate prepare his first foreign policy speech, which began, "The time has come for us to seek a partnership between North America, Western Europe and Japan."[15] With several of his trilateral advisors leading the applause, Carter emphasized the importance of encouraging closer cooperation between advanced industrial nations. In the ensuing months, the Democratic candidate continued to espouse other foreign policy recommendations proposed by the Trilateral Commission. In fact, Carter's growing dependence on an elite group of trilateral advisors, including Zbigniew Brzezinski and Cyrus Vance, convinced some campaign observers that "Carter's entire foreign policy, much of his election strategy, and at least some of his domestic policy [came] directly from the Commission and its leading members."[16]

It is difficult to determine the extent to which various trilateral advisors influenced Carter's views on foreign and domestic policy, but there is little doubt that membership on the commission left a lasting impression on him. As Carter noted, "In order to insure the continuing opportunity for penetrating analyses of complicated, important, and timely foreign policy questions, there is an organization known as the Trilateral Commission. A group of leaders from the three democratic developed areas of the world meet every six months to discuss ideas of current interest to Japan, North America and Europe ... Membership on this commission has provided me with a splendid learning opportunity, and many of the other members helped me in my study of foreign affairs."[17]

Zbigniew Brzezinski, the Trilateral Commission's first director and later national security adviser to President Carter, agrees that the commission offered Carter an invaluable learning experience but denies that it advised him on domestic and foreign affairs:[18]

The Commission did not play any role in advising [Carter] whatsoever. But I think the commission was of importance to him in two ways. One, it provided the framework for his generally first extensive exposure to international affairs. Prior to his membership on the commission, he had no exposure to international affairs. It was through the commission that he really became exposed to foreign affairs. Secondly, on the commission, he met a number of people interested in foreign affairs, some of whom he recruited to work for him when he was making the appointments for his administration. I believe that someone once counted, I don't remember the exact number, but I sort of vaguely remember that up to eighteen senior appointees in his administration were from members of the commission.[19]

Brzezinski could not recall the exact number of trilateral commissioners who were appointed by President Carter,[20] but he stated that "all the key foreign policy decision makers of the Carter administration had served in the Trilateral Commission."[21] Other than Brzezinski, several Trilateral members received appointments in the Carter administration, including Walter Mondale, Paul Volcker, and Paul Warnke.

Carter depended heavily on several trilateral commissioners to fill key posts in his administration, yet his search for policy advice did not end there. The Trilateral Commission quickly established a reputation as one of the premier policy research institutions in the United States. However, the president-elect could not afford to ignore the elite group of policy specialists at other distinguished think tanks, such as the Council on Foreign Relations. Moreover, since many trilateral commissioners were also members of the CFR, Carter's access to some of the nation's most prominent decision makers was greatly facilitated.[22]

At Carter's invitation, at least fifty-four members of the CFR joined his new administration. Among them were P.R. Harris, secretary of housing and urban development (HUD) and health, education and welfare (HEW); Philip Habib, under-secretary of state; Stansfield Turner, director of the CIA; D. Aaron, deputy to the national security advisor; A. Solomon, under-secretary of the treasury; and Donald McHenry, ambassador to the United Nations. Having assembled an impressive team of policy advisors from the Trilateral Commission and the Council on Foreign Relations, Carter finally turned to the Brookings Institution to complete his "brain trust."

Recognizing the invaluable contribution that several Brookings scholars had made to the formulation of various governmental policies during previous democratic administrations, Carter first approached the institution in July 1975 for advice. During his brief visit, he attended two informal luncheons on foreign policy and economics and began to establish ties to many of Brooking's most distinguished residents. Following his election victory, Carter invited several Brookings scholars to join his staff. In addition to Stephen Hess, who advised him on how to restructure his White House staff, Carter appointed over a dozen other members of the Brookings Institution to administrative posts, including Charles L. Schultze, chairman of the Council of Economic Advisors; C. Fred Bergsten, assistant secretary of the treasury for international economic affairs; Henry Aaron, assistant secretary of health, education and welfare for planning and evaluation; Karen Davis, deputy assistant secretary of health, education and welfare; Emil Sunley Jr, deputy assistant secretary of the treasury; Barry Blechman, assistant director of the Arms Control and Disarmament Agency (ACDA); Barry Bosworth, director of the Council on Wage and Price Stability; Henry D. Owen, special White House representative for economic summits; L.N. Cutler, White House counsel; L.W. Benson, under secretary of state; Gerard C. Smith, ambassador at large; and Nancy H. Teeters, Federal Reserve Board.

With the support and advice of over one hundred policy analysts from three of America's most prestigious think tanks, Carter rose from relative obscurity to occupy the oval office. Although several factors contributed to his election victory, the vital role think tanks played during his campaign cannot be overlooked. Carter's dependence on think tank specialists did not end when he entered the White House. On the contrary, as the newly installed president sought to chart a new course for America in the latter half of the decade, he began to rely even more on his advisors for direction and guidance. While Carter solicited the advice of his top economic advisors to enhance America's position in the international economy, his preoccupation with resolving tensions in Latin America and the Middle East provided foreign policy analysts, both in and out of government, with unique opportunities to capture the president's attention. In fact, on several occasions Carter's policies toward these particular regions appeared to be shaped and moulded by prominent members of Washington's think tank community.[23]

Carter depended on several prestigious Northeastern think tanks to gain national exposure, but his successor turned to other policy research institutions to transform his set of conservative beliefs into a winning election platform. Reagan had occasionally solicited the advice of policy analysts from prominent think tanks and universities during his tenure as governor of California, but, it was not until he launched his bid for the presidency in 1980 that he began to surround himself with some of the nation's most respected conservative policy intellectuals.[24]

RONALD REAGAN AND THE THINK TANKS THAT ADVISED HIM

Despite finishing second to Gerald Ford at the 1976 Republican National Convention in Kansas City, Missouri, Ronald Reagan wasted little time preparing for the 1980 presidential campaign. As one of his campaign advisers observed during the candidate's return flight to California, Reagan stared out the plane's window for a few seconds and then proceeded to write the following note on the back of a ticket to the national convention, "We dreamed – we fought & the dream is still with us."[25]

In those few words, Reagan expressed his commitment to return to the campaign trail in the hope of securing the presidential nomination. And on 17 July 1980 in Detroit, Michigan, four years after his narrow defeat, Reagan won the Republican nomination by an overwhelming majority. One hundred and eleven days later, he won the general election, and on 20 January 1981 Ronald Wilson Reagan became the fortieth president of the United States.

Reagan's sweeping victory over an increasingly despondent and frustrated president is often attributed to the failure of the Carter administration to safeguard U.S. economic and political interests in the international community. Carter's inability to prevent the overthrow of the shah of Iran, the installation of the Sandinista government in Nicaragua, the seizure of the U.S. embassy in Tehran, and the Soviet invasion of Afghanistan did little to instill confidence in the electorate. Nonetheless, his foreign policy failures alone did not ensure a Republican victory. The ability of Reagan's advisors to translate a set of conservative beliefs into an appealing political agenda also contributed to the outcome of the 1980 campaign.

Before Reagan's plane had even landed in Southern California following his acceptance speech in Detroit, some of his campaign advisors began to map out a new strategy to promote their candidate's views on domestic and foreign policy. And just as Reagan had undergone a political conversion by leaving the Democratic party to join the Republican cause following Kennedy's narrow election victory over Nixon in 1960, his campaign advisors now had to determine how to expedite the American electorate's conversion to conservatism.[26]

For Martin Anderson, a senior fellow at the Hoover Institution and a key member of Reagan's inner circle of policy advisors, the most effective way to communicate his candidate's political agenda to the American public was to attract the support of some of the nation's leading intellectuals. Convinced that "ideas move nations"[27] and that policy ideas arise primarily in universities and think tanks, Anderson set out to assemble an impressive team of academics who could promote Reagan's vision of America.[28] As Anderson points out in his memoirs of the Reagan years, "[A]s early as 1975, after I agreed to join his presidential campaign, I started a systematic effort to introduce the nation's best economists to Reagan. Most of them were selected from my personal file of leading policy experts I began collecting during Nixon's campaign in 1967. This was part of a more general effort to recruit an army of intellectuals to advise and counsel Reagan on the entire range of policy issues."[29]

After inviting such prominent economists as Milton Friedman, William Niskanen, and Murray Weidenbaum to join Reagan's campaign team, Anderson began to set his sights on creating several policy task forces to advise Reagan on domestic and foreign policy.[30] Anderson first recognized the importance of establishing policy task forces to advise presidential candidates when he was in charge of policy research for Nixon in 1968. He notes, "I learned that policy advisers from the intellectual world could be a tremendous asset to a campaign ... the very existence of a large group of distinguished intellectuals gave a powerful boost to the credibility of the candidate. In effect, those intellectuals were co-signing the ideas of the candidate."[31]

Anderson was in charge of organizing the domestic and economic policy task forces, and Richard Allen, a fellow Hoover colleague, was entrusted with overseeing the foreign and defence policy groups.[32] Reflecting on how his policy groups channelled information to Reagan, Allen stated, "I had a total of 120 people; 80 foreign policy advisers and 40 defence and national security advisers. These people were typically specialists in the field, either academic specialists or retired or departed specialists from government, including people from the Pentagon and the Department of State, former diplomats and the like. [They] produced information, opinions, parts of speeches that would be included in the speeches of the candidate ... That's the way that part of the system worked. [The policy groups] were extremely useful in providing background information and general data."[33]

A press release issued by Reagan on 23 October 1980 documented the scope and function of the policy task forces: "Governor Reagan today announced the completion of 23 domestic and economic policy task forces with 329 advisers who have been asked to address the important issues that will have to be faced by a new administration ... These task forces join 25 foreign policy and defence working groups with 132 advisers that are examining, in detail, the major questions that relate to these two important areas."[34]

The active involvement of policy task forces during the Reagan campaign was commented on by transition team director Edwin Meese III: "Reagan's 1980 campaign had been served by policy task forces that comprised 'the largest and most distinguished group of intellectuals ever assembled for an American political campaign.' Nearly fifty groups, with over 450 advisors, studied numerous areas of foreign, defence, domestic, and economic policy and provided hundreds of recommendations."[35] By producing detailed studies on topics ranging from welfare reform to missile defence, and by outlining several policy recommendations, the policy task forces had, in effect, established a blueprint for the incoming administration. As Martin Anderson points out, "[w]hen Reagan took power in 1981, the battle plan for what to do with that power was largely written."[36]

Two weeks before president-elect Reagan took the oath of office at a dinner in honour of the Hoover Institution's Board of Overseers, Meese elaborated on the important contribution the policy development teams made in assembling information for the new administration. "We have already had a series of meetings ... with [the] Heritage [Foundation] and others to make recommendations to the new President-elect as to the course his administration should follow. By the time January twentieth comes around, there will already be an agenda of initial action projects which will carry the administration through its first year of operation and which will set major and intermediate goals so that there will always be an eye on the blueprint of what the administration seeks to accomplish."[37]

The president-elect wasted little time rewarding advisers who made important contributions to his campaign. Among those participating on Reagan's policy task forces who received high-level government appointments were Alan Greenspan, chairman of the board of governors of the Federal Reserve; Antonin Scalia, appointed to the Supreme Court; George Shultz, secretary of state; Caspar Weinberger, secretary of defence; William Howard Taft IV, deputy secretary of defence; Richard Allen, national security adviser; James Miller, chairman of the Federal Trade Commission and later director of the Office of Management and Budget (OMB); Edwin Harper, deputy director of the OMB; Murray Weidenbaum and Beryl Sprinkel, chairmen of the Council of Economic Advisers (CEA); William Niskanen and Thomas Moore, CEA; Norman Ture and Paul Craig Roberts, undersecretary and assistant secretary for economic policy in the Department of the Treasury; Arthur F. Burns, ambassador to Germany; Darrell Trent, deputy secretary of transportation; Rudolph Penner, head of the Congressional Budget Office; and Martin Anderson, chief Domestic and economic policy adviser.[38]

Of these, over half were members of think tanks before joining the Reagan administration. Their institutional affiliations were as follows: Richard Allen, the Center for Strategic and International Studies, the Heritage Foundation, and the Hoover Institution; Martin Anderson, Thomas Moore, and Darrell Trent, the Hoover Institution; Norman Ture, the Heritage Foundation; Caspar Weinberger, the Institute for Contemporary Studies;[39] Murray Weidenbaum, James Miller, and

Arthur Burns, the American Enterprise Institute; and William Niskanen, RAND and the Institute for Defence Analyses.[40]

The number of individuals belonging to think tanks who decided to join the Reagan crusade is far more extensive. Between 1981 and 1988, close to two hundred members from America's leading conservative think tanks participated in the Reagan administration in a full-time consulting or advisory capacity.[41] Five think tanks in particular were well represented during the Reagan years; fifty-five scholars came from the Hoover Institution, thirty-six from the Heritage Foundation, thirty-four from the American Enterprise Institute, thirty-two from the Committee on the Present Danger,[42] and eighteen from the Center for Strategic and International Studies.[43]

Until the 1980 campaign records at the Reagan Presidential Library become available, it will be difficult to provide a more detailed examination of the relationship between think tanks and the Reagan administration. Nonetheless, a preliminary search of available materials indicates that some think tanks played a crucial role in the transition period following the 1980 election. Although several think tanks were actively involved in the campaign, few assumed more importance during the transition than the Heritage Foundation.

In the fall of 1979, in anticipation of a Republican presidential victory, Heritage president Edwin Feulner began to consider how his organization could assist in the transition to a conservative administration. After consulting several of his colleagues in the policy research community, Feulner decided to launch an extensive research project to produce a study that could, in effect, serve as a manual for conservatives to follow in implementing domestic and foreign policy initiatives. According to Feulner, "our strong feeling was that people who came into the administration should have some source of information and guidance other than what you get from the incumbents that you replace."[44]

With the assistance of over three hundred academics, consultants, lawyers, and former government officials divided into twenty project teams, the Heritage Foundation produced an eleven-hundred-page "blueprint for the construction of a conservative government."[45] In its *Mandate for Leadership: Policy Management in a Conservative Administration*, the Heritage Foundation outlined two thousand proposals on issues ranging from how to streamline the government bureaucracy to ways to improve U.S. national security.[46]

Delighted with the results of Heritage's year-long study, not to mention the outcome of the 1980 campaign, Feulner presented a copy of the manuscript to Edwin Meese III at the Hay-Adams Hotel in mid-November 1980.[47] After scanning the extensive report, Meese said that the *Mandate for Leadership* study was very impressive and that the

Reagan team "will rely heavily on it."[48] It was "one of the most meaningful and best things that President Reagan and those associated with him will have to guide them in the next few years."[49] According to Meese, "President Reagan gave a copy of the book to each member of his cabinet and directed them to read it."[50]

In his memoirs of the Reagan years, Meese, currently the Ronald Reagan fellow in Public Policy at the Heritage Foundation, stated that the *Mandate for Leadership* study was largely responsible for the growing influence of the Heritage Foundation: "This major accomplishment put Heritage 'on the map' as far as Washington decision makers were concerned. Indeed, many leaders in the federal government were appointed from among the Heritage staff and the contributors to *Mandate for Leadership*. [Moreover] Edwin Feulner provided expert advice to the new administration in varying capacities."[51] Meese's overwhelming endorsement of the Heritage study may in part explain why it appeared on the *Washington Post*'s best-seller list for three weeks in early 1981. It may also explain why observers of Washington politics began referring to the study as the bible of the Reagan administration – even a year after *Mandate for Leadership* was released, journalists and policy analysts were speculating on the extent to which President Reagan's domestic and foreign policies were influenced by the publication.

However, few individuals paid more attention to how closely government officials followed the policy recommendations outlined in the Heritage study than Edwin Feulner, who estimated in early 1982 that more than 60 percent of Heritage's proposals had been adopted by the Reagan administration.[52] In flaunting this statistic, Feulner neglected to explain that a number of the policy recommendations included in his organization's study did not originate there but were developed and refined by other policy research institutions over several years. According to Glenn Campbell, former director of the Hoover Institution, many of Heritage's recommendations were extracted from an earlier Hoover publication, *The United States in the 1980s*.[53] Even former Soviet President Mikhail Gorbachev was convinced that several of the Reagan administration's policies were borrowed from the Hoover Institution's three-and-a-half-pound study. Waving a copy of the publication in front of Secretary of State George Shultz and Robert McFarlane, Reagan's third national security adviser,[54] Gorbachev shouted, "We have read this book and watched all its programs become adopted by the Reagan administration."[55]

Notwithstanding the discrepancy over where the majority of policy recommendations outlined in the Heritage study originated, it is difficult to ignore the integral role this organization played during Reagan's transition to power. As journalist Bernard Weinraub points out, "Working from an out-of-the way, white brick building in north-east Washington that once housed a Korean grocery and a halfway house for drug addicts, a group of little-known academics and congressional aides ... emerged as a major force in Ronald Reagan's transition to the presidency."[56]

The *Mandate for Leadership* study had propelled the Heritage Foundation into the national spotlight, and from its new headquarters located just two blocks from the Capitol Building, the "feisty new kid on the conservative block" as President Reagan called it, continued to shape America's political agenda.[57] By 1984 Heritage's clout in Washington's policy-making community had grown to the point that New Republic columnist James Rosenthal, writing of the impact of *Mandate for Leadership II*, commented, "Heritage helps shape what people in Washington talk about after they read the morning paper. It helps set the agenda."[58]

Riding the new wave of conservatism that was quickly sweeping across the United States, the Heritage Foundation soon became immersed in Washington's decision-making establishment. While several liberal policy research institutions were simply concerned with remaining afloat during the Reagan years, the Heritage Foundation, with the financial support of a growing number of individuals and corporations, began to transform itself into one of Washington's leading think tanks. Yet, despite its increasing visibility and overt desire to shape the political agenda, the Heritage Foundation did not monopolize the attention of decision makers. By making their way through Washington's policy-making labyrinth, members of the Center for Strategic and International Studies, the Committee on the Present Danger, the Hoover Institution, and the American Enterprise Institute were also able to advise key government officials on a host of domestic and foreign policy issues in various capacities.

Like his predecessor, Reagan surrounded himself with some of the nation's most distinguished scholars. By doing so, he not only broadened his base of intellectual support throughout the academic community but, more importantly, attracted individuals who could translate his conservative beliefs into a set of viable policy options. In the process of advancing Reagan's political mandate, several think tanks that had previously observed the mechanics of government from the sidelines became firmly integrated into the decision-making network; as active participants in the political arena, many took advantage of new opportunities to shape governmental policies. The extent to which various think tanks were ultimately responsible for directly influencing American domestic and foreign policy during Reagan's terms in office is difficult to measure. What is clear, however, is that during the 1980s think tanks assumed a more visible profile on America's political landscape. Indeed, it was not until George Bush assumed the presidency in 1989 that the presence of think tanks in key policy-making circles began to diminish.

Unlike Reagan, Bush did not invite dozens of academics from think tanks to participate in his 1988 or 1992 presidential campaigns, nor did he rely heavily on them to fill high-level positions in his administration. On the contrary, Bush made a concerted effort to insulate himself from think tanks that had established and maintained close ties to his predecessor. As Annelise Anderson, a senior fellow at the Hoover Institution and former adviser to Vice-President Bush points out, "President Bush wanted to climb out of Reagan's shadow and [therefore] distanced himself from most Republican experts attached to Reagan. He also treated neo-conservatives much like President Carter did. They both discounted their importance as intellectuals ... In doing so, they excluded a lot of intellectual firepower, people like Jeane Kirkpatrick, Norman Podhoretz and Irving Kristol who had inspired and invigorated the Reagan administration."[59]

The visibility and prominence of think tanks in Washington appeared to temporarily fade during the Bush years; however, when Governor Clinton announced his bid for the presidency in 1991, they began to attract considerable attention once again. As Clinton's campaign gained momentum, journalists began to pay more attention to the individuals and organizations who were advising the Arkansas governor. What they discovered was that Clinton, like Carter and Reagan, had established close ties to a handful of think tanks.

BILL CLINTON AND A PLACE CALLED THE PROGRESSIVE POLICY INSTITUTE

In the winter of 1991 few Democrats on Capitol Hill or, for that matter, throughout the United States, could have predicted that the Republicans decade-long reign in the White House would soon come to an end. Enjoying unprecedented popularity in the polls, largely as a result of the overwhelming support for the u.s. – led coalition to "liberate Kuwait," President Bush appeared destined to win a second term in office.[60] As a former Washington insider and long-time resident at a think tank confidently remarked at the time, "Jesus Christ could run on the Democratic ticket and he still wouldn't beat George Bush."[61] Yet, as the growing frustration and concern of American voters over worsening economic conditions overshadowed their initial enthusiasm for Operation Desert Storm, Bush's political future no longer seemed assured. In fact, in the ensuing months it became apparent that unless he could convince the u.s. public that an economic recovery plan for America constituted an integral part of his vision for a New World Order, the oval office would soon have a new occupant.

Anxiously anticipating a Democratic victory on election day, several think tanks began preparing blueprints for the next administration. Modelling their ambitious research projects on the Heritage Foundation's *Mandate for Leadership*,[62] several think tanks outlined a series of recommendations for the next president to follow on issues ranging from health care and educational reform to international trade agreements and defence procurement programs.[63] By the spring of 1992, as Bill Clinton began to accumulate enough delegates to secure the presidential nomination, it appeared to many think tanks that if they were to have any discernible impact on shaping his campaign platform, they would have to capture the governor's attention.

For Clinton, the five-term governor of Arkansas who easily secured his party's nomination at New York's Madison Square Garden in July 1992, there was little question about which think tanks and policy advisors he would turn to for advice throughout his campaign and during his transition to the presidency.[64] Dozens of academics, interest groups, business leaders, and representatives from a range of non-governmental organizations conveyed their ideas to Clinton in the months preceding the November election. However, it appeared to many journalists covering the campaign that Bill Clinton would rely predominantly on the Washington-based Democratic Leadership Council (DLC) and on its policy arm, the Progressive Policy Institute (PPI), to develop his election platform.[65]

Making this prediction hardly required a crystal ball. After all, in addition to being one of the forty founding members of the DLC, which was created in 1985 following Walter Mondale's humiliating defeat in the election of 1984, Clinton was its chairman from 1990–91.[66] Throughout his association with the DLC, Clinton, along with approximately three thousand other members, invested considerable time and energy to move the Democratic party from the left to the centre of the political spectrum, the principal mandate of the DLC.[67] In an attempt to broaden the Democratic Party's base of political support by appealing to disillusioned voters, particularly in the southern and western regions of the United States, Clinton participated in the creation of the PPI in 1989 to convince Americans that Democrats, like Republicans, could successfully compete in the marketplace of political ideas. By the 1992 election, the PPI was prepared to spread its message across the country, and fortunately for the institute, it found the right messenger. According to Achenbach, "After creating the DLC, their next move was to create an idea arm, the PPI ... The solution was to come up with new ideas, and find someone to embody them – which happened when Clinton became chairman of the DLC and then carried the group's agenda into the presidential campaign."[68]

Clinton did far more than just carry some of the PPI's policy ideas into the campaign, however. Once in office, he tried to translate several of the institute's suggestions into concrete public policies, often with the assistance of a handful of staff from the DLC and the PPI that had joined his administration.[69] Several administration policies, including reforming America's health care system, linking student aid to national service, helping communities cope more effectively with crime, demanding that welfare recipients perform a variety of community services, and injecting an entrepreneurial spirit into the federal government, are among the many program initiatives that bear a striking resemblance to the recommendations made by various contributors to the PPI's study *Mandate for Change*.[70] Some of these ideas had been advocated by other individuals and organizations, but few institutions in the 1992 campaign offered a more comprehensive guide to reforming government than the PPI.

In addition to drawing heavily on the recommendations made by the DLC and the PPI, Clinton also consulted formally and informally with several other individuals to solicit their advice on a wide range of policy initiatives before assuming office. For instance, during the Clinton-Gore economic conference held in Little Rock, Arkansas, on 14–15 December 1992, Clinton listened to 329 of the nation's leading economists, corporate executives, and labour leaders comment on how to address the economic problems confronting the United States.[71] In a less formal setting he also mingled with several hundred members of America's elite during the now famous Renaissance Weekend held at Hilton Head, South Carolina, over New Year's.[72]

The involvement of think tanks in the campaigns that propelled Carter, Reagan, and Clinton to office reveals one of the most visible channels think tanks rely on to shape the policy direction of incoming administrations. It also demonstrates how candidates can benefit from the considerable policy expertise available at some of America's leading policy institutes and the potential rewards those institutes can earn by being so closely linked to a winning campaign. This may explain why George W. Bush, unlike his father, enlisted the support of policy experts from several think tanks and why so many think tanks were willing to help shape his policy ideas.

PLANTING NEW IDEAS: GEORGE W. BUSH AND HIS QUEST FOR THE PRESIDENCY

As a U.S. congressman, former director of the CIA, ambassador to the United Nations and vice-president and president of the United States,

George Bush was the consummate Washington insider. By contrast his first son, George W. Bush, had little first-hand experience with the types of issues he had to confront as president. In the Texas state legislature in Austin, Bush became familiar with a host of local concerns ranging from education and health care to the environment and transportation, but as president, he required insight into a multitude of domestic and international issues that until then he had demonstrated little knowledge of.[73] Like Carter, Reagan, and Clinton before they declared their intention to run for the presidency, Bush possessed a limited understanding of foreign affairs, an observation not lost on several journalists and political opponents. In fact, his inability to pass a journalist's pop quiz on foreign policy in November 1999 raised serious concerns about his intellectual grasp of America's international priorities.[74]

In an attempt to allay concerns about his ability to lead the world's remaining superpower and to promote America's economic interests in the twenty-first century, Bush assembled a team of over one hundred policy experts, many from the Hoover Institution,[75] to advise him on economic, foreign, and defence policy. During his campaign, he also set up policy advisory committees on issues such as education and technology to help deepen his knowledge of domestic policy issues. Bush's team of economic advisers was headed by Lawrence Lindsey of the American Enterprise Institute (AEI), who has since been appointed assistant to the president for economic policy.[76] Joining Lindsey were several prominent economists, including John Taylor, a Hoover fellow who served on President George Bush's Council of Economic Advisers, Harvard Economics professor Martin Feldstein; J.D. Foster, executive director of the Washington-based Tax Foundation and R. Glenn Hubbard of Columbia University's Business School.[77]

Bush's thirteen-member education policy advisory committee was also well stocked with experts from several leading think tanks. Among those who agreed to take some time away from their institutes to assist Bush were Lynne Cheney, a senior fellow at the AEI and wife of Richard Cheney, and her colleague Lynne Munson; Williamson Evers, a senior fellow at the Hoover Institution; and Diane Ravitch, who holds research posts at the Brookings Institution and the New York – based Manhattan Institute for Policy Research.[78]

The foreign policy and defence policy teams Bush assembled were even more impressive, reading, as James Kitfield observed, "like a Who's Who of the Reagan and Bush foreign policy establishments."[79] Heading the foreign policy brain trust were Condoleeza Rice, Bush's national security adviser, who, in addition to being a fellow at the Hoover Institution, also served in the National Security Council under President George Bush;[80] Rice's colleague at Hoover, former secretary of state George Shultz; and Vice-President Richard Cheney, a former secretary of defense. Other prominent defence and foreign policy analysts included Paul Wolfowitz, Richard Perle, and Robert Zoellick former Pentagon and State Department official; dean of the Johns Hopkins School for Advanced International Studies (SAIS); former assistant defence secretary and director of the American Enterprise Institute's Commission on Future Defenses and former president of the Center for Strategic and International Studies and U.S. trade representative.[81]

Although it is premature to predict how much impact these and other advisers will have on shaping Bush's policy ideas during his tenure as president, it is clear that during the campaign he relied heavily on his battle-hardened team of experts for advice. Particularly in foreign policy, where Bush admitted he had much to learn, policy experts were well positioned to articulate their views to a novice hungry for ideas. As Bush stated in an interview with the *New York Times* during the campaign, "I may not be able to tell you exactly the nuance of the East Timorian situation, but I'll ask people who've had experience, like Condi Rice, Paul Wolfowitz, or Dick Cheney. I am smart enough to know what I don't know, and I have good judgement about who will either be telling the truth, or has got some agenda that is not the right agenda."[82]

Unlike his brother Jeb Bush, governor of Florida, George W. Bush does not see himself as a "policy wonk," a phrase often used in the media to describe political leaders who enjoy immersing themselves in the intricacies of policy formulation.[83] And according to Tim Adams, a veteran of President George Bush's administration who organized a briefing for the Texas governor on technology, he does not want to be. As Adams observes, George W. Bush "believes a chief executive should set out principles, a vision of where you want to go, and then surround yourself with very smart people and listen to them and work with them."[84] If he is correct, then Bush's management style will be similar to Reagan's, who, unlike Clinton and Carter, preferred to leave the details of policy development to his subordinates.

For Governor Bush, there was much to be gained and little to lose by developing an extensive network of policy experts. While Bush was under no obligation to accept anyone's policy advice, he had at his disposal dozens of leading economists, political scientists, and former policy-makers who could give substance to his vision of how America should be governed. As the final section of this chapter illustrates, for think tanks there may be some cost to becoming too closely affiliated with presidential candidates – although the potential benefits may far outweigh any drawbacks.

AN OFFER TOO TEMPTING TO RESIST

Establishing close ties to the White House is an opportunity few think tanks appear willing to pass up. Indeed, since they are organizations committed to shaping public opinion and public policy, being in a position to influence the policy direction of the president may be the best opportunity some have to market their ideas. Yet in the process of finding an appropriate messenger to translate their ideas into concrete policies, think tanks are becoming increasingly aware of the potential costs of becoming publicly involved in presidential campaigns.

Aside from the obvious concern of having their tax-exempt status under the Internal Revenue Code revoked for engaging in inappropriate political activities, think tank directors realize that their institute's credibility can be damaged in some academic and policy-making circles if they are perceived as leading spokespersons for a particular candidate.[85] As a result, although several think tank staff have participated and will likely continue to participate in presidential campaigns in various capacities, directors like John Raisian of the Hoover Institution acknowledge "that we have to be very careful about how we handle it."[86] How Raisian and other think tank directors, including Edward Crane of the Cato Institute and Edwin Feulner of the Heritage Foundation, "handle it" is by making sure that their staff are willing to provide policy advice, not political advice, to any candidate willing to listen. In this way they attempt to create the impression that, contrary to the views of their critics, they are nonpartisan.

Reinforcing their image as nonpartisan research institutes is not only necessary to keep the Internal Revenue Service at bay but also critical in cultivating their reputation as independent and objective centres for research and analysis. After all, unless think tanks can demonstrate that they produce sound and balanced policy-relevant research, few policymakers, including aspiring presidential candidates, will need their services. As the 2000 presidential campaign confirmed, there are plenty of organizations that lobby on behalf of various causes. But what policymakers require is sound policy ideas, not more political lobbyists.

How think tanks balance the need to create a credible research program with the desire to influence public policy will inevitably determine which institutes are called upon to advise presidential candidates. For the think tanks that are able to achieve an effective balance, the rewards can be vast. Not only do close ties between think tanks and presidential candidates often translate into more funds from admiring donors, but such an association can result in high-level job offers for think tank staff. Alternatively, for think tanks that are more interested in the cachet that comes from advising a presidential candidate than providing informative and well-balanced policy advice, the costs can be significant. Being associated with a winning presidential campaign may result in short-term benefits, but the long-term damage to their credibility may be far more significant.

In examining the involvement of think tanks in the four presidential elections discussed in this chapter, two observations come to light. First, Jimmy Carter, Ronald Reagan, Bill Clinton, and George W. Bush had much in common before embarking on their road to the presidency: in addition to being governors, none of the candidates had any formal experience in foreign policy, which may explain why they all turned to think tanks for insights on defence and foreign policy issues. Second, and perhaps more importantly, the candidates were drawn to think tanks because they could provide the candidates with credible and independent policy advice. Probably the most significant function of think tanks for the presidential candidates was their ability to enhance the legitimacy of the candidates' policy ideas.

Much has been written about the extent to which think tanks in the United States and, to a lesser extent, in Canada have become engaged in political advocacy, often at the expense of producing solid policy research. While it is difficult to ignore how think tanks have become more advocacy-oriented, we cannot assume that the institutes most adept at marketing their institutional mandate will necessarily be of the greatest assistance to policymakers. As demonstrated in this chapter and in the chapter that follows, policymakers may at times be more inclined to enlist the support of think tanks that are known more for their policy expertise than for their ability to capture the spotlight.

Policy Experts or Policy Instruments? Think Tanks and the Debate over Constitutional Reform in Canada

In their annual reports and promotional materials, think tanks in Canada, like their American counterparts, frequently highlight their achievements. Among other things, they list their recent publications, provide information on the research programs they are engaged in, and summarize their contributions to various policy issues. To put it simply, think tanks, like corporations, have a vested interest in convincing their target audiences that they offer a useful product. It is not surprising, therefore, that they often exaggerate their impact in the policy-making process.

Think tanks try to create the impression that they play a critical role in injecting new and innovative ideas into the public arena. However, the handful of scholars in Canada who have closely scrutinized their contributions to various public policy debates have been less willing to embrace their image as indispensable repositories of policy expertise. For instance, rather than portraying think tanks as organizations that have had a decisive impact on shaping policy decisions, Lindquist and Tupper claim that Canadian think tanks have made only modest contributions to important policy debates. In his comprehensive analysis of Canadian think tanks, Lindquist examines the contributions of several research institutes to three policy debates (energy policy, pension reform, and tax policy process reform) that took place from the early 1970s to the mid-1980s. He concludes that while some think tanks may have played important roles during the initial stages of these debates, policymakers have not been impressed by their contributions. As Lindquist observes:

The general finding ... is that institute public inquiry was not of direct relevance to actors interviewed in the case studies; the institutes rarely appeared to challenge senior officials in their deliberations and preparation for their political masters. This finding is of considerable interest because institutes had significant early roles in the debates on pension reform and tax policy process reform. Each case study revealed different aspects of this more general finding. The energy policy case revealed that institute studies were monitored more for political considerations. Officials were hard put to recall any influential work by the institutes, although there is evidence that indicates some of the more technical activities were viewed as being somewhat useful. The pension reform case study showed that senior officials labeled the institutes as interest or advocacy groups, yet none of the institutes were considered to be particularly effective advocates. Nor were they repositories of technical expertise and data on pension issues. The tax policy process reform case study suggests that even when the institutes appeared to have had the ear of senior officials, their work failed to provide insightful analysis of the issues at hand.[1]

Lindquist's conclusions about the relevance of think tanks in the policy-making process have been supported by other scholars in the field, including Allan Tupper. Tupper agrees that think tanks are becoming more visible, but, like Lindquist, questions how much impact they have had in shaping major policy debates. Although he admits that some institutes, including C.D. Howe, may have played a critical role during the Canada-U.S. free trade debate, he is less convinced that think tanks in general produce the type of research that is necessary to provide the basis for informed policy discussions on critical issues. In his study, which examines the research contribution of three Canadian think tanks, the C.D. Howe Institute, the Canadian Centre for Policy Alternatives and the Western Centre for Economic Research, on the "vexing problem of the public debt," Tupper concludes that little of value was added to resolving this ongoing issue confronting policymakers. He notes, "I am critical of think tanks' contribution to our understanding of the public debt. Their research is short-sighted, too polemical, and in the main too wedded to the perspectives of modern economics. It adds little to our understanding of a contentious issue."[2]

In this chapter I explore the contribution of think tanks to yet another important policy issue, constitutional reform. The findings of this case study, which is intended simply to illustrate the involvement of think tanks in one policy area, are consistent with Lindquist's and Tupper's skepticism about the contribution of think tanks to policy development. However, as this case study reveals, I am skeptical, not because of the questionable quality of some think tank publications, but because of the willingness of a handful of think tanks to jeopardize their institutional autonomy by advancing the political interests of policymakers.

During the winter of 1992 five think tanks – the C.D. Howe Institute, the Institute for Research on Public Policy (IRPP), the Canada-West

Foundation, the Niagara Institute, and the Atlantic Provinces Economic Council (APEC), were unexpectedly thrust into the public debate over the future of constitutional reform in Canada. Although some of these institutes had written extensively on various aspects of the constitution, it was not a particular publication or a speech given by a staff member that propelled them into the spotlight. Ironically, it was the collapse of a parliamentary committee established to consult with Canadians on the proposed changes to the constitution leading up to the Charlottetown Accord that brought them national attention.

When the committee proved incapable of carrying out its responsibilities, Prime Minister Brian Mulroney and Joe Clark, then minister of constitutional affairs, relied on these five institutes to help revive public interest in the constitution. In what was dubbed the Renewal of Canada, the think tanks were contracted to organize a series of constitutional conferences focusing on specific themes and recommendations outlined by the federal government in its 1991 report Shaping Canada's Future Together. Interestingly enough, the institutes were expected not to contribute policy ideas, their raison d'être, but to help transmit those of the government to an increasingly disillusioned public. According to most accounts, they performed this function extraordinarily well.[3] By serving as conference organizers and facilitators, they not only established a legitimate forum for public discussion but played a critical role in preventing the constitutional reform process from being completely derailed. Unfortunately, in the process of providing this crucial public service some of the think tanks involved may have compromised their own legitimacy as independent and credible centres for research and analysis. As this chapter will demonstrate, rather than promoting themselves as policy experts, the think tanks which participated in the constitutional conferences served as policy instruments of the government.

The involvement of think tanks in the constitutional conferences enables scholars to bypass some of the many obstacles they encounter in trying to assess the impact of these organizations. Unlike their behaviour during the vociferous debate over free trade and the goods and services tax (GST), when several think tanks and other nongovernmental organizations sought to convey their views through government and nongovernment channels, only a handful of think tanks were responsible for organizing the Renewal of Canada initiative. Identifying them does not therefore pose a problem, nor does isolating the group of scholars who were seconded to the Federal-Provincial Relations Office (FPRO) in 1991 to draft the government's twenty-eight recommendations on constitutional reform. In short, the involvement of think tanks in the constitutional conferences provides a unique opportunity to evaluate the impact of several think tanks at the height of their public visibility.

This case study has been selected because in addition to avoiding some methodological hurdles, it provides insight into the role several think tanks played in what might be the most important public policy debate in Canada of the last quarter of the twentieth century. With the exception of the Canada-US Free Trade Agreement (FTA) and the North American Free Trade Agreement (NAFTA), it is difficult to think of another policy issue the Canadian government has assigned a higher priority. If think tanks with expertise in constitutional issues could not play an important role in shaping the outcome of this critical policy debate, when could they be expected to have an impact?

Although the temptation to base observations about the nature of think tank influence on one case study must be resisted, much can be gained by looking more closely at the primary role these organizations played during the constitutional conferences. In examining their involvement, three major questions will be addressed. First, why did the federal government hire think tanks to facilitate public discussions on the constitution? Are they uniquely qualified to perform this role, or were there other factors that motivated the government's decision? Second, why did the think tanks agree to serve as conference organizers and facilitators when it was clear from the outset that they would not enjoy complete independence in running the conferences? Did they become involved to enhance their public visibility (all the conferences were televised by the CBC's *Newsworld*), or was the lure of large sums of government money sufficient to entice them? Third, and perhaps most importantly, if the federal government was not asking think tanks to generate their own policy ideas but simply to transmit the ideas of the government, what does this tell us about the role of these organizations in policy-making?

The government's decision to rely on think tanks, or what Clark referred to as "credible independent organizations," was clearly not influenced by their resources.[4] A constitutional conference secretariat, headed by Arthur Kroeger, an experienced deputy minister, had to be established to handle most of the logistics related to the conferences.[5] Rather, the decision to hire think tanks instead of professional consultants, for instance, was motivated by the government's desire to ensure the integrity and legitimacy of the conferences and of the constitutional reform process. Confronted by intense and often harsh media scrutiny, not to mention a public that had grown tired and increasingly skeptical of the government's handling of constitutional issues, Mulroney and Clark had to rely on organizations generally perceived as operating at arm's length from government. Because it

had lost much of its own credibility, the government hoped, by enlisting the support and tacit endorsement of think tanks, to draw on some
of their credibility. Tapping into the reservoir of think tanks gave the
government the much-needed transfusion of legitimacy it required to
revive the constitutional reform process.

On the other hand, the decision of the five think tanks to serve as
conference organizers was likely motivated by several factors, not the
least of which was to increase their cash flow. With the exception of
the IRPP, which draws on interest generated from its hefty $40 million
endowment, the other institutes have modest budgets. Securing access
to funds that could help subsidize their research for a long period of
time had to have been a major consideration. In addition, the desire
of many think tanks to increase their public exposure also influenced
their decision, as may have the prospect of increased access to key
policymakers. However, even more important than the question of why
think tanks agreed to participate are the implications of the role they
willingly agreed to undertake.

While a handful of journalists still cling to the view of think tanks
as research institutions of high-powered intellectuals committed to
addressing society's most pressing economic, political, and social
issues, this image has long been overturned by many think tank
directors and political scientists who work in these organizations. For
several think tanks, particularly the more advocacy-oriented ones,
policy research is only one of their functions. Indeed, for some it is
not even the most important. Stimulating debate on domestic and
foreign policy issues through public workshops and seminars and by
giving interviews to the media, rather than producing scholarly studies,
is often seen as a main priority. If this view of think tanks is accepted,
then the role of the five policy institutes in the constitutional conferences should not be regarded as unusual. After all, if think tanks are
no longer perceived as repositories of policy expertise, why would we
expect the government to turn to them for policy advice? Moreover,
why would they refuse to serve as conference organizers for the
government, a role that they are clearly qualified to assume and one
that many are prepared to accept?

Had the government turned to think tanks like the Fraser Institute
or the Canadian Centre for Policy Alternatives (CCPA), which are
known for engaging in more sharply ideological advocacy and
research, or to one of several others in Canada that perform contract
work for departments and agencies, there would be little need to
pursue this inquiry further. However, given Mulroney and Clark were
concerned with preserving the integrity and legitimacy of the conferences, they intentionally avoided selecting think tanks that were

perceived as overtly partisan or too closely linked to the government. Instead of inviting think tanks like the Fraser Institute, which has often been subjected to negative media coverage, the government turned to the Canada West Foundation and the C.D. Howe Institute, which are widely recognized as highly competent research institutes. Yet despite their expertise, the government did not ask them for independent policy advice but simply asked them to help spark public interest in the constitution – the government was interested not in the insights they could offer but in the public relations services they could provide.

As will be revealed, the five think tanks clearly played an important role for the government, but perhaps not the role one might have imagined. They did stimulate public debate over constitutional reform, something the government was clearly incapable of doing, and several of the conferences generated support for, or opposition to, some of the recommendations of the federal government, a clear benefit to the provincial premiers negotiating the Charlottetown Accord. Nevertheless, despite these contributions think tanks did not appear to have much impact in shaping the initial recommendations for constitutional change.

In this chapter, background information on the events leading up to the creation of the constitutional conferences will be discussed, followed by a brief profile of the five think tanks that participated in the Renewal of Canada initiative and the factors that may have motivated their involvement. Finally, their contribution in the constitutional conferences will be evaluated.

PLAN B: THE CREATION OF THE CONSTITUTIONAL CONFERENCES

In September 1991 the federal government released Shaping Canada's Future Together, a blueprint of twenty-eight recommendations or proposals for constitutional reform that would, if implemented, "revise the rules that shape the country's political life."[6] To ensure that Canadians would have sufficient opportunity to react to the government's vision of a new constitutional framework, something the government had been harshly criticized for not doing prior to the Meech Lake negotiations, a Special Joint Committee of the House of Commons and the Senate (the Castonguay-Dobbie Committee, later to become the Beaudoin-Dobbie Committee) was established.[8] The committee, as Kroeger points out, "was to hold hearings across the country and submit a report by February 28 [1992]. The government would then make decisions about constitutional changes, taking into account the Committee's findings."[9]

Shortly after the committee began its public hearings, however, it appeared that it might not be able to spark the interest of citizens who had grown tired of what seemed like a never-ending debate over the constitution. Moreover, the government's desire to engage the public in a comprehensive and constructive dialogue on constitutional reform was threatened by the committee's "carnival of blunders." According to David Milne, "After an ill-prepared plunge into townhall meetings in several provinces that seemed to offer either empty halls or ready platforms for redneck comments damaging to national unity, after consequent demands for the resignation of co-chairperson Ms. Dobbie, and the departure of her counterpart, respected Quebec Senator Claude Castonguay, the Parliamentary Committee had literally sputtered to a complete stop."[10]

Peter Russell offers an equally scathing indictment of the constitutional hearings: "The trail of Canada's constitutional odyssey is littered with the wreckage of constitutional vehicles that went off the rails, but for sheer disaster nothing can top the miserable performance of the Castonguay-Dobbie Committee."[11] By early November 1991 the committee appeared to have come to a complete standstill when no one showed up at its hearings in Manitoba. According to Milne, at that stage "the government needed to reassert its control over the constitutional process, or face irreparable damage to the constitutional package and its own reputation. Politically, the question was not simply one of finding some other vehicle for testing public attitudes, but rather of finding a means of restoring public confidence in the constitutional process itself."[12]

The Mulroney government clearly understood the important role the parliamentary committee was asked to play and the potential repercussions its implosion could bring. Public input into the constitutional reform process was vital for the conservative government that had been harshly criticized for excluding Canadians from discussions leading up to the Meech Lake Accord. Sensitive to these and similar criticisms, Mulroney recognized the importance of generating public interest and public views on constitutional reform. But equally critical for the government was arriving at an accord that was acceptable both to Quebec and to western provinces, key constituencies for Mulroney. Not only was the Meech Lake Accord unpopular with the West, but its failure spurred a growth in separatist sympathies in Quebec, where Mulroney's promise of constitutional reform had secured his electoral victories in 1984 and 1988.[13] Faced with these considerable pressures before an election, it was critical for Mulroney to arrive at a deal; the collapse of the Castonguay-Dobbie Committee was nothing short of a disaster.

While the government recognized the need to restore public confidence in the constitutional reform process, which, according to most observers, had come almost completely unraveled, it also acknowledged that it had little time to reflect on what had gone wrong. With the parliamentary committee's February 28 deadline approaching, Mulroney had to quickly reconsider his options. Canceling the public hearings would be suicidal for the government, but so would allowing the parliamentary committee to continue playing to sparsely attended audiences. By mid-November the government had decided that instead of terminating the faltering hearings, it would resuscitate them by organizing "five Constitutional Conferences on five consecutive weekends in five different major cities across the country."[14] Referred to by Peter Harrison as Plan B, the constitutional conferences would, they hoped, provide a more legitimate forum for public discussion on the constitution.[15]

On November 14 1991 the cabinet invited Arthur Kroeger to assume responsibility for the initiative. In conveying the government's invitation to Kroeger, Paul Tellier, secretary to the cabinet, indicated that although many of the details had to be worked out, five independent organizations, or public policy institutes, had been contracted to help share in the management of the constitutional conferences.[16] On 2 December 1991 the government formally announced the creation of the conferences and provided the names of the five institutes contracted to assist. The news release from the Privy Council Office on that day read, in part: "The Right Honourable Joe Clark, Minister of Constitutional Affairs and President of the Privy Council, today announced that arrangements have been made to hold a series of conferences on constitutional renewal in early 1992. Each of the first four conferences will be sponsored by an independent institute, and will deal with a particular set of the Government's constitutional proposals. It has been agreed that the institutes will be responsible for the conferences, including selection of the participants, chairpersons and rapporteurs."[17]

Surprisingly, however, the News Release made no reference to why the five had been selected or to why, for that matter, the government had decided to enlist the support of think tanks. Other than identifying the organizations as independent institutes, the government gave no explanation for this change in the constitutional consultative process. Why did the government select a group of think tanks to save the sinking constitutional ship? Were think tanks a logical choice, or could it have turned to other public or private organizations instead? And why did it select the Atlantic Provinces Economic Council (APEC) and the Niagara Institute, organizations not generally known for their expertise on constitutional matters?

At first glance, the government's decision appears logical. As organizations committed to influencing public opinion and public policy, think tanks frequently organize conferences and invite policymakers, academics, journalists, and representatives from the private sector to participate. In doing so, they decide on the format of the conference, arrange for speakers and determine whether and in what form to publish the proceedings. Although few had organized conferences on such a scale, the arrangements that had to be made were not completely foreign to them.

It is unlikely, however, that their ability to organize conferences was sufficient incentive for government to invite their participation. As will be discussed in more detail later in this chapter, since the think tanks lacked the resources to effectively run the conferences, the government had to create a constitutional affairs secretariat at a cost of $8.96 million,[18] to provide "logistic and operational assistance ... and information on the policy substance of the proposals."[19] Not only was the secretariat expected to ensure that the conferences ran smoothly, but it was also responsible for providing the participants with background papers on the proposals under consideration.[20] If the think tanks were not expected to assume full responsibility for running the conferences or even to supply participants with independent appraisals of the constitutional proposals (although some, including C.D. Howe, did), why did the government solicit their assistance?

The simple answer is that what the government desperately needed was something that consulting firms and a host of other organizations capable of organizing conferences could not provide – instant credibility and legitimacy with the public.[21] As independent, non profit, non-partisan organizations, the think tanks had reputations as institutions that operate at arm's length from the government. They attempted, though not always successfully, to portray themselves as organizations committed to improving government decision making, not to advancing a particular ideological agenda or the interests of one political party. It is this perception of think tanks that Clark and Tellier hoped would play particularly well to the media, which had seized on the total breakdown of the Castonguay-Dobbie Committee to predict the imminent failure of future constitutional negotiations. They also hoped that selecting think tanks to help manage the conferences might not only reignite public interest in the constitutional reform process but would, at least in the short-term, provide a new focus for the media. To their delight, it did both.

Once the decision to enlist the support of think tanks was made, deciding which would sponsor the conferences did not likely create much difficulty. Unlike in the United States, where policymakers must rely on directories to keep track of the hundreds of think tanks, in Canada less than three dozen independent think tanks exist, and of these, only a handful of those specializing in domestic policy have made their presence felt in policy-making circles.[22] According to Ron Watts, a constitutional adviser to Joe Clark during this period, after the limited pool of think tanks the government could draw on was identified, two important criteria influenced the selection process: credibility and regional representation.[23] It is unclear what factors were considered in determining which think tanks were deemed credible and which ones were not. However, the decision makers clearly wanted to avoid selecting organizations whose reputation for political advocacy overshadowed their commitment to policy research. In selecting the C.D. Howe Institute (Toronto), the Institute for Research on Public Policy (Montreal), the Canada West Foundation (Calgary), the Atlantic Provinces Economic Council (Halifax), and the Niagara Institute (Niagara on the Lake), the government satisfied both criteria. It found think tanks that generally attracted favourable exposure in the media and that could offer regional representation.

The government's decision to pursue Plan B proved to be an important one. Not only did organizing the constitutional conferences save the parliamentary hearings from imminent disaster, but it renewed public interest in the debate over constitutional reform. By hiring think tanks to serve as conference facilitators, the government achieved what it clearly set out to do. It was able to significantly influence the public consultation process, something the parliamentary committee was incapable of doing, while creating the impression that "independent institutes" were running the show. Ironically, in the process of making the conferences a more legitimate public relations exercise for the government, the think tanks sacrificed some of their own independence, as will be explored more fully in the sections below.

THE CHOSEN FEW

The Atlantic Provinces Economic Council

Of the five think tanks invited to help organize the constitutional conferences, the Atlantic Provinces Economic Council is the oldest. Created in 1954 "as a partnership between the provincial governments and the private sector," APEC's objective is "to promote the Economic Development of the Atlantic Region of Canada."[24] With a research staff of five, together with two administrative assistants, APEC draws on its meager $270,000 budget to analyze and evaluate current and emerging economic trends and policies. Before the constitutional conferences, APEC had published approximately a dozen newsletters and background papers on how a new constitution could affect the Atlantic region.[25]

The Canada West Foundation

Although APEC is not generally known for its expertise in constitutional affairs, the Canada West Foundation is. From its offices in Calgary, the CWF has been a strong advocate for promoting and protecting western Canada's economic, political, and social interests in the Canadian federation. Founded in 1970, the CWF draws on support from various corporations, foundations, and government departments to maintain its active research program, and in 1996 it received two endowments totaling $1.5 million.[26] By the time David Elton, former president of the CWF, had been invited to participate in the Renewal of Canada initiative, his institute had released close to two dozen publications on constitutional issues, ranging from how to reform the Canadian Senate to the possible repercussions of Quebec separation, and it had organized a handful of major conferences on constitutional reform.

The Niagara Institute

The Niagara Institute, established in 1971, stands in stark contrast to the CWF. Unlike CWF, the Niagara Institute does not claim to have expertise in constitutional affairs or in any specific policy area, for that matter. According to Garry Rawson, director of business development at the Niagara Institute, before the 1992 conferences his institute had never focused on constitutional issues. Niagara became involved, Rawson stated, "because of their skill in managing search conferences."[27] Although the institute has clearly benefited from the research programs undertaken by the Conference Board of Canada, which it merged with in 1994, the institute does not engage in public policy research. Rather, it seeks "to enhance the quality of Canadian leadership in business, government and non-governmental organizations [by offering] specialized programs designed to help leaders identify, understand and address the issues of our time."[28] Of the five think tanks, the Niagara Institute was clearly the anomaly.

The C.D. Howe Institute and the Institute for Research on Public Policy

The two remaining institutes, the C.D. Howe Institute (1973) and the Institute for Research on Public Policy (1972), have similar institutional profiles.[29] Both have about fifteen members and budgets in the range of $2 million or more, and both institutes were created to improve public policy in Canada by providing objective and sound analysis of policy issues. However, unlike C.D Howe, the IRPP has a sizeable endowment to support its activities. Of the two, C.D. Howe enjoys greater public exposure, a result no doubt of its more extensive research program.[30] C.D. Howe had published no less than twenty studies on constitutional issues before becoming involved in the conferences, more than twice the number produced by the IRPP.

THE CONSTITUTIONAL CONFERENCES

When the federal government approached the five institutes to help organize the constitutional conferences, it made clear that it did not expect them to produce independent appraisals of the twenty-eight proposals on constitutional reform. Nor did it expect them to assume full responsibility for running the conferences. Instead, the institutes were contracted to perform six specific functions: to define the conference agenda and format, identify chairs and co-chairs for conference sessions, select appropriate participants, prepare conference material, offer on-site supports and submit a conference report.[31]

Initially, it appeared that the institutes would exercise considerable independence in organizing the conferences, something they had apparently demanded in exchange for agreeing to participate. A closer look at the government's criteria, however, reveals that in several instances the government dictated how it wanted the conferences run. In addition to determining which of its twenty-eight proposals in *Shaping Canada's Future Together* would be the "primary thematic focus of each conference" (the conference agenda), the government had considerable input into the individuals who would be invited to participate. According to the News Release of 2 December 1991, "The institutes are to invite to the Conferences on an *ex-officio* basis:

- all members of the Joint Parliamentary Committee,
- two individuals selected respectively by each of the caucuses of the three federal political parties with Parliamentary status,
- two individuals from each province and territory, to be selected by the Premier/Head of Government, and
- one representative of each of the four national aboriginal organizations."[32]

Moreover, the government specified that although the "Institutes are responsible for determining the manner in which [members of the public] are selected ... individuals selected should have a demonstrated interest in, and some knowledge of constitutional matters, and should have a significant record of service to their communities." Furthermore, it indicated that "experts invited by the Institutes to participate in panels and workshops must, taken together, represent a broad and balanced cross-section of views."[33]

The government also went to great lengths to outline the format of the conferences. Among other things, it stated that at each conference, institutes had to provide "an opportunity for a government spokesperson to outline the constitutional proposals and underlying rationale with particular reference to those which are the subject of each conference."[34] Apparently the government had little confidence in the ability of experts from independent think tanks to explain the nature of the constitutional proposals under discussion. Government officials did not demonstrate much confidence in their ability to prepare final reports on the conference proceedings either. The Constitutional Conferences Secretariat arranged with the Privy Council and the Federal-Provincial Relations offices "to have a team of 'note-takers' available at each conference." As Harrison notes, "in summarizing what had been the gist of discussion in the various forums, this assisted rapporteurs in providing summaries to plenary sessions, and report writers in pulling together the sense of the conferences."[35]

Judging by the arrangements agreed to before the conferences began, it was clear that the institutes would not be permitted to exercise complete independence. This was a price, however, that some institutes were prepared to pay. Asked why their institute became involved in the 1992 conferences even though they would not be permitted to enjoy complete independence, a senior analyst from one think tank remarked, "We did not want to get involved in the conferences but figured we had to. It would have been perceived as bad PR to not want to save the country" (off-the-record telephone interview). Some institutes on the other hand, did not believe that their institutional independence was compromised at all. Despite the amount of government intervention, they continued to insist that they, not Ottawa, were ultimately in charge. In a report on the constitutional conference it helped organize, the Canada West Foundation stated: "The Conference was organized and managed by the Canada West Foundation, with assistance from a Conference Secretariat set up by the Government of Canada to aid in logistics and media coverage. Canada West Foundation exercised complete independence in the selection of conference participants, the organization of the program, the setting of the agenda, the selection of co-chairs and speakers, the preparation of pre-conference materials, and the writing of final report. There was no interference or direction, direct or indirect, on the part of the government."[36]

While these and similar statements were no doubt comforting to the government, the institutes were deluding themselves if they believed they had complete independence.[37] But for the think tanks, sacrificing some independence may have been a small price to pay in return for the potential benefits derived from their participation, including, of course, establishing greater credibility with the government. Becoming more firmly entrenched in policy-making circles could pay handsome dividends for think tanks committed to shaping public policy. In addition, by helping to organize the conferences, the institutes were able to attract considerable media exposure. The importance of generating media attention cannot be understated – not only does increased media coverage help foster the illusion of policy influence, but directors of several think tanks can often parlay their organization's media visibility into corporate and private donations.[38]

Generating free publicity was only one of the factors that would have motivated their decision to participate. Being centre stage at what might be the most important public policy debate in a quarter-century was also a strong incentive. For organizations committed to influencing public policy and public opinion, the opportunity to help put the constitutional reform process back on track would be difficult to pass up. Although they ran the risk of participating in conferences that could become public relations disasters, the government, not the institutes, would probably have been held accountable.[39] If, on the other hand, the conferences succeeded, the think tanks would forever be linked to a pivotal period in Canada's constitutional development.

The financial rewards of accepting a generous government contract may also have convinced several of the think tanks that had modest financial resources to take on the task. For its efforts, the Atlantic Province Economic Council received $314,000;[40] the C.D. Howe Institute and the Institute for Research on Public Policy shared $200,00 for co-organizing a conference; and the Canada West Foundation received $315,000. These figures, however, pale in comparison to the $760,000 cheque the Niagara Institute received.[41] Perhaps even more lucrative than accepting the government's offer was the potential for additional contracts in the future, an enormous benefit, since the majority of Canada's think tanks constantly struggle to keep afloat.

Each institute may have been motivated to participate in the Renewal of Canada conferences for different reasons, but in the final analysis, they all shared the government's commitment to move the constitutional process forward. The potential benefits and some of the costs associated with this decision have been outlined. What needs to be discussed now is what contribution the think tanks made to this critical

issue. I will now evaluate the role the institutes played at critical stages
leading up to and during the conferences.

SOME CAUSE FOR CONCERN: AN ASSESSMENT OF THE IMPACT OF THINK TANKS

Well before the federal government made its twenty-eight proposals
on constitutional reform known, most of the think tanks that participated in the constitutional conferences had given considerable thought
to the future of the Canadian federation. With the exception of the
Niagara Institute, the institutes involved had published studies detailing the economic, social, and political issues associated with a changed
constitution. In examining several controversial issues ranging from
the potential ramifications of introducing a triple E Senate to granting
Quebec distinct status within the constitution, they had articulated
their views. The "independent credible organizations" that the government was hoping would provide legitimacy to the public consultation
process on constitutional reform had already staked out their positions.
Nevertheless, when the government began considering how to reform
the constitution after the failure of the Meech Lake Accord, it did not
turn to these think tanks to draft a new blueprint but to a small group
of academics in universities.

Shortly after Professor Ron Watts was seconded from Queen's University to the Federal-Provincial Relations Office in April 1991 to serve
as a constitutional adviser to Joe Clark, a select group of constitutional
experts consisting of Kathy Swinton (University of Toronto), Roger
Gibbins (University of Calgary), Peter Leslie (Queen's University), and
Doug Purvis (Queen's University) were called upon to assist him in
drafting the government's constitutional reform proposals.[42] In addition, Watts was asked to edit a series of background papers intended
to explain in a clear and straightforward manner the government's
proposals for reforming the constitution. So, when the government was
formulating its vision of a new federation, the views of a handful of
academics were clearly heard; the recommendations of private think
tanks, on the other hand, were barely noticed.

Directors of think tanks often credit their institutes with helping
formulate government legislation and initiatives, but in this particular
case they appear to have had little impact. It was not until the parliamentary hearings on the constitution failed that they became part of
the consultation process, and not as transmitters of knowledge but as
conference organizers and facilitators, so they could not legitimately
claim that their ideas on how to reform the constitution mattered.

Think tanks made a difference in this later phase of constitutional discussions, but not in the way one might imagine.

The absence of think tanks during this critical stage of policy-making raises important questions about their role in policy research. If policy makers were aware of the institutes' research on various constitutional issues after Meech Lake, why were they not asked to help draft the government's proposals? Did policymakers question the quality of their publications or the credentials of their staff? If they did, why did the government regard them as sufficiently credible to organise their conferences? Were they simply selected because they were perceived by the *media* as credible institutions? Alternatively, if the government was unaware of their research, what does this say about the ability of think tanks to convey their ideas?

For some of the think tanks, organising the constitutional conferences was a mixed blessing: it may have increased their exposure, but it did little to advance their reputations as scholarly research organizations. It demonstrated that at times some of the country's most talked-about think tanks have little influence in shaping policy issues. The role of the five think tanks in the constitutional conferences should encourage scholars to think more critically about the contribution research institutes make to public policy. If they are simply expected to serve as policy instruments of government and provide tantalizing morsels of information to the media, then there should be little cause for concern. On the other hand, if think tanks are expected to serve as sources of policy expertise, then their participation in the Renewal of Canada conferences should raise some eyebrows.

LESSONS LEARNED?

The federal government clearly learned some important lessons from soliciting the assistance of think tanks in the winter of 1992. Among other things, it realized the potential benefits of enlisting the support of independent policy research institutes to facilitate discussions on important issues, particularly when the government's handling of those issues was being called into question. Policymakers also realized that the reputation think tanks have cultivated as independent centres of policy expertise could work to their advantage. By drawing on their credibility, the government could enhance its own.

The success of the constitutional conferences did not go unnoticed by the federal Liberal government that handily defeated the Conservatives in 1993. In preparation for the 1994 budget, Minister of Finance Paul Martin called for a more open process of budget consultations, which included four public conferences. Martin announced that the public conferences would be held in Halifax, Montreal, Toronto, and Calgary in January 1994 and would be hosted by four think tanks, all but one of which, the Public Policy Forum, had participated in the 1992 conferences. The other think tanks involved were the Atlantic Provinces Economic Council, the Institute for Research on Public Policy, and the Canada West Foundation.[43]

In accepting Martin's invitation, the four institutes requested and received more control over the selection of the approximately one hundred participants who attended each conference than they had enjoyed in 1992. Some institutes, including the IRPP and the Canada West Foundation, also distributed materials their institutes had prepared to the participants shortly before the conferences began.[44] However, even though the think tanks were more conscious of playing a hands-on role at the 1994 conferences, many of the same issues surrounding their involvement remained.

As in 1992, the think tanks that became involved in the 1994 pre-budget consultations were looked to not for their expertise as policy analysts but as organizations that could make the public consultation process work for the government. Once again they seemed to perform this function admirably. Nonetheless, in the wake of the 1994 conferences it is important for think tanks to re-evaluate what their priorities are and how they can best be advanced. While think tanks can serve the government's interests by acting as facilitators, they may not necessarily be advancing the public's interests or their own. Think tanks, according to their own promotional material, are in the business of developing and promoting ideas. They exist to think critically about important policy issues, not simply to advance or market the ideas of policymakers.

The case study presented in this chapter, like the studies prepared by Lindquist and Tupper, offers some insight into how think Canadian think tanks have become involved in particular policy areas. The picture that emerges may not be favourable, particularly for the think tanks singled out for examination. Nonetheless, the findings reinforce the central argument of this book that think tanks cannot be expected to play a decisive role at each stage of the policy cycle or, for that matter, in every policy area. While some think tanks may help to frame the parameters of key policy debates through their publications and media commentary, they may be less effective, as Lindquist and Tupper observe, in influencing specific policy decisions. Or as the constitutional conferences revealed, policymakers may not even be aware of the publications think tanks have produced, preferring instead to rely on them as conference facilitators.

The advantage of developing case studies that examine the participation of think tanks in specific policy areas is that it enables scholars to go beyond simple data sets to more accurately assess their relevance. The disadvantage is that it is difficult to make general observations about their impact in the policy-making process by relying on a handful of cases. Indeed, by focusing on Ken Battle's contributions to the development of social welfare policy in Canada, one might conclude – and justifiably so –, that the president of the Caledon Institute has had a profound impact in shaping public policy. A similar conclusion might be reached in examining the contribution of the C.D. Howe institute to the free trade debate and to the future of the Canada Pension Plan. Depending on the specific policy issue that is under consideration and the particular stage of the policy-making process that one is focusing on, scholars may walk away with the impression that think tanks are either extremely influential or entirely irrelevant. Both impressions would be right.

CHAPTER EIGHT

Conclusion:
Policy Influence, Policy Relevance, and the Future of Think Tanks in Canada, the United States, and Beyond

This book began with a seemingly straightforward question – do think tanks matter? Unfortunately, after surveying the think tank population in Canada and the United States and examining their involvement in the policy-making process, there does not appear to be a simple answer. Depending on who the question is directed to, responses may range from yes to no, and from at times to more than you can possibly imagine. In some respects all these answers are accurate. Indeed, as this study has demonstrated, several conclusions can be drawn regarding the role and significance of think tanks in policy-making.

Notwithstanding the considerable differences in their political systems, think tanks in the United States and Canada have often played an important role in contributing to the public dialogue. Through their publications, interviews with the media, appearances before legislative committees, and participation in conferences and seminars, think tanks have clearly made their presence felt. Moreover, in both countries think tanks have relied on less visible channels to convey their views to policy-makers. However, largely due to differences in their political structures, think tanks in the United States and Canada often attempt to exercise policy influence at different times and at different stages of the policy cycle.

The highly decentralized and fragmented political system of the United States, combined with its weak party system, helps explain why American think tanks assign a high priority to sharing their ideas with members of Congress. Since members of Congress are not constrained by party unity, think tanks have an incentive to establish contact with as many Democrats and Republicans as possible. The more predictable electoral cycle in the United States, and the absence of party-based research institutes also helps to explain why think tanks regard presidential elections and the transition periods that follow as opportune times to influence the policy direction of government. By contrast, the presence of strong party unity in Canada and the prime minister's long-standing tradition of relying on the Prime Minister's Office, the Privy Council Office, and senior bureaucrats for policy advice may account for think tanks in Canada often relying on different channels to reach policymakers.

Differences in the institutional structures of the two countries may explain why think tanks in the United States have more opportunities or access points to influence policymakers than think tanks in Canada. However, they do not explain why some are far more effective at marketing their message than others. Several factors, including their financial resources, the number and quality of their staff, the strong connections some think tank directors have to policymakers, and their ability to convey their ideas to multiple audiences may influence how much or how little impact think tanks have.

The willingness of office holders to embrace the ideas of certain think tanks is also important in explaining why some enjoy tremendous visibility while others languish in obscurity. As chapter 6 showed, several presidential candidates, particularly those regarded as Washington outsiders, have helped to elevate the profile of several think tanks. Similarly, in Canada one sees periods when the visibility and prominence of some think tanks has either been significantly enhanced or greatly diminished. As chapter 7 demonstrated, at no other time have Canadian think tanks generated as much public attention as during the constitutional conferences in the winter of 1992. Ironically, less than two weeks after the last constitutional conference organized by a think tank ended, several other think tanks in the policy research community were forced to close their doors.

While it is not difficult to observe where in the policy cycle think tanks in the United States and Canada appear to be most active, determining how influential they are at different stages of policymaking remains problematic, since to assess how much or how little influence they have, several methodological barriers must be overcome. One major barrier is how to measure policy influence. Should it be measured by recording media citations, appearances before legislative committees, the number of publications, or the number of staff appointed to high-level positions in the government? Or are there other tangible and intangible indicators that should be considered? Do some indicators provide a more accurate measurement of policy influence than others?

Although data on each indicator may provide insight into the amount of exposure think tanks and their staff generate, they cannot confirm how much or how little influence they have in shaping public opinion and the preferences and choices of policymakers. For instance, several

think tanks tally how often their organizations are referred to in the
media and the number of times their staff are called on to testify before
legislative committees. But what conclusions can be drawn from these
data? Not surprisingly, think tanks that register the most media citations
and appearances before committees conclude that they are the most
influential. Those studying these institutions must, however, be a bit
more circumspect. Data on media citations may tell us which institutes
are effective at making the news, yet it tells us little about whether their
views have helped shape, reinforce, clarify, or change the minds of
policymakers and the public. It cannot be assumed that policymakers
or members of the general public are even familiar with what certain
think tanks have stated in the media. Similarly, when think tanks testify
before legislative committees, we cannot be certain that their statements
made a difference in how policymakers approached particular issues.
At times their testimony may influence the views of some policymakers;
at other times, however, their input may simply reinforce the views of
policymakers or, as is often the case, experts from think tanks might
simply be ignored. Other indicators, such as the number of their publications or how many of their staff receive high-level appointments,
may reveal even less about their influence in policy-making. Put simply,
it is virtually impossible to assign a numerical value to the amount of
influence think tanks wield. We cannot, for instance, conclude that think
tanks have influence 20 percent or 50 percent of the time. We cannot
even say for certain how much impact specific think tanks have had at
particular stages of policy debates or whom exactly they have influenced. At best, by assessing their involvement in specific policy areas,
we can obtain a better sense of how relevant or irrelevant they were.

    In addition to considering how to measure policy influence or
whether, in fact, it can be measured at all, other obstacles must be
overcome to evaluate the impact of think tanks: for instance, determining how to isolate the views of think tanks from dozens of other
individuals and governmental and nongovernmental organizations that
actively seek to influence public policy. As the policy-making community becomes increasingly congested, tracing the origin of an idea to a
particular individual or organization creates its own set of problems.

    Examining the organizations and individuals who coalesce around
particular policy issues or who congregate at a certain stage in the
policy cycle can offer a useful point of departure for studying the interaction between policymakers and representatives of nongovernmental
organizations in specific policy communities.[1] In addition to identifying
the organizations and individuals most actively involved in discussing
a particular policy concern with government officials, which views generated the most attention can be determined through interviews and

surveys. Yet, unless policymakers admit that their policy decisions were based primarily on recommendations from a particular individual or organization, something they are rarely inclined to do, it is difficult to determine how much influence participants in the policy process had.

Since it is unlikely that these and other methodological obstacles will be overcome, it may be more appropriate to discuss the relevance of think tanks in the policy-making process than to speculate about how much policy influence they wield. In other words, rather than trying to state categorically on the basis of a handful of indicators that some think tanks are more influential than others, it should be determined if, when, and under what conditions they can and have contributed to specific public policy discussions and to the broader policy-making environment. At the very least, scholars studying these institutions should acknowledge that given their tremendous diversity, all think tanks do not possess the resources, the expertise, or the desire to become embroiled in every policy debate. They should also acknowledge that think tanks assign different priorities to becoming involved at different stages of the policy-making process. Thus, while some think tanks may play an active role in discussing the implications of a specific government policy with the media, others may be trying to convey their views to policymakers through less visible channels.

There will be ample opportunity to assess the relevance of think tanks in the future. As the following section indicates, in Canada and the United State and in the global community, policymakers are turning increasingly to think tanks to provide expertise and to stimulate informed debate on a range of issues. The question that remains is whether think tanks possess the resources and desire to make a difference.

THE FUTURE OF THINK TANKS:
A VIEW FROM CANADA, THE UNITED STATES,
AND THE GLOBAL COMMUNITY

The future of publicly funded think tanks in Canada looked bleak when Conservative finance minister Don Mazankowski handed down the 1992 federal budget. Within minutes of getting up on the floor of the House of Commons, Mazankowski announced that forty-six government agencies, boards, commissions, corporations, and advisory bodies would be dismantled. After the shock of the drastic cost-cutting set in, several journalists commented on what the 1992 budget would mean for the state of policy research in Canada. What they and others discovered was that contrary to Mazankowski's assertions, there were few other sources of independent expertise in Canada that could fill the void left by some of Canada's leading domestic and foreign policy think tanks.[2]

Had Mazankowski and his advisors looked more closely at the external policy research community, they would have realized that there were no private institutes, university departments, or other non-governmental sources of policy expertise that possessed the resources to undertake the extensive long-term research being conducted by the Economic Council of Canada (ECC). Not even the Conference Board of Canada and the C.D. Howe Institute, which the finance minister considered viable replacements for the ECC, were prepared or qualified to assume this role.[3] Moreover, there did not appear to be many organizations that could carry out the type of work initiated by the Science Council of Canada. At the time of its closure, several other scientific bodies existed, including the National Advisory Board on Science and Technology, the National Research Council, the Natural Sciences and Engineering Research Council, and the Council of Science and Technology Ministers, but unlike the Science Council of Canada their mandate was not to provide long-term thinking on issues of science and technology. As Janet Halliwell, head of the Science Council remarked shortly after the budget, without the Science Council, "the Canadian economy loses its reflective foresight capacity."[4]

In foreign policy the Mulroney government did not demonstrate much foresight either. There were no institutes that had the staff or the financial resources to mount the type of research program on peace and security conducted by the CIIPS. Indeed, except for the small and poorly funded research centres on defense and security issues at a dozen Canadian universities and except for a handful of think tanks that dealt with international affairs in some fashion, the foreign-policy research community remained relatively barren.[5]

The 1992 budget called into question the importance policymakers gave to policy research institutes, but in recent years high-level policymakers have once again recognized the contribution think tanks can make to improving public policy. In July 1996 Jocelyne Bourgon, former clerk of the privy council office and secretary to the cabinet, launched the Policy Research Initiative (PRI), an ongoing project that has involved several think tanks across Canada. Overseen by the Policy Research Secretariat of the Privy Council Office, the PRI is intended to help government departments and agencies determine the most effective ways to enhance the policy capacity of the federal public service, an important concern in the wake of government downsizing. Recognizing the dual needs of providing greater policy coordination in an increasingly complex policy environment and helping government think more strategically about the long-term implications of particular policies, the PRI has taken a profound interest in the state of the policy research community. Think tanks have figured prominently in the

Policy Research Secretariat's discussions on building stronger networks between organizations engaged in policy analysis and federal department and agencies. While it is premature to predict how worthwhile the PRI will be, it is clear that think tanks have been presented with a significant opportunity to showcase what they can contribute to policy-making.

Unlike several think tanks in the United States, the majority of policy institutes in Canada cannot impress policymakers with high-profile staffers or multimillion dollar budgets, nor will they likely be able to in the foreseeable future. Nonetheless, as this study has shown, think tanks do not require millions of dollars or dozens of staff members to convey their ideas. As Ken Battle of the Caledon Institute and David Zussman of the Public Policy Forum, among others, have demonstrated, using some ingenuity to communicate ideas to policymakers and putting important and valuable ideas on the table can go a long way in establishing think tanks as relevant players in policy-making.

As in the past, Canadian think tanks in the coming years will be faced with important challenges, not the least of which is securing access to sufficient funds and qualified staff. To survive, some may have to merge or occasionally pool their resources with other institutes. This may be the only way a number of smaller think tanks can remain open. Others may elect to merge to simply enhance their overall profile.[6] Still, unless philanthropic foundations and affluent donors in Canada become as enamoured with think tanks as have several leading philanthropists in the United States, it is unlikely that many Canadian policy institutes will ever enjoy financial security.

Besides constant funding concerns, think tanks in Canada will have to give serious thought to what their mission is and how it can best be achieved. If think tanks are truly committed to improving governmental decision making, as many claim they are, they have to provide policymakers with what they require most – long-term strategic thinking about key domestic and foreign policy issues. On the other hand, if they are more interested in advancing a particular ideological agenda than in supplementing the policy needs of government, they should pay closer attention to the strategies pursued by more advocacy-oriented institutes in the United States. Although a handful of think tanks in Canada have adopted this mode, it has yet to become the dominant trend.

The tendency of think tanks in the United States to become more advocacy-oriented will, however, likely continue. As more institutes enter the already crowded policy-research community, they will rely on a wide range of strategies to capture the attention of the public, the media, and the policymakers. Moreover, if the Democratic and

Republican parties become increasingly divided in the coming years, members of Congress will likely be even more willing to listen to those think tanks whose views strike a responsive chord with their constituents. However, the ever watchful eye of the Internal Revenue Service could interfere with the efforts of advocacy think tanks to achieve their goals. If the IRS revoked the tax-exempt status of a high-profile think tank for engaging in inappropriate political activities, it would send a strong message to other think tanks to curtail some of their more aggressive marketing techniques.

Despite the likelihood that the IRS will pay closer attention to the activities of think tanks, there is little to suggest that the growth rate of policy institutes in the United States will come to a halt. Think tanks have continued to spring up throughout the country. So long as there are policy entrepreneurs willing to create them and philanthropists prepared to fund them, there is no reason to believe that the explosion of policy institutes witnessed over the past two decades will fizzle out. However, while a handful in the United States will likely continue to dominate the headlines, it must be remembered that the majority of American think tanks closely resemble those in Canada in size and scope. Like the majority of Canadian think tanks, most in the United States will have to think about how to establish their niche in the policy-research community, a job made difficult by the presence of several institutes with multimillion dollar endowments.

The growth and evolution of think tanks in Canada and the United States will provide those engaged in the study of comparative political institutions with much to think about in the coming years, and students of international relations will likely begin to pay closer attention to the role and impact of think tanks on the world stage. Recently, the World Bank Institute, in partnership with several other organizations, including the Washington-based Center for International Private Enterprise (CIPE), organized a series of meetings with think tanks in the Middle East, Africa, and Europe to consider, among other things, how think tanks in emerging democracies could, with financial assistance from the World Bank and others, promote social, economic, and political reform.[7] This theme resurfaced at the World Bank's inaugural conference of the Global Development Network (GDN) in Bonn in December 1999. As part of its ongoing efforts to become a "knowledge bank," the World Bank is asking think tanks to help build policy networks between researchers and policymakers both within and across countries.[8] In the process, the bank hopes that think tanks will become vehicles that can help transform the political landscape of the international community. What remains to be seen is whether these organizations are up to the challenge.

The growing involvement of think tanks in the policy-making process at the national and international levels will give rise to a new set of intriguing questions. Undoubtedly one that will be asked from time to time is, Do think tanks matter? Judging by this analysis of Canadian and American think tanks, it is unlikely that a simple answer will be found.

NEXT STEPS

As the literature on think tanks continues to grow, scholars must keep abreast of what ground has been covered and what still needs to be studied. While much has been written on the think tank landscape in many industrial and developing nations, we still know relatively little about the internal workings of think tanks or how they assess their own impact in the policy-making community. Indeed, as difficult as it is for scholars to arrive at some consensus about how to measure policy influence, think tanks also struggle over how to evaluate their performance. For think tank directors, who must explain to their boards of directors and donor agencies how their resources are being spent and what results they have achieved, providing accurate and worthwhile performance indicators is not merely an academic exercise.

The reality facing think tank directors and those who study their institutions is that there is no single performance indicator that will provide an accurate assessment of what they have achieved relative to other institutes in the policy-making community, an observation consistent with the findings in chapter 5. Under ideal conditions we could assume that all think tanks agree on the same set of indicators and allocate a roughly equal percentage of their budgets to enhancing their performance in each category. After adjusting for differences in revenues and expenditures, scholars could then provide an annual ranking of institutes, perhaps similar to the *Maclean's* ranking of Canadian universities and colleges, which could in turn be passed on to think tanks. The job of think tank directors would then be done. Or would it? What directors of think tanks would be left with is some indication of where they ranked relative to other institutes – for instance, in media citations generated or in testimonies given. Unfortunately, while some think tanks might find comfort in these numbers, others would still be left with the lingering question of how much difference their institutes really made.

A potential solution to this nagging question would be for think tanks not to compare themselves to other policy institutes, although there might be external and internal pressures to do so, but to set out their own measurements of success. By reviewing their mission statements, think tanks could begin the process of identifying what policy issues they believed were important to study and the various channels they needed to rely on to convey their insights to selected target audiences. Once they had done this, they could then set out the performance indicators that would provide them with some insight into whether they were making progress toward achieving their specific objectives.

In examining the internal workings of think tanks, future researchers in this field will undoubtedly discover that policy institutes will rely on very different benchmarks for success. Some will continue to emphasize the importance of enhancing their media exposure and will closely monitor the number of media citations they receive. Others, however, will likely focus on less visible but potentially more influential channels, such as meetings and conferences with key policymakers. What will be interesting to discover is how think tanks seek to implement their goals while constantly confronting the financial pressures of staying afloat.

Scholars should also pay more attention to what policymakers think about the contribution think tanks have made at different stages of the policy-making process. They could do so either through interviews with or through surveys distributed to policymakers throughout government. A comprehensive survey of the attitudes of policymakers and journalists toward u.s. think tanks was conducted by Andrew Rich, but a similar survey has yet to be released in Canada.[9] Although some policy institutes have apparently commissioned private polling firms to survey Canadians about their views of think tanks, a more extensive survey of policymakers is needed. The obvious benefit of a survey is that policymakers can be asked specifically which think tanks have contributed to public policy and in what ways. They can also be asked to give examples of where think tanks may have made a difference. Among other things, those examples would allow scholars to develop more complete case studies.

In the case studies included in this book we are left with the impression that by virtue of participating in presidential campaigns some think tanks in the United States have become firmly entrenched in the policy-making process. While this is certainly true for a handful of institutes, the vast majority have not had the privilege of establishing such close ties to government. We are also left with the impression that unlike their American counterparts, think tanks in Canada, have rarely played a critical role in policy development. Although this finding is consistent with the observations made in chapter 7, there are countless other policy issues in which Canadian policy institutes may have played a more decisive role. A survey of policymakers would go a long way toward identifying these areas.

For those looking for a definitive answer to the question posed at the beginning of this book, the conclusion that I have reached may be disappointing. But as in other avenues of scholarly inquiry, we are often left with far more questions than answers. Think tanks are interesting organizations worthy of further scholarly attention, and as their visibility continues to increase, more people will likely question how much impact they have. I anxiously await their responses.

A Profile of Selected American Think Tanks

- The Carnegie Endowment for International Peace
- The Hoover Institution on War, Revolution and Peace
- The Council on Foreign Relations
- The American Enterprise Institute
- The Center for Strategic and International Studies
- The Institute for Policy Studies
- The Urban Institute
- The Cato Institute
- The Manhattan Institute for Policy Research
- The Progressive Policy Institute

THE CARNEGIE ENDOWMENT FOR INTERNATIONAL PEACE

Located adjacent to the Brookings Institution on Washington's Massachusetts Avenue, the Carnegie Endowment for International Peace (CEIP) has become one of America's premier foreign policy think tanks. With a $10 million endowment, the CEIP was established by Andrew Carnegie in 1910 as a nonpartisan institute to educate the public about peace, "to spread arbitral justice among nations and to promote the comity and commerce of the world without the dangers of war."[1] Acting on the advice of several leading pacifists, including then secretary of state Elihu Root, Carnegie stated that the annual income derived from the endowment should be used in any way "appropriate to hasten the abolition of war." Moreover, he directed that when "the establishment of peace is attained ... the revenue shall be devoted to the banishment of the next most degrading evil or evils, the suppression of which would most advance the progress, elevation and happiness of man."[2]

In accordance with the wishes of its founder, Carnegie's three-dozen researchers examine a wide range of issues that fall under two main programs: global policy and Russia/Eurasia. Some of these issues include worldwide migration, nuclear nonproliferation, economic reform and inequality, regional conflicts, and transparency and civil society. Although the institute publishes several studies each year, it is best known for its quarterly journal, *Foreign Policy*. The journal, along with the many seminars and workshops the CEIP conducts, is intended to stimulate debate among leading foreign-policy makers. The Carnegie Endowment also relies on other channels to convey its ideas. Staff from the institute frequently submit articles to major newspapers and regularly appear as guests on American television networks.

In 1993 the Carnegie Endowment decided to expand its reach even further by creating a public policy research centre in Moscow. Designed "to promote intellectual collaboration among scholars and specialists in the United States, Russia, and other post-Soviet states," the Carnegie Moscow Center sponsors workshops, seminars, and study groups that bring together academics, journalists, and representatives from the private, public, and nonprofit sectors to exchange views. The centre also provides a forum for international leaders to discuss various issues with audiences in Moscow.

THE HOOVER INSTITUTION ON WAR, REVOLUTION AND PEACE

Known for its commitment to pursuing traditional conservative principles, the Hoover Institution at Stanford University has rarely strayed from the mission its founder laid out for the institute decades ago. Established in 1919 by Herbert Hoover to protect and house valuable historical records acquired during World War I, the Hoover Institution's primary mission has been to reduce the role of government in economic and social affairs and to promote the national security interests of the United States.[3] As Herbert Hoover noted in founding the institute,

The Institution supports the Constitution of the United States, its Bill of Rights and its method of representative government. Both our social and economic systems are based on private enterprise from which springs initiative and ingenuity ... Ours is a system where the Federal Government should undertake no governmental, social or economic action, except where local government, or the people, cannot undertake it for themselves ... The overall mission of this Institution is, from its records, to recall the voice of experience against the making of war, and by the study of these records and their publication, to recall man's endeavors to make and preserve peace, and to sustain for America the safeguards of the American way of life. This institution is not, and must not be, a mere library. But with these purposes as its goal, the Institution itself must constantly and dynamically point the road to peace, to personal freedom, and to the safeguards of the American system.[4]

With an initial donation of $50,000 from Herbert Hoover, the institute has evolved into a leading centre for research and analysis on domestic and foreign policy. The institute's three main research areas are American institutions and economic performance, democracy and free markets, and international rivalries. In addition, its research program includes six international area studies that coincide with its library and archival collections. The areas of study are Russia and the other republics of the former Soviet Union, Europe, East Asia, Africa, the Middle East, and the Americas. The Hoover Institution's active research program results in the publication of several books and public policy essays each year.

Relying on a budget in excess of $20 million, the Hoover Institution has assembled a talented staff consisting of over seventy resident scholars, including several former high-level policymakers and Nobel prize winners. However, despite the contributions many of its scholars have made to the fields of economics, history, and political science, the institute has had a stormy relationship with Stanford faculty and administrators for years. The turbulent relationship between Hoover and Stanford is in large part fueled by the active role Hoover scholars have played in assisting several Republican presidential candidates to win office, a subject that was explored in chapter 6. The presence of an openly conservative think tank at a predominantly liberal university has resulted in several heated exchanges between the two bodies.

Like many think tanks based in Washington, Hoover relies on several strategies to communicate its research to policymakers, including organizing workshops and seminars for elected officials and scholars to debate various policy issues. Yet, unlike some think tanks located outside the Beltway, including the Hudson Institute and RAND, Hoover has resisted the temptation of opening a Washington office. Concerned that such a move would distract the institute from pursuing its research agenda, Hoover prefers to remain somewhat detached from the vicissitudes of Washington politics. Nonetheless, Hoover, like many advocacy-oriented think tanks, relishes the attention it receives in the media. It is particularly fond of quoting from a 1991 article in the *Economist*, which noted in its evaluation of think tanks that "The Hoover Institution on War, Revolution and Peace is hard to match for sheer intellectual firepower."[5]

THE COUNCIL ON FOREIGN RELATIONS

The origin of the New York–based Council of Foreign Relations (CFR) can be traced to an elite monthly dinner club that was established in the spring of 1918 to discuss various aspects of foreign affairs. Headed by Elihu Root, who

had played an important role in convincing Andrew Carnegie to create the
Carnegie Endowment for International Peace, the distinguished group of thirty
participants created a forum in which leaders from finance, industry, education,
government, and science could share their thoughts on pressing international
issues. However, it was not until 1921 that the monthly dinner club was
transformed into a permanent institution committed to the study of foreign
affairs.

The idea of creating an organization dedicated to an "improved understanding
of American foreign policy and international affairs" emerged when twenty-
one members of a select group called The Inquiry were invited to accompany
Woodrow Wilson to the Paris Peace Conference in 1919. Frustrated by
Wilson's refusal to accept their advice and disillusioned with several of the
provisions in the Treaty of Versailles, members of the American delegation
began to discuss the prospects of creating a transatlantic research organization
with their British counterparts. Despite their initial enthusiasm for the joint
venture, however, the American and British delegates made little progress in
achieving their goals over the next two years. Indeed, after it appeared that
the venture would not move forward, two members of the American delegation
approached Root and asked if he would be prepared to merge his Council of
Foreign Relations with the body the American delegates had established at the
Paris Peace Conference. With Root's consent, the two groups consolidated and
incorporated the Council on Foreign Relations on 29 July 1921.[6]

The primary mission of the Council on Foreign Relations is "to foster America's understanding of other nations – their peoples, cultures, histories, hopes,
quarrels, and ambitions – and thus to serve our nation through study and
debate." It seeks to accomplish this mission by pursuing three goals: improving
understanding of world affairs and providing new ideas for U.S. foreign policy,
transforming the council into a truly national organization, and finding and
nurturing the next generation of foreign policy leaders and thinkers.[7]

The Council on Foreign Relations publishes the quarterly journal *Foreign
Affairs,* as well as a wealth of studies on various aspects of world affairs. Yet
it is perhaps best known for its distinguished and exclusive group of members.
Among its thirty-five hundred members nationwide (they must be nominated
before they can join) are former presidents, secretaries of state, and other high-
level policymakers. At its headquarters in New York and at its several branches
throughout the United States, prominent policymakers and scholars are regularly invited to present lectures before members. Although the Council on
Foreign Relations has cultivated a reputation as an elite club for policymakers,
it has also developed a wide-ranging research program. Over sixty-five scholars
or research fellows comprise the CFR's Studies Department, which conducts
research in several areas, including Asia, Africa, peace and conflict, science
and technology and international economics.

THE AMERICAN ENTERPRISE INSTITUTE

Established in 1943 by Lewis H. Brown, president of the Johns-Mansville Corporation, to promote the virtues of "free-market economics in the face of a rising tide of Keynesianism," the American Enterprise Association (AEA), as it was then called, existed in relative obscurity for over a decade. By 1954 the AEA had only four full-time employees and an annual budget barely exceeding $80,000.[8] It was not until 1962, when William Baroody Sr, who had been the AEA's executive vice president, became president, that the organization began to make its presence felt.

Using the marketing skills he had developed while working at the U.S. Chamber of Commerce, Baroody transformed the newly named American Enterprise Institute into what Patricia Linden has called "the MGM of Washington think tanks."[9] In addition to devoting considerable resources to marketing the AEI's products, a trademark of advocacy-oriented think tanks, Baroody began recruiting some of America's leading conservative intellectuals, including Milton Friedman, Jeane Kirkpatrick, and the late Herbert Stein.

After suffering some financial setbacks during the mid-1980s under the leadership of Baroody's son, William Baroody Jr, the AEI has once again emerged as a strong voice in conservative policy-making circles. With over fifty resident scholars, including Kirkpatrick, Robert Bork, and former speaker of the house Newt Gingrich, and with over one hundred adjunct scholars at universities and policy institutes throughout the United States, the AEI ranks among the most talked about and written about think tanks in Washington. With a budget approaching $20 million, the AEI has managed to establish a comprehensive research program that covers economic and policy studies, social and political studies and foreign and defense studies. In addition to publishing dozens of books each year, the AEI also publishes the *American Enterprise*, an opinion magazine that examines a host of current policy issues.

THE CENTER FOR STRATEGIC AND INTERNATIONAL STUDIES

The directory of scholars at the Center for Strategic and International Studies (CSIS) reads like a who's who? in Washington's foreign-policy-making community. Home to several former ambassadors, secretaries of defense, and national security advisers, CSIS is among the most respected defense and foreign policy think tanks in the United States. Founded in 1962 by David Abshire, former assistant secretary of state for congressional affairs, and by Arleigh Burke, former chief of naval operations, CSIS's mission is "to inform and shape selected policy decisions in government and the private sector by providing long-range, anticipatory, and integrated thinking over a wide range of policy issues."[10]

With ninety policy experts, eighty support staff, and seventy interns and with a budget of $17 million, CSIS is well-placed to put its mission statement into action. Each year the organization convenes approximately seven hundred to eight hundred meetings, seminars, and conferences with policymakers and scholars in the United States and abroad and generates hundreds of media appearances. CSIS also publishes several books, journals, and conference papers. Its marquee publication is the *Washington Quarterly*.

Over the years CSIS has developed an extensive research program that covers every region of the world. It is also among the few American think tanks that has taken an active interest in Canada: there are currently eight scholars studying various issues relating to Canadian politics. In addition, CSIS has established specific initiatives within regions that address issues of current relevance. Examples include the National Commission for Retirement Policy, the Global Organized Crime Project, and the Enterprise for the Environment.

THE INSTITUTE FOR POLICY STUDIES

Often regarded as Washington's think tank of the left, the Institute for Policy Studies was founded by Marcus Raskin and Richard Barnett, two former staffers in the Kennedy administration. Convinced that steps had "to be taken to combat the over-militarized ways of thinking in foreign and national policy,"[11] Raskin and Barnett decided to establish their own institute, and with $200,000 in grants, the IPS opened its doors in October 1963.[12]

The fundamental purpose of the IPS is to provide the country's most important social movements with the intellectual ammunition they require to transform "their moral passion into a sensible public policy." To this end, the IPS has developed five principal programs that are intended to stimulate public debate and to help social movements succeed: global economic justice, sustainable communities, economic and social rights, real security, and culture.

The IPS, like other advocacy-oriented think tanks, relies on several channels to influence political change. In addition to conveying its ideas to policymakers and the public through the media, the institute has established links to several members of Congress and individuals in the executive branch. It has also advised several presidential candidates, including George McGovern, Jesse Jackson, Bob Kerrey, and Tom Harkin.

The IPS relies on other strategies as well. For instance, to better equip leaders of social movements to articulate their views to policymakers, the IPS has created a Social Action and Leadership School for Activists (SALSA) where organizers can meet to discuss strategy. The IPS also works closely with various national and transnational social organizations to mobilize opposition to various public policies. With a budget of $1 to $2 million and approximately fifteen staff members, the IPS does not enjoy the visibility of Washington's larger and better-funded think tanks. Nonetheless, because of its publications and networks with other nongovernmental organizations, its views have not been ignored.

THE URBAN INSTITUTE

The Urban Institute, according to Paul Dickson, "had a typically long bureaucratic birth."[13] Although its conception can be traced to the Kennedy Administration, it was not until President Johnson put his weight behind the initiative that the prospect of creating a think tank that could address the many domestic problems plaguing the United States during the 1960s gained momentum. As noted in its annual report of 1998, "the Urban Institute got its start in 1968 as the brainchild of a blue-ribbon panel set up by President Lyndon Johnson to monitor and evaluate the Great Society Initiatives that sprang from some 400 laws that had been passed since 1964."[14] President Johnson believed that the Urban Institute could bridge "the gulf between the scholar in search of truth and the decision-maker in search of progress."[15]

Answering the need "for independent analysis of government performance and for data-driven research on America's cities and their residents in the wake of widespread urban unrest," the Urban Institute devoted its early years to examining persistent domestic problems such as poverty, education finance, unemployment, urban housing shortages and decay, urban transportation gaps, and the need for welfare reform.[16] Since then it has greatly expanded its research program. With over two hundred staff members and a budget exceeding $50 million, the Urban Institute conducts research in several areas, including education, population, health, and human resources. It is currently involved in research projects with partners in more than forty-five states and twenty countries. Although 85 percent of its research agenda is financed by public agencies and foundations, the Urban Institute has made a concerted effort to broaden its base of support over the years. It lists dozens of private supporters as contributors. Moreover, the Urban Institute's $50 million endowment provides added financial security.

The Urban Institute, like many think tanks created during the Progressive Era, jealously guards its institutional independence. Despite relying heavily on government support, the institute has been able to insulate itself from outside interference. According to its former president, William Gorham, the government has largely refrained from interfering in work that it has funded.[17] The Urban Institute continues to publish dozens of studies each year, and its staff members are often quoted in the mainstream media.

THE CATO INSTITUTE

Founded in 1977 by Edward Crane, former national chairman of the Libertarian Party, the Cato Institute has become something of an anomaly in Washington.

Named for "*Cato's Letters,* libertarian pamphlets that helped lay the philo-
sophical foundation for the American Revolution,"[18] the institute, which
moved from San Francisco to Washington in 1981, promotes an odd mix of
conservative and liberal ideas. On the one hand, Cato recommends scrapping
the social-security system in favour of a private retirement program, a sugges-
tion embraced by many Republicans. On the other hand, it supports gay rights
and the legalization of marijuana, and it takes a liberal view of pornography,
positions generally held by the Democratic left.[19] What Cato consistently
opposes, however, is virtually all forms of government intervention.

Initially bankrolled by Kansas oil baron Charles Koch, a steadfast contributor to libertarian causes, Cato has since broadened its base of financial
support. Although some of its donors withdrew their funding after Cato
criticized the U.S. role in the Gulf War, it has since found support among
several powerful corporations, including Coca-Cola, Citibank, Shell Oil, Philip
Morris and Toyota.[20] In 1999 Cato's budget was $13 million, all of which
was raised from private sources.

Cato has grown considerably since its founding. It now has approximately
seventy-five employees, fifty-five adjunct scholars, and fourteen research fellows.
Among its many publications are the *Cato Journal*, published three times a
year; a quarterly magazine, *Regulation* and a bimonthly newsletter, *Cato Policy
Report*. In addition to holding conferences on a regular basis, Cato staff frequently convey their views to the media. Between 1991 and 1997, only a handful of Washington-based think tanks generated more media attention than Cato.

THE MANHATTAN INSTITUTE
FOR POLICY RESEARCH

Located near Grand Central Terminal in the heart of Manhattan, the Manhattan Institute has become Mayor Rudolph Giuliani's favourite think tank.
Created in 1978 by the late William Casey, former director of the Central
Intelligence Agency under President Reagan, the institute has been credited
with helping Giuliani sell his conservative agenda in a city known for its liberal
leanings.[21] The Manhattan Institute's conservative credentials are well
deserved. In 1980 it helped launch George Gilder's *Wealth and Poverty*, "a
paean to tax cuts and freewheeling capitalism," and four years later it aggres-
sively promoted Charles Murray's study *Losing Ground*, "a tough-minded
attack on social welfare programs."[22] Murray would attract even more attention later with his best-selling and controversial co-authored book, *The Bell
Curve*, which examined the relationship between class and intelligence.

The Manhattan Institute has advocated a number of policies intended to
move New York more to the right. Among other things it has supported the
privatization of hospitals and actively promoted school choice. It has also
spoken out against rent control. The institute uses several channels to market

its ideas. In addition to its quarterly magazine, *City Journal*, it publishes books and articles and holds lavish lunches several times a month at the Harvard Club with journalists, politicians, bureaucrats, and business leaders.

The institute's staff of twenty senior fellows includes David Frum, the Toronto-born neoconservative and author of several best-selling books, and Diane Ravitch, a former United States assistant secretary of education. Institute staff conduct research on a wide range of municipal issues of interest to officials both in New York and in other cities throughout the United States. The institute also houses two research centres: the Center for Civic Innovation and the Center for Legal Policy. In 1997 it had a budget of $5 million.

THE PROGRESSIVE POLICY INSTITUTE

Created as an offspring of the Democratic Leadership Council (DLC) in 1989, the Progressive Policy Institute (PPI) did not have to wait long to attract the attention of policymakers in Washington. When Bill Clinton, former chair of the DLC, decided to run for the presidency in 1992, the PPI found the right messenger to deliver its progressive message. Indeed, when president-elect Clinton endorsed the PPI's blueprint, *Mandate for Change*, a comprehensive study of how to reform government, it became clear to many journalists covering Washington politics, that the PPI's views would be well received in key policymaking circles. As Thomas Friedman of the New York Times stated, "*Mandate for Change* is as good a crib sheet as any for Mr Clinton's first State of the Union Message, and the recommendations are expected to become standard-issue bedtime reading for the 'new kind of Democrats' about to take over Washington."[23]

Several ideas that the PPI helped to formulate made their way onto Clinton's political agenda, including national service in exchange for college loans. Moreover, several other issues that the PPI explored, including crime prevention, health care, educational excellence, and environmental safety, found a receptive audience in the Clinton White House, which had become home to a handful of former PPI staffers.[24]

The PPI's research continues to advocate a new progressive politics for the United States. Among other things, the PPI believes in restoring the American dream by accelerating economic growth, expanding opportunity, and enhancing financial and personal security. It also maintains that global order can be sustained by building new international structures based on economic and political freedom. With approximately one-dozen staff members and a budget between $1 million and 2 million, the PPI has attempted to model its marketing strategy on the strategies employed by the Heritage Foundation and the Cato Institute.[25]

A Profile of Selected Canadian Think Tanks

- The Canada West Foundation
- The Institute for Research on Public Policy
- The C.D. Howe Institute
- The North-South Institute
- The Canadian Institute of Strategic Studies
- The Canadian Centre for Policy Alternatives
- The Mackenzie Institute
- The Public Policy Forum
- The Canadian Policy Research Networks, Inc.
- The Atlantic Institute for Market Studies

THE CANADA WEST FOUNDATION

Established in 1971, the Calgary-based Canada West Foundation traces its origins to the One Prairie Conference held in Lethbridge in 1970. A consensus developed at the conference that research on Western Canadian concerns should not only continue but be expanded. This decision led to the formation of the Canada West Council, which in turn developed the mandate for the Canada West Foundation. The Canada West Foundation is governed by the Canada West Council, "which provides direction on the current and future education and research activities of the Foundation."[1]

With a budget of less than $1 million, the Canada West Foundation pursues three main objectives: "to initiate and conduct research into the economic and social characteristics and potentials of the West and North within a national and international context; to educate individuals regarding the West's regional economic and social contributions to the Canadian federation; and to act as a catalyst for informed debate."[2]

Despite its modest financial resources, Canada West has established an active research program over the past several years. Between 1980 and 1997 Canada West published over one hundred studies on issues ranging from the effects of free trade on the Western economy to the regulation of charities in Alberta. Since it is a leading proponent of greater Western representation in Parliament, several of its publications and conferences have focused on the prospects for constitutional reform in Canada. Recently, however, Canada West has tried to diversify its research program by moving beyond the West's role in the Canadian federation. In addition to maintaining an active interest in Senate reform, the foundation's nine-member research team is currently conducting research on the nonprofit sector, gambling, Western cities, Tax reform, health care and the economy of Western Canada. The current president of Canada West is Roger Gibbins, formerly of the Department of Political Science at the University of Calgary.

THE INSTITUTE FOR RESEARCH ON PUBLIC POLICY

The Institute for Research on Public Policy (IRPP) is unique among Canadian think tanks. To begin with, it is one of the few think tanks in the country whose financial security has been guaranteed by a sizeable endowment. With a current market value of $40 million, the IRPP's "endowment fund was built up in the 1970s and 1980s by $10 million from the private sector and provincial governments, matched by $10 million from the federal government."[3] Since the interest earned from the endowment covers most of the IRPP's operating expenses, the IRPP, unlike other think tanks in Canada, does not have to mount annual fund-raising campaigns. The IRPP is also unique because it is among the few independent English-language public-policy research institutes in Quebec. After the IRPP opened its doors in Montreal in 1972, its head office moved to several cities, including Ottawa, Halifax, and Victoria, before relocating to Montreal in 1991. The IRPP currently has approximately fifteen full-time staff members.

The IRPP's creation was inspired by the eminent Canadian economist Ronald Ritchie, who in 1968 was commissioned by Prime Minister Trudeau to examine the feasibility of creating an independent multidisciplinary research institute in Canada. After surveying the think tank landscape in several countries, including the United States, and after interviewing dozens of think tank directors and policymakers, Ritchie recommended that an institute similar to the Brookings Institution be established in Canada to provide long-term strategic analysis. Although Ritchie's report did not result in the creation of a think tank on the scale of the Brookings Institution, it did lead to the founding of the IRPP and several other policy research institutes.

Remaining loyal to Ritchie's vision of an institute conducting independent policy analysis, the IRPP has undertaken a "measured approach to public policy, which revolves around informing policy debates rather than advancing a particular ideological position."[4] It seeks to inform and educate policymakers and the public, primarily through its magazine, *Policy Options,* which is published ten times a year, and through its book-length studies. While staff members from the IRPP have also testified before parliamentary committees and submitted op-ed articles to Canadian newspapers, the institute claims that enhancing its media profile is not a priority. This position may change, however, under the leadership of former conservative advisor Hugh Segal, who recently became president of the IRPP.

Despite allocating 77 percent of its $3 million budget to research, the IRPP has not developed significant in-house expertise. Indeed, rather than hiring several researchers, the institute has used its small staff to coordinate research projects that are undertaken largely by academics at various universities. The IRPP's current research activity focuses on four main areas: governance, family and social policy, labour market and human capital, and cities-regions.

THE C.D. HOWE INSTITUTE

Few think tanks in Canada have attracted more attention in the media and in policymaking circles than the Toronto-based C.D. Howe Institute. Named after the Liberal cabinet minister, Clarence Decatur Howe, the institute's origins can be traced to the Private Planning Association of Canada (PPAC), which was established in 1958 "by business and labor leaders to undertake research and educational activities on economic policy issues."[5] In 1973 the PPAC merged with the C.D. Howe Memorial Foundation (1961) to become the C.D. Howe Research Institute (HRI). Eight years later, when the HRI dissolved, the "Foundation again became a separate entity and the reconstituted PPAC was renamed the C.D. Howe Institute."[6]

Known for its expertise on Canadian economic, social, and trade policy, C.D. Howe has published hundreds of studies on virtually every major policy initiative the federal and provincial governments have embarked on. Many of these studies have been written by its small staff of in-house experts, including William Robson and Wendy Dobson. Countless others have been prepared by some of the country's leading economists, including David Laidler, Judith Maxwell, and Thomas Courchene. The institute, which devotes 90 percent of its $1.5 to $3 million budget to research, does not try to overwhelm readers with monographs of several hundred pages but relies on brief studies or commentaries to highlight the implications of particular government policies.

The C.D. Howe Institute, like many other think tanks, does not assess its influence by the number of publications it produces or by the many prominent business leaders who serve on its board of directors. Rather, it evaluates its impact by the contribution it makes to stimulating informed public debate. According to a recent annual report, "The Institute monitors whether its output measures up to the high standards of its members, the media, policymakers, and the public. Key indicators of success are strong attendance at Institute meetings, wide news coverage of Institute publications, an improved quality of public debate, and, ultimately, the willingness of policymakers to listen."[7]

The fifteen full-time staff at C.D. Howe follow a simple formula to ensure that policymakers listen: it outfits "influential decision-makers with concrete research, [and] provide[s] a forum in which they can interact, and mix vigorously."[8] This formula seems to have paid off. Over the years, C.D. Howe has received dozens of endorsements from policymakers, journalists, and business leaders who have acknowledged the valuable work of the institute.

THE NORTH-SOUTH INSTITUTE

Established in 1976 with a start-up grant from the Donner Canadian Foundation, the North-South Institute (NSI), located in Ottawa's Byward Market, assesses "the needs and demands of developing countries, and the strategies and policies open to Canadians in meeting these challenges."[9] The institute was founded by Bernard Wood of the Parliamentary Centre for Foreign Affairs and University of Toronto economics professor Gerald Helleiner at a time when no existing institution in Canada had assigned a high priority to examining North-South issues. Wood, who currently serves as director, development co-operation, at the Organization for Economic Development and Co-operation in Paris, obtained additional experience working at a think tank after resigning as president of the North-South Institute in 1989. After leaving the NSI, he replaced Geoffrey Pearson as executive director of the now-defunct Canadian Institute for International Peace and Security.[10]

The objectives of the North-South Institute are clearly stated in the organization's letters-patent: "to conduct policy-relevant research of high quality on important issues in the field of world development ... to stimulate other institutions and individuals in Canada to conduct collaborative research on such problems ... to provide a non-governmental centre through which groups and individuals can exchange views and information on world development issues ... and to take other necessary steps to keep the urgent importance of world development issues before the Canadian public and policy-makers."[11]

Through its many publications, including the *Canadian Development Report*, and through seminars and conferences with policymakers, academics, business leaders, representatives from various nongovernmental organizations, and the media, the North-South Institute seeks to generate "greater understanding and informed discussion of the problems and opportunities facing Canada and countries in the developing world." To this end, its eighteen-member staff conducts research on four broad themes: strengthening cooperation between developing countries and multilateral financial institutions;

improving governance or "promoting civil society," that is, encouraging nongovernmental organizations to solve enduring development problems; enhancing gender equity; and preventing regional ethnic conflicts.[12]

The NSI relies on a budget of approximately $2 to $3 million to conduct its activities. Approximately half its revenue is provided by a grant from the Canadian International Development Agency (CIDA). The NSI's current president, Roy Culpeper, like many other think tank directors, is attempting to diversify the institute's sources of funding. However, as he has discovered in recent years, securing access to additional funds is far more problematic than conveying the NSI's views to policymakers and the public.

THE CANADIAN INSTITUTE OF STRATEGIC STUDIES

The Canadian Institute of Strategic Studies (CISS) is the smallest think tank specializing in foreign and defence policy in the country, but it is also among the most visible. With one full-time staff member and an intern, the Toronto-based institute has become a favourite source among journalists covering issues ranging from bombing raids in Bagdad to the refusal of a Canadian officer to take the anthrax vaccine. The CISS is a private think tank dedicated to the study and discussion of national and international strategic issues, including foreign and defence policy, economic strategy, Canadian-American security arrangements, Canadian security and sovereignty, arms control and disarmament, peacekeeping, and conflict resolution.

Created in 1976 by a group of World War II veterans led by Professor George Bell of York University, the CISS was established to provide a focus for independent strategic thinking in Canada. Bell, according to Jim Hanson, associate executive director of the CISS, was aware that two other institutes, the Canadian Institute of International Affairs (CIIA) and the Atlantic Council of Canada, existed at the time. However, he wanted to create a think tank that did not deal with general matters of foreign affairs, as the CIIA did, or with such narrow issues as Canada's participation in NATO, the mandate of the Atlantic Council. For Bell what was needed in Canada was a think tank that could bridge the gap between the two organizations.[13]

With modest financial resources ($100,000 to $500,000) generated primarily through the Department of National Defence's Strategic Defence Forum (SDF) and membership donations, the CISS has managed to establish a strong presence in Canada's foreign and defence policy research community. In addition to conducting seminars and lectures, the CISS publishes the *McNaughton Papers* twice a year and regularly publishes its conference proceedings.

THE CANADIAN CENTRE FOR POLICY ALTERNATIVES

The Canadian Centre for Policy Alternatives was founded in 1980 by a group of academic and labour economists, including Steven Langdon, Peter Findlay, and Robert Clarke, who, along with a cross-section of representatives from labor unions and left-leaning political organizations, "saw the need for an independent left-of-centre research agency to counterbalance the right-wing Fraser and C.D. Howe Institutes."[14] Unlike the free market-oriented C.D. Howe and Fraser Institutes, the CCPA believes that "social and economic issues ... are not something to be left to the marketplace or for governments acting alone to decide." The centre "is committed to putting forward research that reflects the concerns of women as well as men, labour as well as business, churches, cooperatives and voluntary agencies as well as governments, minorities and disadvantaged people as well as fortunate individuals."[15]

Since its inception, the CCPA has published hundreds of reports, studies, and books on a wide range of social and economic policy issues. It also publishes a monthly journal, the CCPA *Monitor*, and since 1995 has released the *Alternative Federal Budget*, an edited collection of articles that, as the book's title implies, suggests different ways the government could spend its revenue. In addition to conveying its ideas through its many publications, the CCPA often works closely with policymakers and representatives from unions and other nongovernmental organizations to advance its agenda.

The CCPA's budget of between $500,000 and $1.5 million is generated primarily from the contributions of its five thousand organizational and individual members and donors. The institute performs contract work for various governmental and nongovernmental organizations as well. The CCPA's national headquarters is based in Ottawa, where it has nine staff members. In 1997 it expanded its operations beyond the nation's capital by opening branch offices in Manitoba, British Columbia, and Nova Scotia.

THE MACKENZIE INSTITUTE

Named for the famous Canadian explorer Alexander Mackenzie, "the first to trace the river that bears his name to the Arctic Ocean," the Mackenzie Institute in Toronto "also follows lines of inquiry and explore issues that others suspect exist but have not yet dared to take."[16] Founded in 1986, the Mackenzie Institute is a small think tank that specializes in defence, security/intelligence, and policing issues. It has attracted some notoriety in recent years for its research on terrorist organizations, low intensity warfare, and propaganda and right-wing extremist factions. It has also generated attention because of a series of threats made against its handful of employees. As a result, its office is not open to the public.

The institute's budget of under $1 million is raised primarily by foundations and individual and corporate donations. It does not accept any government funding. The institute does, however, perform contract work for large and small companies. In addition to publishing a quarterly newsletter, the Mackenzie Institute publishes a series of occasional papers and briefing notes.

THE PUBLIC POLICY FORUM

Unlike most think tanks in Canada, the Public Policy Forum (PPF), created in 1987, does not rely on the media or on its publications to influence policymakers. Rather, the fifteen staff members of the Ottawa-based think tank pursue less visible strategies to help shape public policy. The PPF does not regard itself as an advocacy think tank that seeks to impose its agenda on policymakers. Indeed, in its promotional literature the institute emphasizes that it does not take positions on any policy issues. It was founded not to advance a particular set of ideological goals, but "to provide a neutral venue where the private sector and the public sector could meet to learn from one another."[17] According to the PPF, "In the 1980s, it became clear that, in the global arena where the quality of government directly affected the competitiveness of the nation, Canada suffered from the isolation of government from the private sector."[18] To remedy this problem, the PPF's president, David Zussman, notes, "we help to bridge the gap between the two solitudes – government and the private sector – in order to deal more effectively with issues of common concern."[19] The PPF has recently expanded its mandate to include representatives from the voluntary, or "third," sector in its policy forums.

The PPF's emphasis on organizing conferences and workshops for policymakers and representatives from the private and nonprofit sectors is reflected in the allocation of its resources. Sixty percent of the institute's operating budget of $1 to $2 million, raised almost entirely from membership donations, is set aside for this purpose. Among its more than one hundred members are the Bank of Montreal, Bell Canada, Canada Post Corporation, and several provincial governments. Only 20 percent of its budget is allocated for research, a function that the PPF has only begun to devote more attention to.[20] The Forum, which has done considerable work in economic, social and trade policy, has recently identified four themes that it will concentrate on between 2000 and 2002. They fall under the broad categories of globalization and Canadian governance, competitiveness, productivity and the quality of life, trust and confidence in public institutions, and public sector management.

THE CANADIAN POLICY RESEARCH NETWORKS, INC.

The Canadian Policy Research Networks, Inc. (CPRN) is the brainchild of Judith Maxwell, the CPRN's president and former head of the Economic Council of Canada (ECC). After the ECC closed in June 1992, a victim of the Mulroney government's cost-cutting budget of that year, Maxwell decided to teach part-time at Queen's University while she completed a number of research projects. However, having worked at the C.D. Howe Institute in the 1970s and at the ECC since 1985, Maxwell was eager to return to a think tank. For Maxwell, what the Canadian policy research community desperately needed was an interdisciplinary research institute that could encourage fruitful exchanges between senior-level public servants, academics, and representatives from the private and nonprofit sectors. Since no think tank like the one she envisaged existed at the time, Maxwell began to assemble a team of individuals who would be prepared to work at such an organization and set out to raise the necessary start-up funds. As Maxwell recently observed, "we felt like pioneers, except we had no tent to sleep in."[21]

Funds to shelter Maxwell's new think tank for its first five years were secured in 1994 when Jocelyn Bourgon, former clerk of the Privy Council and secretary to Cabinet and now president of the Canadian Centre for Management Development (CCMD), was able to obtain financial support from six federal government departments. The CPRN's core funding of $2 to $3 million has since been renewed. The CPRN's mission "is to create knowledge and lead public debate on social and economic issues important to the well-being of Canadians. [Its] goal is make Canada a more just, prosperous and caring society."[22]

With two dozen staff members, the CPRN has established three major policy networks – health, work, and the family – to coordinate its research and to facilitate exchanges among key stakeholders. The institute has already held several meetings with policymakers and representatives from the private and nonprofit sectors in these areas and has published a number of studies highlighting important issues. Although Maxwell agrees that assessing the impact of a think tank's work is difficult, she has nonetheless set out a number of indicators to evaluate the CPRN's success.[23] These include the participation of policymakers in the CPRN's activities, the quality of research produced under the institute's auspices, and the sustained interaction between the CPRN staff and engaged communities.

THE ATLANTIC INSTITUTE FOR MARKET STUDIES

The Halifax-based Atlantic Institute for Market Studies (AIMS), like the North-South Institute, received a generous start-up grant from the Donner Canadian Foundation. Created in 1994 by a group of Atlantic Canadians committed to broadening "the debate about realistic options available to build [the Atlantic] economy, AIMS pursues four main objectives. These include initiating and conducting research that identifies current and emerging economic and social issues confronting Atlantic Canada; investigating a full range of options for public and private responses to these issues; communicating its research to regional and national audiences in a non-partisan manner; and sponsoring seminars, lectures, and training programs."[24]

Reflecting on the need to create a think tank in Atlantic Canada that examines current and emerging policy issues in the region, AIMS President Brian Lee Crowley remarked:

There are other national think-tanks that aim to stimulate people to think in new and better ways about economic and social policy, to take the long strategic view, to speak out on controversial issues ... The C.D. Howe Institute, the Fraser Institute, the Institute for Research on Public Policy and the [Canadian] Centre for Policy Alternatives spring to mind. But these national organisations can devote little of their time and effort to the particular challenges and circumstances of Atlantic Canada ... Regionally, there are other groups, like the Atlantic Provinces Economic Council, that gather and publish the most complete and up-to-date economic data on our current economic state, while others, like the Canadian Institute for Research on Regional Development, publish academic treatises ... AIMS seeks to do more than provide useful factual information on what's going on in the economy today ... Rather, AIMS exists to offer a platform for the best and brightest to put forward their own thoughts and analysis about what to do about our challenges and opportunities, about how we can think and act strategically, and for the long term, to build a more prosperous future for the region.[25]

AIMS relies on several channels to convey its thoughts on how best to confront the many challenges confronting Atlantic Canada. In addition to producing a quarterly newsletter, the *Beacon*, and several other publications, AIMS regularly holds conferences and seminars to promote exchanges between policymakers, academics, and leaders from the private and nonprofit sectors. With a full-time staff of five and a budget under $1 million, AIMS has managed to carve a niche for itself in the policy-research community. Its staff are regularly quoted by journalists covering regional and national affairs.

Notes

INTRODUCTION

1 For a comprehensive directory of American think tanks, see Hellebust, *Think Tank Directory*. A database of over three thousand think tanks around the world was compiled by James McGann for a report submitted to the Tokyo-based National Institute for Research Advancement (NIRA). See his *Think Tanks*.

2 For a detailed comparison of American and British think tanks see Stone, *Capturing the Political Imagination*, and Higgott and Stone, "The Limits of Influence." On some of the fundamental differences between Canadian and American think tanks see Abelson and Carberry, "Following Suit?" For detailed analyses of think tanks in several different countries and regions see Stone, Denham, and Garnett, *Think Tanks across Nations*; McGann and Weaver, *Think Tanks and Civil Societies*; and Langford and Brownsey, *Think Tanks*.

3 Abelson and Carberry, "Following Suit?" 525–6.

4 For instance, Ernst suggests that the C.D. Howe Institute played a critical role in reinforcing and advancing the Conservative government's free trade agenda during the 1980s. See his article "Liberal Continentalism." Moreover, Brodie and Jenson have noted that several Canadian think tanks, including the Fraser Institute, C.D. Howe Institute, and the Economic Council of Canada, have contributed to the new "neoliberal" orthodoxy. See *Crisis, Challenge and Change*, 312.

5 Several scholars studying think tanks in the United States have attempted to show how think tanks shape policy issues and legislation as diverse as the Strategic Defence Initiative (SDI, or Star Wars Project) and the creation of a national budget system. For a discussion of the contribution of the Heritage Foundation to the debate over SDI, see Edwards, *The Power of Ideas*. On the impact of the Brookings Institution in

helping to create a national budget system see Critchlow, *The Brook-ings Institution*, and Smith, *Brookings at Seventy-Five*. By contrast, the handful of scholars studying Canadian think tanks have provided a less than enthusiastic endorsement of the impact of policy institutes on key policy debates. See, for instance, Lindquist, *Behind the Myth*, and Tupper, "Think-Tanks."

6 Some commentators have suggested that the sheer number of think tanks, interest groups, and other organizations committed to influencing public policy in the United States may constitute a constraint. See, for example, Denham and Garnett, *British Think-Tanks*, 19. However, since not all think tanks have comparable resources, it is questionable how much constraint the think tank population imposes on these organiza-tions. If, for instance, there were dozens of think tanks on the scale of the Brookings Institution, then perhaps this argument would be more persuasive. Yet, as this study demonstrates, the Brookings Institution and the handful of other think tanks in the United States that possess comparable resources face little competition from the majority of much smaller policy institutes.

7 In his assessment of the impact of societal groups on Canadian foreign policy, Nossal draws a distinction between influencing policy-making and the policy-making environment. See *Canadian Foreign Policy*, 117. This distinction is important when one is evaluating the impact of think tanks. As Pal notes, while think tanks in Canada "have enlarged the terms of political discourse," it is important not to exaggerate their impact on policy-making. See his *Public Policy Analysis*, 92- 4.

8 See, for instance, Kitschelt, "Political Opportunity Structures," 57–85, and Kriesi et al., "New Social Movements."

9 Stone, *Capturing the Political Imagination,* 38–52.

10 For examples of how scholars have attempted to assess the impact of ideas on policy-making see Yee, "Causal Effects of Ideas"; Campbell, "Institutional Analysis"; and Goldstein and Keohane, *Ideas and Foreign Policy*.

11 The media coverage a select group of American think tanks has gener-ated and the various factors that account for their visibility are exam-ined by Rich and Weaver, "Think Tanks." Useful data on how often American think tanks testify before Congressional committees is pro-vided by Rich, "Think Tanks." For a discussion of the relationship between the public visibility of a cross-section of Canadian think tanks and their relevance in policy-making, see Abelson, "Public Visibility."

12 Jérôme-Forget, "Institute for Research on Public Policy," 99.

13 Interview with author, 16 December 1998.

14 Smith, *The Idea Brokers*; Stone, Denham, and Garnett, *Think Tanks across Nations*.

15 McGann and Weaver, *Think Tanks,* 2.
16 McGann, *Competition for Dollars,* 9.
17 For more on the role of public think tanks such as the Congressional Research Service see Robinson, "Public Think-Tanks."
18 For more on the restrictions placed on the political activities of charitable organizations in Canada see Revenue Canada, *Information Circular 87–1: Registered Charities – Ancillary and Incidental Political Activities.* For information on restrictions on registered charities in the United States see *Internal Revenue Code of 1986,* 1077–96.
19 Sundquist, "Research Brokerage."
20 Peschek, *Policy Planning Organizations,* 7.
21 See, for instance, McGann and Weaver, *Think Tanks and Civil Societies;* Stone, *Political Imagination;* Stone, Denham, and Garnett, *Think Tanks across Nations;* Smith, *The Idea Brokers;* and Abelson, *American Think Tanks.*
22 The most comprehensive directory of American think tanks is Hellebust, *Think Tank Directory.* For a listing of conservative, or classical liberal, think tanks, see Atwood and Mead, *Directory of Public Policy Organizations.* While no comprehensive directory of Canadian think tanks has been produced, there are some international directories that should be consulted. The National Institute for Research Advancement's (NIRA) *World Directory of Think Tanks* is the most extensive. On think tanks specializing in defence and security issues see Van Der Woerd, *World Survey of Strategic Studies Centres.*
23 Peschek, *Policy Planning Organizations.* Also see Domhoff and Dye, *Power Elites;* and Saloma, *Ominous Politics.* Several other studies have examined think tanks from an elite theory perspective. Among them are Silk and Silk, *The American Establishment;* Shoup and Minter, *Imperial Brain Trust;* and Sanders, *Peddlers of Crisis.*
24 Heclo, "Issue Networks," and Lindquist, "Think-Tanks?"
25 See Kitschelt, "Political Opportunity Structures"; Kriesi et al., "New Social Movements."

CHAPTER ONE

1 Smith, *Idea Brokers.*
2 See Hellebust, *Think Tank Directory.* See also McGann, *Think Tanks.*
3 On my calculation of the data provided in Hellebust, *Think Tank Directory,* less than 4 percent of the estimated twelve to fifteen hundred think tanks in the United States have budgets in excess of $10 million. Less than 16 percent of all American think tanks have budgets exceeding $1 million.
4 Lindquist, "A Quarter-Century of Think Tanks," 130.

5 See, for instance, Weaver, "Changing World," and McGann, *Competition for Dollars*. See also Wallace, "Between Two Worlds."

6 Weaver, "Changing World," 564.

7 Despite portraying themselves as scholarly institutions, both the Brookings Institution and the Hoover Institution have been criticized for their partisan leanings. In part this stems from the contributions individuals at these institutions have made to supporting particular presidential candidates. For more on this see Abelson and Carberry, "Policy Experts."

8 Weaver, "Changing World," 567.

9 Lindquist, "Think Tanks?" 576.

10 For more on the role of think tanks during the Progressive Era, see Smith, *The Idea Brokers*, and Critchlow, *The Brookings Institution*.

11 Several scholars have argued that philanthropists often support research institutions to advance their own political and ideological interests. See, for example, Sealander, *Private Wealth*, and Culleton Colwell, *Private Foundations*.

12 For a more complete chronological listing of think tanks created during this period see McGann, "Academics to Ideologues," 739–40.

13 See Abelson, *American Think Tanks*, especially chapter 2, and "From Policy Research to Political Advocacy." For more on the political agendas of philanthropic donors see Freund, *Narcissism and Philanthropy*.

14 Abelson, *American Think Tanks*, 35.

15 Among the many factors that could account for the fact that Canada, unlike the United States, did not develop several prominent research institutions during the early 1900s is the absence of large-scale philanthropic foundations dedicated to social science research. For more on this see Richardson and Fisher, *The Development of the Social Sciences*, especially the introduction.

16 Lindquist employs the term "club" to describe the goals and functions of many Canadian policy institutes. See his "Think Tanks?"

17 For more on the early history of these organizations see Manny, "The Canadian Institute of International Affairs"; Osendarp, "A Decade of Transition"; Holmes, "The CIIA," 9–10; Demson, "Canadian Institute of International Affairs"; and Greathead, "Antecedents and Origins."

18 The history of the CCSD is examined in Splane, *75 Years of Community Service*.

19 The Rand Corporation is now referred to simply as RAND. There are several other institutes, including the Center for Naval Analyses and the Institute for Defense Analyses, that advise the U.S. government on defence issues. In recent years RAND has expanded its research program to include, among other things, health care reform. RAND also offers a joint graduate program with the University of California at Los Angeles,

and it maintains a smaller office in Washington, DC. For a detailed analysis of RAND, see Kaplan, *Wizards of Armageddon.*

20 The Hudson Institute was founded by Kahn and a handful of his former colleagues at RAND in 1961. Although originally based in Westchester County, New York, Hudson moved to Indianapolis following Kahn's death in 1984. It also maintains an office in Washington, DC. The Hudson Institute's major clients include the Departments of Defense (including the u.s. Navy), Labor, State, and Commerce. Former vice-president Dan Quayle and Elliot Abrams, former assistant secretary of state for human rights, took up residence at Hudson after leaving public office. The Urban Institute was created in 1968 at the request of President Lyndon B. Johnson and his domestic policy advisers. It was originally conceived as the domestic policy equivalent of RAND. From its inception, the Urban Institute has relied extensively on government contracts from the Department of Housing and Urban Development (HUD), the Department of Transportation, and several other departments and agencies at the state and federal level. It also receives financial support from various private donors and philanthropic foundations.

21 For more on CSIS see Smith, *Strategic Calling.*

22 Several studies have been written on the Institute for Policy Studies. See, for instance, Powell, *Covert Cadre*; Muravchik, "The Think-Tank of the Left"; and Yoffe, "IPS Faces Life."

23 Abelson and Carberry, "Following Suit?" 534.

24 C.D. Howe Institute, home page (www.cdhowe.org), "A History of the Institute."

25 Abelson and Lindquist, "Think Tanks in North America," 41.

26 Vanier Institute of the Family, home page (www.familyforum.com).

27 For a discussion of how task forces and royal commissions have been used as sources of policy expertise for the Canadian government, see Bradford, *Commissioning Ideas*, and Jenson, "Commissioning Ideas."

28 The Economic Council of Canada was formerly known as the National Productivity Council, created in 1961.

29 The Economic Council and the Science Council were disbanded following the February 1992 federal budget. Other victims of budget constraints included the Canadian Institute for International Peace and Security and the Law Reform Commission. On the demise of the Science Council of Canada, see De La Mothe, "A Dollar Short," 873–86.

30 Abelson and Lindquist, "Think Tanks in North America."

31 Ibid.

32 For more on the PRI, see Anderson, "The New Focus."

33 On the AEI's influence on Heritage see Abelson, *American Think Tanks,* 54–5.

34 On the strategies of advocacy think tanks, see Abelson, "In Search of Policy Influence," "Policy Experts and Political Pundits,"and "Think Tanks in the United States."

35 For more on the involvement of the Heritage Foundation during the 1980 presidential campaign and the transition period that followed see Abelson, *American Think Tanks.*

36 See Weaver, "The Changing World," 567.

37 Abelson and Lindquist, "Think Tanks in North America." See Ritchie, *An Institute for Research on Public Policy.*

38 Ibid. The Private Planning Association of Canada was created in 1957 as the Canadian counterpart to the u.s. National Planning Association; its creation was a condition for receiving foundation support to establish the Canadian-American Committee (CAC), a council of one hundred private sector leaders and representatives who were to meet two or three times a year to discuss common problems, sponsor research, and develop consensus positions. For some additional information on the C.D. Howe Institute, see Beigie, "Economic Policy Analysis," and Ernst, "Liberal Continentalism."

39 Canadian Centre for Philanthropy, home page (www.ccp.ca).

40 Ibid. In addition to pursuing its research program, the Fraser Institute has found innovative ways to promulgate its values: the widely reported Tax Freedom Day, the Poleconomy board game, a contest for reducing wasteful government expenditures, and syndicated radio spots that are transcribed and published in the *Fraser Forum* are just some of the methods Fraser uses to convey its ideas.

41 The term vanity think tank was coined by Landers in "Think-Tanks."

42 For information on Jimmy Carter and the Carter Center see Troester, *Jimmy Carter,* and Brinkley, "Jimmy Carter's Modest Quest."

43 See Gellner, "Political Think-Tanks."

44 Chisolm, "Sinking the Think Tanks Upstream."

45 As a result of a growing controversy over the legality of creating an organization that on the surface appeared to be used to circumvent campaign finance laws, Dole pulled the plug on this project. For more on this see Melton, "Closing of Dole's Think Tank."

46 On the Progress and Freedom Foundation see Regan, "A Think Tank with One Idea"; Dickerson, "Newt Inc."; Weisskopf, "New Political Landscape"; and Simpson, "New Addition." After resigning his position as speaker of the house, Newt Gingrich decided that in addition to undertaking some consulting work, he would strengthen his ties to conservative think tanks. He is currently a senior fellow at the American Enterprise Institute and a distinguished visiting fellow at the Hoover Institution.

47 For more on the Canadian Centre for Foreign Policy Development, see Lee, "Beyond Consultations."

48 See, for instance, Abelson and Lindquist, "Who's Thinking about International Affairs?"

49 Abelson and Lindquist, "Think Tanks in North America," 45.

50 For a history of the Brookings Institution see Critchlow, *The Brookings Institution*; Saunders, *The Brookings Institution*; and Smith, *Brookings at Seventy-Five.*

51 Robert S. Brookings extraordinary life is chronicled in Hagedorn, *Brookings.*

52 See Saunders, *The Brookings Institution.*

53 Brookings Institution, *Annual Report 1998.*

54 Brookings is one of only a handful of American think tanks that has the luxury of drawing on a sizeable endowment. The others include RAND, the Hoover Institution, the Carnegie Endowment, and the Russell Sage Foundation. While its endowment and fund-raising activities cover about 30 percent of the cost of running its research departments, the directors of these departments are required to cover the remaining 70 percent. See Morin and Deane, "The Ideas Industry," 7 December 1999, a29.

55 On the Center on the US and France, see Morin and Deane, "The Ideas Industry," a13.

56 Orlans, *The Nonprofit Research Institute,* 19.

57 On the removal of Project Rand from Douglas Aircraft, see Smith, *The Rand Corporation,* 51–74.

58 Orlans, *The Nonprofit Research Institute,* 21.

59 RAND's contribution to America's nuclear strategy is examined in Kaplan, *Wizards of Armageddon.*

60 Budget sources are based on 1998 figures. RAND also receives funding from the Department of Health and Human Services/National Institutes of Health, other federal and government agencies, private firms, associations and international agencies, foundations, and individuals. It also draws on its sizeable endowment to support its research. See publication by RAND entitled *An Introduction to RAND.*

61 Tyman, "A Decade-Long Heritage."

62 For an interesting history of the Heritage Foundation, see Edwards, *Power of Ideas.*

63 Taken from the Heritage Foundation's mission statement.

64 Quoted in McCombs, "Building a Heritage." For more on Heritage's goals see, Feulner, "Heritage Foundation."

65 Center for International Private Enterprise, "Think Tanks as Advocates of Change," 6.

66 Heritage Foundation, *1998 Annual Report.*

67 Kaiser and Chinoy, "Scaife's Money," a01. For more on the financing of conservative foundations and think tanks see report by the Washington-based National Committee for Responsive Philanthropy entitled *$1 Billion*

for Ideas; and Covington Colwell, *Moving a Public Policy.* In addition, see Stefancic and Delgado, *No Mercy.*

68 Empower America mission statement.

69 Ibid.

70 Demson, *A Brief History,"* 1.

71 Ibid., 2.

72 Lindquist, "Think Tanks?"

73 After spending over two decades at the University of Toronto, the CIIA relocated to Glendon College in May 1998.

74 Lindquist, "Behind the Myth," 347.

75 Ibid.

76 Ibid.

77 Ibid.

78 Conference Board of Canada, "Who We Are."

79 Conference Board of Canada, "Leveraging Knowledge."

80 Fraser Institute, *Challenging Perceptions,* 2.

81 Ibid., 3.

82 Ibid., 4.

83 Ibid., 8.

84 When the institute was founded in 1974, it had 65 supporters. It now enjoys the support of over 2,500 individuals, corporations, and foundations. Eighty-three percent of Fraser's revenues are raised from donations by corporate members (39 percent), foundations (31 percent), and individual donations (13 percent). The remaining 17 percent is generated from sales of publications and miscellaneous services. See The Fraser Institute's home page (www.fraserinstitute.ca).

85 For more on Michael Walker's impressions of the work of the Fraser Institute see his "What's Right, Who's Left?" and Lorinc, "Hold the Fries," 11–15, 61.

86 Interview with Ken Battle, 16 December 1998.

87 Ibid.

88 Caledon Institute of Social Policy, *An Overview,* home page (www.caledoninst.org)

89 Interview with Ken Battle.

90 Abelson, "Public Visibility and Policy Relevance."

CHAPTER TWO

1 See, for instance, Peschek, *Policy Planning Organizations;* Dye, *Who's Running America?* Domhoff, *Power Elite;* Domhoff and Dye, *Power Elites and Organizations;* and Saloma, *Ominous Politics.*

2 Judis, "Japanese Megaphone."

3 Domhoff, *Power Elite.*

4 See Newsom, *Public Dimension*, 141–62.
5 The American pluralist tradition is strongly rooted in the belief that society is composed of individual groups that compete for power and status in the policy-making community. Two studies, in particular, have had a major impact on shaping this perspective: Truman, *The Governmental Process*, and Bentley, *The Process of Government*.
6 See Critchlow, *The Brookings Institution*; Schulzinger, *Wise Men*; Edwards, *Power of Ideas*; and Smith, *Rand Corporation*.
7 For instance, see Dickson, *Think Tanks*; Smith, *Idea Brokers*; Ricci, *Transformation of American Politics*; Lindquist, "Canadian Think Tanks"; McGann and Weaver, *Think Tanks*; and Stone, *Capturing the Political Imagination*.
8 For an example of information on research projects, see Dobuzinskis, "Trends and Fashions."
9 For a more detailed discussion of epistemic and policy communities, see Haas, *Knowledge*; Pross, *Group Politics*, especially chap. 5; and Coleman and Skogstad, *Public Policy and Policy Communities*.
10 See Heclo, "Issue Networks"; Lindquist, "Think Tanks?" and Stone, *Capturing the Political Imagination*.
11 See Kingdon, *Agendas*, and Stairs, "Public Opinion and External Affairs."

CHAPTER THREE

1 For more on this, see Weiss, *Organizations for Policy Analysis*; Stone, *Political Imagination*, especially chap. 3, and Weaver, "Changing World."
2 Interview with David Zussman, 14 September 1999.
3 Stone, *Political Imagination*.
4 See Kitschelt, "Political Opportunity Structures."
5 For an interesting examination of the involvement of think tanks in several government departments and agencies during the Reagan-Bush years, see Burch, *Research in Political Economy*.
6 The Rutherford Institute's support of Paula Jones in her case against President Clinton is an example of a think tank trying to influence the judicial process. The chair of the Rutherford Institute, John Whitehead, has appeared on several American talk shows and newscasts supporting Jones's legal actions. For a more detailed discussion of the ties between think tanks and the judiciary, see Burch, *Research in Political Economy*.
7 Several articles have been written on think tanks specializing in state politics. See, for instance, Scott, "Intellectuals Who Became Influential," and Moore, "Local Right Thinkers."
8 For a comprehensive discussion of the many factors that have contributed to the rise of think tanks, see Weiss, *Organizations for Policy Analysis*.

9   In addition to 100 senators and 435 elected members of the u.s. House of Representatives, there are 3 nonvoting members representing the District of Columbia who sit in the House.

10 For more on this, see Abelson, "Think tanks in the u.s."

11 For more on the Congressional Policy Advisory Board, see the House Policy Committee, "Congressional Policy Advisory."

12 Ibid.

13 The role of think tanks and party foundations in Germany is examined in Gellner, "Think Tanks in Germany."

14 The role and function of public think tanks is the focus of Robinson's paper "Public Think Tanks in the u.s."

15 See Abelson, *American Think Tanks.*

16 Ibid.

17 On the role of advisors in the Bush campaign, see Van Slambrouck, "California Think Tank"; Hager, "Bush Shops for Advice"; Swanson, "Brain Power"; and Schmitt, "Foreign Policy Experts."

18 Abelson, *American Think Tanks.*

19 With the Canada Elections Act of 1996 the minimum election period was shortened from forty-seven to thirty-six days. A sitting government may run a longer election period, but politically it has rarely been in its interest to do so. A longer election period provides opposition parties with more time to criticize government policies.

20 For more on this see Baier and Bakvis, "Think Tanks and Political Parties."

21 Guy, *People, Politics and Government,* 215.

22 For more on the use of royal commissions and commissions of inquiry, see Bradford, *Commissioning Ideas,* and Jenson, "Commissioning Ideas."

23 Think tanks in Canada are registered as tax-exempt organizations under the Income Tax Act. This tax privilege is conferred by Revenue Canada on organizations that perform educational functions, but it is extended with certain limitations. Think tanks are prohibited from engaging in certain political activities, including supporting or opposing political parties and their members and furthering the political platforms of parties. Similar limitations are placed on think tanks in the United States by the Internal Revenue Service. Think tanks in the United States are also concerned about the potential political repercussions of being too closely linked to one party. Not only might such an association threaten a think tank's tax-exempt status but it would likely undermine its ability to engage in objective scholarly analysis. For more on this see Morin and Deane, "The Ideas Industry," 8 June 1999.

24 Interview with author, 15 December 1998.

25 Interview with author, 17 December 1998.

26 In the fall of 1999 the PPF began a research project on managing transitions. The PPF was created in 1987 to strengthen the dialogue between government and the private and nonprofit sectors in the hope of improving public-policy decision-making. Information obtained during interview with David Zussman, president of PPF, 14 September 1999.

27 This point is reinforced by Lindquist in "Transition Teams and Government Succession," 49.

28 Guy, *People, Politics and Government,* 215.

29 The directors of the research offices of Canada's five political parties are well aware of the work being conducted by the country's leading think tanks. In interviews with the author on December 14, 15, and 17 December 1998, all the directors indicated that they regularly receive publications from Canadian policy institutes and occasionally meet with some of their staff.

30 Interview with author, 16 December 1998. Several independent sources, including Jonathan Murphy, director of the National Liberal Caucus Research Bureau (interview with author, 14 December 1998), have acknowledged Battle's access to cabinet and his significant impact in helping shape legislation on several social policy issues. For more on Battle's influence in key Liberal policy circles, see Greenspon and Wilson-Smith, *Double Vision,* especially chap. 9.

31 Ibid.

32 Interview with author, 16 December 1998.

33 Ibid.

34 *Associations Canada,* 1999–2000.

35 For more on the role of the Conference Board of Canada, see Lindquist, *Behind the Myth.*

36 u.s. data appears in u.s. Department of Education, "Degrees and Other Formal Awards Conferred." Data on social science phds in Canada appears in Statistics Canada, "Earned Doctorates, by Field of Study and Sex."

37 There have been several recent reports in the media suggesting that over the next ten years there will be a significant shortage of faculty to staff universities and colleges in Canada.

38 Figures obtained from personal correspondence with IRPP staff.

39 Figures provided by Caledon president Ken Battle.

40 Interview with author, 14 September 1999. The North-South Institute currently receives $1 million annually from a government body called the Canadian International Development Agency (CIDA). This amount represents 65 percent of its budget.

41 For more on the role of foundations in the United States, see Berman, *Influence,* and Sealander, *Private Wealth.*

42 The AEI's financial crisis during the mid-1980s was also a result of poor management. See Abelson, *American Think Tanks,* 53–4.

43 Morgan, "Think Tank or Hired Gun?" For more on the relationship between think tanks and corporate donors, see Stefancic and Delgado, *No Mercy.*

44 Abelson and Carberry, "Following Suit?" 546–7.

45 Kingdon, *Agendas,* 129.

46 Ibid., 130.

47 Harrison and Hoberg, "Setting the Environmental Agenda."

48 Abelson and Carberry, "Following Suit?" 547. For more on theories of entrepreneurship, see Schneider and Teske, "Political Entrepreneur." On the role of institutional structures in influencing policy entrepreneurship, see Checkel, *Ideas.*

49 Ibid, 548.

50 For more on the origins of the Fraser Institute, see Lindquist, *Behind the Myth,* 377–80.

51 Drawing on their extensive service in the public sector, Kirby and Pitfield played an important role in recognizing the need for policymakers to draw on policy expertise both inside and outside government. Pitfield served as deputy secretary to the Cabinet (Plans) and deputy clerk of the Privy Council (1969–73). He also served as clerk of the Privy Council and secretary to Cabinet (1975–79). Kirby was assistant secretary to the prime minister (1974–76), secretary to the Cabinet for federal-provincial relations (1980–82), and deputy clerk of the Privy Council Office (1981–82). On the contribution of senior civil servants to think tank development, see Lindquist, *Behind the Myth.*

52 Abelson and Carberry, "Following Suit?" 548.

53 Ibid.

54 Gray, "Think Tanks."

55 Lipset, "Canada and the u.s.," 110. For other treatments of u.s.-Canadian comparisons, see Presthus, *Cross-National Perspectives,* and Merelman, *Partial Visions.*

56 Lipset, *Continental Divide,* 136.

57 The Saskatchewan Institute of Public Policy (sipp), based in Regina, was created "to engage the academic, government, private business, and non-profit sectors in meeting the public policy challenges of our time." Its current budget of $250,000 is provided entirely by the province.

58 Ibid.

59 See Abelson, *American Think Tanks.*

60 For a detailed examination of the types of presidential candidates most inclined to rely on advocacy think tanks, see Abelson and Carberry, "Policy Experts in Presidential Campaigns."

61 Data on the educational and professional experience of researchers at think tanks was obtained from current annual reports. Some think tanks are able to recruit and retain more phds than others. The

North-South Institute, for instance, currently has five staff members with doctorates. Moreover, the majority of experts at C.D. Howe possess PHDs. The same, however, cannot be said of several other think tanks, including the Institute for Research on Public Policy, the Atlantic Institute for Market Studies, the Canadian Institute of Strategic Studies, and the Mackenzie Institute.

62 Information obtained from institute web sites.

63 There are some exceptions to this trend. For instance, Gordon Robertson, who held several important government positions, including clerk of the Privy Council and secretary to Cabinet (1963–75) and secretary to Cabinet for provincial-federal relations (1975–79), was president of the Institute for Research on Public Policy from 1980 to 1984 and remained as a fellow in residence until 1990. Another exception is Hugh Segal, a former staff member of Ontario Premier Bill Davis and federal Conservative leaders Robert Stanfield and Brian Mulroney, who became president of the IRPP in 1999.

64 Interview with David Zussman, 14 September 1999.

65 Lindquist, *Behind the Myth*. A similar sentiment is expressed by Tupper in his assessment of the contribution of a select group of Canadian think tanks to the debate on public debt in Canada. See his "Think Tanks."

66 Quoted in Stone, *Political Imagination*, 43.

CHAPTER FOUR

1 For more on the increased competition among think tanks, see McGann, *Competition for Dollars*.

2 Abelson, *American Think Tanks*, 57.

3 Ibid.

4 Some presidents have relied far more heavily on scholars from think tanks to serve on presidential advisory boards than others. For instance, President Reagan invited several scholars from the Hoover Institution to sit on the President's Foreign Intelligence Advisory Board (PFIAB). Conversely, of the eleven members PFIAB appointed by President Clinton and chaired by Warren Rudman, none had permanent positions at a think tank. For more on the role of these boards, see Abelson, *American Think Tanks*, 75–9.

5 Ibid., 68.

6 Linden, "Powerhouses of Policy," 100.

7 Judith Maxwell appeared on the CBC and CTV evening news on 24 January 2000.

8 Fraser Institute, *Challenging Perceptions*, 12.

9 Heritage Foundation, *1998 Annual Report*.

10 Based on 1997 figures. Data obtained from a survey distributed to Canadian think tanks by the author in the fall of 1997.

11 Heritage Foundation, *1998 Annual Report.*

12 See Weaver and Rich, "Think Tanks." See also Dolny, "What's in a Label?"

13 See Abelson, "Public Visibility."

14 Heritage Foundation, *1998 Annual Report.*

15 Crowley, "How Can Think Tanks Win Friends?"

16 Abelson, *American Think Tanks*, 88.

17 Ibid.

18 Ibid, 86.

19 Ibid.

20 Abelson, "Policy Experts and Political Pundits."

21 Abelson, "Public Visibility and Policy Relevance," 241.

22 Quotations drawn from Fraser Institute promotional material. Before assuming office, Margaret Thatcher helped establish the Centre for Policy Studies, in London. For more on this and other British think tanks, see Stone, *Capturing the Political Imagination,* and Denham and Garnett, *British Think Tanks.*

CHAPTER FIVE

1 Some think tanks consider these and other indicators in assessing their own performance. However, for the purposes of this chapter, they will not be included.

2 Weaver and Rich, "Think Tanks."

3 Rich, "Perceptions of Think Tanks."

4 There is no consensus, nor, for that matter, are there many reliable estimates, on how many think tanks exist in Canada. Lindquist has estimated that there are likely a hundred, although this number may vary, depending on one's definition of a policy institute. This study focuses on twenty-two think tanks, a sizeable cross-section of the think tank population.

A think tank receives one citation per article even if several references are made to it. English-language newspapers were selected for their broad national and regional coverage of domestic and foreign policy issues. Since an index listing individuals and organizations who have appeared before various parliamentary committees and subcommittees has yet to be produced, the names of witnesses were taken from each committee report. A complete list of the committees covered in this study is included in table 5.11. Data are from the parliamentary sessions from 1980 to 1999, a period closely corresponding to the time when media data became available, were used, along with the federal government's report on policy consultants.

5 Weaver and Rich, "Think Tanks," 1.

6 Despite including twenty-two think tanks not based in the District of Columbia in their study, Weaver and Rich did not examine how much media attention regional newspapers devoted to think tanks.

7 Although the Hoover Institution generates far less media coverage than several DC-based think tanks, it received the highest overall score from the *Economist* in its ranking of think tanks. Interestingly enough, the *Economist* did not refer to Hoover's media visibility in evaluating its performance. Several other factors, including its funding, library, and high-profile staff, helped the magazine to make its assessment. See "The Good Think-Tank Guide."

8 Ibid., 23.

9 The conservative *Washington Times* quotes scholars from the Heritage Foundation, the American Enterprise Institute, CSIS, and the Cato Institute far more than any other newspaper in Rich and Weaver's study.

10 Rich and Weaver, "Advocates and Analysts," 249. See also Rich, "Think Tanks as Sources of Expertise."

11 Ibid. See also Rich, "Perceptions of Think Tanks."

12 Ibid. The Fraser Institute has accepted public sector money only once, during the mid-1980s, when the federal government asked it to undertake a three-year joint project with the Institute for Research on Public Policy to study the service industries. According to executive director Michael Walker, "the funding received ... was a self-contained grant [and] the institute retained full editorial control and publication copyright." Survey distributed by the author in the fall of 1997.

13 Data on the size and budget of the Conference Board was obtained from *Associations Canada 1996*.

14 Data on the size of these institutes was obtained from a questionnaire distributed by the author in the fall of 1997.

15 Ibid.

16 See Kingdon, *Agendas*.

17 For background information on the creation of this task force, see Anderson, "The New Focus."

18 This finding is not surprising, since six federal government departments fund CPRN, Inc.

19 Individuals not invited to testify before a parliamentary committee may request to appear by contacting the clerk of the appropriate committee. For guidelines on how individuals are selected to testify, see Dawson, *Government of Canada*, 348–51. For a more recent examination of the rules and procedures of parliamentary committees, see Docherty, *Mr. Smith*.

20 With few exceptions, majority and minority members of congressional committees and subcommittees have the authority to call witnesses to

testify. However, in practice the party in power will have more input into which individuals and organizations will appear to comment.

21 Remarks made to author by staff members of the Canadian Tax Foundation, 7 April 1998.

22 A Spearman Correlation is a nonparametric correlation coefficient based on the ranks of data rather than the actual values. Values of the coefficient range from −1 to +1. The absolute correlation coefficient indicates the strength of the relationship between the variables, and the sign of the coefficient indicates the direction of the relationship. Definition obtained from SPSS for Windows Release 6.1 (24 June 1994).

23 Pal, *Public Policy Analysis*, 92–4.

CHAPTER SIX

1 Van Slambrouck, "California Think Tank."

2 Swanson, "Brain Power."

3 Judis, "Taking Care of Business."

4 Interview with Dr Martin Anderson, 19 March 1990.

5 While presidential candidates must raise their own funds during the primaries, the nominees selected by each party can, should they elect to, draw on public funds for the general election. If presidential nominees accept public funding, they cannot draw on any private sources of money.

6 Abelson and Carberry suggest that two characteristics of presidential candidates – their status as Washington insiders or outsiders and the strength of their ideological views as approximated by voter election studies – can help to explain the recruitment patterns of think tanks by candidates. See their article "Policy Experts."

7 Swanson, "Brain Power." Think tanks have different policies for staff who advise presidential candidates. Some, such as the Cato Institute, actively discourage staff from becoming too closely associated with particular candidates, preferring them to make their advice available to any candidate who wants it. Others, like the Center for National Policy, which are more concerned about keeping the Internal Revenue Service (IRS) at bay, insist that scholars take a leave of absence if they decide to work on a campaign. The IRS expressly forbids nonprofit organizations from participating in political campaigns. For more on this, see Morin and Deane, "The Ideas Industry," 8 June 1999.

8 For an analysis of the 1976 presidential campaign, see Schram, *Running for President*, and Witcover, *Marathon*.

9 Shoup, *The Carter Presidency*, 39.

10 Ibid., 43.

11 For a detailed examination of the Trilateral Commission, see Gill, *American Hegemony*, and Sklar, *Trilateralism*. For more information

on how Carter was selected to become a member of the Trilateral Commission, see Gerard Smith's Personal Files, "Memorandum from George Franklin to Gerard Smith on the Circumstances of Carter Coming with the Commission," Box 4, 1/1/76–6/3/77, Jimmy Carter Library.

12 Perloff, *The Shadows of Power*, 156.

13 Ibid.

14 Shoup, *The Carter Presidency*, 50.

15 Perloff, *The Shadows of Power*, 157.

16 Shoup, *The Carter Presidency*, 51.

17 Carter, *Why Not the Best?*, 164. Although Carter acknowledges the benefits of participating on the Trilateral Commission in his autobiography, he does not even mention the commission in his memoirs, *Keeping Faith*.

18 Contrary to Brzezinski's assertions that the Trilateral Commission did not advise Carter, Brzezinski did discuss several foreign policy issues with Carter in his capacity as director of the Commission. See, for instance, Brzezinski's Personal Files on the Trilateral Commission, Box 8, 7/1/75–8/31/75, and Box 5, 1/1/75–1/31/75, Jimmy Carter Library.

19 Interview with Dr Zbigniew Brzezinski, 30 May 1991.

20 There appears to be little agreement on the exact number of Trilateral Commission members who served in the Carter administration. Figures range from a low of eighteen to a high of twenty-five.

21 Perloff, *The Shadows of Power*, 158.

22 A majority of the trilateral commissioners who served in the Carter administration were also members of the Council on Foreign Relations. For a list of individuals who participated in both organizations, see Shoup, *The Carter Presidency*, 105.

23 Robert Pastor, Carter's Latin American specialist on the National Security Council, claims that the president's foreign policy toward Latin America was significantly influenced by two reports issued by the Commission on u.s.-Latin American Relations; *The Americas in a Changing World* and *The u.s. and Latin America*. The commission, chaired by Ambassador Sol Linowitz, was a bipartisan group of approximately twenty-five leaders from universities, think tanks, and corporations. Pastor, who served as executive director of the commission before joining the National Security Council, states that "The reports helped the administration define a new relationship with Latin America, and twenty-seven of the twenty-eight specific recommendations in the second report became u.s. policy." For additional information on the background of the Linowitz Commission and its contribution to u.s. foreign policy in Latin America, see Pastor, "The Carter Administration and Latin America," 62–5.

24 Reagan was governor of California from 1967 to 1975.

25 Anderson, *Revolution*, 47.

26 The various factors influencing Reagan's decision to leave the Democratic party are discussed in his autobiography, *An American Life*, 132–6.

27 The term "ideas move nations" was coined by Easterbrook and is used as the title of his article on the rise of conservative think tanks, which appeared in the *Atlantic Monthly*, January 1986.

28 Anderson, *Revolution*, 8. Anderson has apparently changed his mind about universities serving as reservoirs for policy ideas. In his book *Impostors in the Temple* Anderson claims that many universities have become inundated by academic frauds unable to maintain acceptable scholarly standards.

29 Anderson, *Revolution*, 165.

30 It is not uncommon for policy task forces to be created during presidential campaigns to provide candidates with information and advice. Several presidents, including John F. Kennedy, have relied on them. For more on this see Campbell, *Managing the Presidency*, and Hess, *Organizing the Presidency*.

31 Anderson, *Revolution*, 166.

32 Seventy-four economists participated on the economic policy task forces. Six chaired issue task forces in various areas of economic policy: Arthur F. Burns (task force on international monetary policy); Alan Greenspan (task force on budget policy); Paul McCracken, former chairman of the Council of Economic Advisers (task force on inflation); Charles E. Walker, former deputy secretary of the treasury (task force on tax policy); Murray L. Weidenbaum (task force on regulatory reform); and Caspar Weinberger (task force on spending control). The other members of the coordinating committee were Milton Friedman; Michel T. Halbouty, former president of the American Association of Petroleum Geologists and chairman of the task force on energy policy; Jack Kemp; James T. Lynn, former director of the Office of Management and Budget; William E. Simon, former secretary of the treasury, and Walter Wriston, chairman of Citi-bank/Citicorp.

33 Interview with Mr Richard V. Allen, 29 May 1991. For a more detailed discussion of the role and function of policy task forces during the 1980 campaign, see Wood, *Whatever Possessed the President?* 140–3.

34 Anderson, *Revolution*, 167.

35 Meese, *With Reagan*, 59.

36 Anderson, *Revolution*, 167.

37 Meese, *Transition*, 11.

38 Anderson, *Revolution*, 170.

39 The Institute for Contemporary Studies (ICS) in San Francisco was established by Caspar Weinberger and Edwin Meese III as a nonprofit organization in 1972. The ICS and its affiliated institutes publish studies

on economic, social, and foreign policy issues. For an interesting analysis on the founding of the ICS, see Beers, "Buttoned-Down Bohemians."

40 Background information on these and other members of the Reagan administration can be found in Brownstein and Easton, *Reagan's Ruling Class*.

41 Since some scholars belonged to one or more think tank before joining the Reagan administration, I have provided an approximate figure only.

42 A list of members of the Committee on the Present Danger who served in the Reagan administration can be found in Saunders, *Peddlers of Crisis*, 287–8. According to Eric Alterman, the Committee on the Present Danger eventually furnished fifty-nine members to the Reagan national security team. See his book *Sound and Fury*, 80. For additional information on the Committee on the Present Danger see Dalby, *Creating the Second Cold War*.

43 Figures for the AEI, the CSIS, and the Heritage Foundation are quoted in Blumenthal, *Counter-Establishment*, 35–8.

44 Weinraub, "Conservative Group's Blueprint for Reagan."

45 Omang, "Heritage Report."

46 Heatherly, *Mandate for Leadership*. In preparation for the 1984 and 1988 presidential campaigns, the Heritage Foundation produced similar volumes that examined a wide range of domestic and foreign policy issues. See Butler et al., *Mandate for Leadership II*, and *Mandate for Leadership III*. The Heritage Foundation also issued an interim report during the first term of the Reagan administration. See Holwill, *Agenda '83*. The Heritage Foundation was not the first think tank to produce detailed "blueprints" for the executive and Congress. Since 1971 the Brookings Institution has published an annual series entitled *Setting National Priorities*, which provides policymakers and scholars with in-depth analyses of domestic and foreign policy issues. Moreover, following the 1992 campaign Will Marshall and Martin Schram of the Progressive Policy Institute produced a blueprint for the Clinton administration entitled *Mandate for Change*, a title apparently borrowed from the Heritage Foundation's series *Mandate for Leadership*.

47 In an interview with the author on 29 May 1991, Richard Allen, President Reagan's first national security advisor, confirmed that Feulner presented Meese and Allen with a copy of *Mandate for Leadership* in mid-November. Allen added that the study "was immediately reproduced and distributed to our entire transition team." It is not surprising that Allen was willing to accept and reproduce Feulner's study. The two had established close ties as early as 1965 through the Intercollegiate Studies Institute, the first national conservative student organization in the United States. Eventually, through Allen, Feulner became a Hoover

Institution Fellow. For a discussion on the relationship between Feulner and Allen see Blumenthal, *Counter-Establishment*, 46–8.

48 Omang, "The Heritage Report."

49 Knickerbocker, "Heritage Foundation's Ideas." Meese also acknowledged receiving studies from the National Academy of Public Administration and from the Kennedy School of Government at Harvard. When asked if he had received a study from the Hoover Institution, Meese remarked, "I don't think so. There's nobody left there; they're all here in Washington working with us, helping out." See Meese, *Transition*, 7.

50 Meese, *With Reagan*, 60.

51 Ibid. On two occasions, Edwin Feulner took leave of the Heritage Foundation to serve as a special consultant in the White House on specific strategic planning projects and throughout the two terms was an informal advisor to President Reagan and members of his cabinet.

52 Ibid. For a discussion of which policy recommendations in the Heritage study were adopted by the Reagan administration during the early 1980s, see Horwill, *Agenda '83*.

53 Duignan and Rabushka, *The U.S. in the 1980s*. Interview with author, 2 May 1990. Campbell added that when Edwin Feulner was a Public Affairs Fellow at the Hoover Institution, he admitted to Campbell that he was "a retailer not a wholesaler of ideas." Campbell remarked jokingly that he would "buy a used idea from Feulner anytime."

54 Richard Allen resigned as National Security Adviser in early 1981 amidst allegations of wrongdoing and was replaced by Judge William Clark. Clark left the National Security Council (nsc) in October 1983 to become secretary of the interior and was replaced by the deputy national security adviser, Robert "Bud" McFarlane. For background information on the transfer of power in the nsc, see Menges, *National Security Council*.

55 Anderson, *Revolution*, 3.

56 Weinraub, "Conservative Group's Blueprint for Reagan."

57 Knickerbocker, "Heritage Foundation's Ideas."

58 Quoted in Wheeler, "Heritage Chiefs."

59 Interview with Dr Anderson, 19 August 1996. Richard Allen agrees that President Bush went to great lengths to distance himself from the Reaganites. Allen stated that by doing so, President Bush had cut himself off from some of America's most important and influential policy experts. Interview with the author, 6 September 1996.

60 For an interesting analysis of president Bush's reaction to public opinion polls during the Gulf War, see Brace and Hinckley, *Follow the Leader*.

61 Interview with Martin Anderson, Hoover Institution, 19 March 1990.

62 Heatherly, *Mandate for Leadership*.

63 The Carnegie Endowment for International Peace, the Citizens Transition Project, and the American Enterprise Institute were among the many organizations that outlined a series of domestic and foreign policy recommendations. See Rosenbaum, "Torrent of Free Advice."

64 David Osborne, a fellow at the PPI and co-author of *Reinventing America*, helped introduce Clinton to the think tank set. See Fineman, "Clinton's Team."

65 Several books have been written on the 1992 presidential election, including Allen and Portis, *The Comeback Kid*; Brummett, *High Wire*; Germond and Witcover, *Mad As Hell*; Goldman et al., *Quest for the Presidency*; Hohenberg, *Bill Clinton Story*; and Moore and Ihde, *Clinton*.

66 Clinton resigned as chair of the DLC shortly before announcing his candidacy for the presidency. The DLC is currently chaired by Louisiana senator John Breaux. Al From is the organization's president and executive director. The DLC currently has a staff of over twenty people and an annual budget of approximately $2.5 million, which is raised from private philanthropists, corporate donors, and grass-roots organizations.

67 The DLC has approximately 3,000 members, including about 750 elected officials nationwide, with 32 u.s. senators and 142 current and former House members. It also has chapters in twenty-eight states in every region of the country. For more on the DLC's membership, see Barnes, "Will DLC Be a Lobbying Heavyweight?"; Grove, "Steering His Party"; and Towell, "DLC Moves into Driver's Seat."

68 Achenbach, "Wonk If You Love Clinton."

69 Although Clinton appeared to draw heavily on the PPI's study *Mandate for Change*, only a few members from the PPI and the DLC received appointments in the Clinton administration. Bruce Reed and Bill Galston received positions in the domestic policy office. Reed was issues director in the campaign and deputy director of the transition for domestic policy. He was later appointed as White House domestic policy advisor. Will Marshall, Al From, and Robert Shapiro, the PPI's vice-president (who later resigned over the Whitewater scandal), were Clinton campaign advisers. From also served in the transition. For more on Clinton's inner circle of policy advisors, see Fineman, "Clinton's Team"; Weisberg, "Clincest"; and Bandow, "New Democrats."

70 Marshall and Schram, *Mandate for Change*. In addition to providing Clinton with several policy ideas to consider during the campaign, the DLC engaged in an active lobbying campaign to support some of the president's policies. For instance, the DLC devoted considerable resources to convincing members of Congress to ratify the North American Free Trade Agreement (NAFTA). For more on this, see Barnes, "Will DLC Be a Lobbying Heavyweight?"

71 For a complete text of the Clinton-Gore Economic Conference, including the list of presenters, see *President Clinton's New Beginning*.

72 Philip Lader, a South Carolina businessman, was the founding father of the annual Renaissance Weekend, which began in 1980. The purpose of the Renaissance Weekend is to provide leaders from various careers with an opportunity to share ideas in an informal setting. Seminars are held during the retreat, and journalists are prohibited from commenting on the proceedings. Bill and Hillary Clinton have attended the Renaissance Weekends since the mid-1980s. For more on Clinton's involvement in the Renaissance Weekend, see two articles by Maraniss, "Letter from Never-Never Land" and "A Weekend With Bill and Friends." Also see Jehl, "Thinking Party," and Baer, "Network for the Nineties."

73 For more on George W. Bush's career as Texas governor, see Ivins and Dubose, *Shrub*; Mitchell, *Bush Dynasty*; and Minutaglio, *First Son*.

74 Russo, "Brain Power." Also see Daalder and Lindsay, "Bush."

75 For more on the relationship between George W. Bush and the Hoover Institution, see Hager, "Bush Shops for Advice," and Healy and Hebel, "Academics."

76 Lindsey also served as an advisor to President George Bush. For more on Lindsey's background see Kessler, "Economic Adviser."

77 Maggs, "Tax Cuts," 2236.

78 Gorman, "Bush's Lesson Plan," 2230–2.

79 Kitfield, "Periphery Is Out," 2293.

80 For more on Rice's background see Mufson, "Daunting Challenge."

81 For more on Zoellick's appointment see Babington, "Bush Names Zoellick."

82 Kitfield, "Periphery is Out."

83 For more on Jeb Bush's fascination with policy development, see Minutaglio, *First Son*.

84 Greenberger, "CAMPAIGN 2000."

85 The majority of think tanks in the United States are registered as chapter 501(c) tax-exempt educational institutes under the Internal Revenue Code. To qualify, they must agree not to engage in certain types of political activities. According to chapter 501(c), subsection 3 of the Internal Revenue Code of 1986, "no substantial part of the activities of [registered organizations can carry] on propaganda, or otherwise attempt, to influence legislation (except as otherwise provided in subsection (h)), and which does not participate in, or intervene in (including publishing or distributing of statements), any political campaign on behalf of (or in opposition to) any candidate for public office." It is this last statement, the inability of registered organizations to participate in political campaigns, that has resulted in IRS audits of some think tanks.

Think tanks like the Hoover Institution, which is located on a university campus, are particularly vulnerable to losing credibility by being perceived as spokespersons for a particular candidate. When several of its staff advised Reagan in the 1980 campaign, the Hoover Institution discovered that close ties with politicians can lead to serious tensions with university faculty. Tensions between Hoover and Stanford arose once again as a result of the involvement of Hoover scholars in the Bush campaign. For more on this controversy, see Manley and Rebholz, "Hoover Institution," and Abelson, *American Think Tanks*, 41–3.

86 Van Slambrouck, "California Think Tank."

CHAPTER SEVEN

1 Lindquist, *Behind the Myth*, 227.
2 Tupper, "Think Tanks," 532.
3 Several journalists covering the constitutional conferences reported favourably on their role in stimulating public discussion. For instance, Jeffrey Simpson commented that "Against the odds, these gatherings in Halifax, Calgary, Montreal, Toronto and Vancouver worked splendidly. Indeed, they rescued constitutional reform, at least temporarily ... Instead of the usual shouting and insinuation, the discussions were civil and constructive, a rediscovery of the much-ballyhooed but infrequently observed Canadian compromise and tolerance." Quoted by Milne in "Innovative Constitutional Processes," 38.
4 Kroeger, "Constitutional Conferences," 2.
5 Ibid.
6 *Shaping Canada's Future Together*, iii.
7 Ibid.
8 This was not the first attempt by the federal government to generate public discussion on constitutional reform following Meech Lake. The Spicer Commission, formally known as the Citizens' Forum on Canada's Future, was established in November 1990 to give Canadians an opportunity to speak out on the future of Canada. For more on this, see Russell, *Constitutional Odyssey*, 154–89.
9 Kroeger, "The Constitutional Conferences," 1.
10 Milne, "Innovative Constitutional Processes," 29.
11 Russell, *Constitutional Odyssey*, 175.
12 Milne, "Innovative Constitutional Processes," 29.
13 See Russell, *Constitutional Odyssey*.
14 Harrison, *Constitutional Conferences Secretariat*, 1.
15 Ibid.
16 Kroeger, "Constitutional Conferences," 2.
17 President of the Privy Council, *News Release*.

18 Department of Finance, *Supplementary Estimates.*

19 President of the Privy Council, *News Release,* 2.

20 A series of background papers on the various themes explored in *Shaping Canada's Future Together* were released by the Federal-Provincial Relations Office (FPRO) before the constitutional hearings began in the fall of 1991. They were edited by Ronald Watts, director of the Institute for Intergovernmental Relations at Queen's University, who had been seconded to the FPRO in April 1991, and they were intended to provide additional information and insights into the constitutional reform proposals outlined by the federal government. Among the titles released were *Responsive Institutions for a Modern Canada, Canadian Federalism and Economic Union,* and *Aboriginal Peoples, Self-Government, and Constitutional Reform.*

21 This observation is confirmed by Harrison, who stated that "If the conferences were to be based on openness, then it was paramount that the process used to develop them be as neutral as possible. A key decision in this regard was the decision to invite five independent institutes to sponsor the first four conferences … It could be argued that the only way in which potential concerns about 'manipulation' could be minimized was by handing considerable authority to these outside bodies." See Constitutional Conferences Secretariat, "Constitutions Conference," 5.

22 See chapter 5.

23 Discussion with Ron Watts, 27 July 1999. David Elton, president of the Max Bell Foundation and former president of the Canada West Foundation made similar remarks to me regarding the selection criteria for think tanks (25 July 1999).

24 Information about mission statement obtained from APEC's home page (www.apec-econ.ca).

25 Correspondence with Patrick Brannon, research analyst, APEC.

26 Canada West Foundation, *Annual Report 1997,* 6.

27 Interview, 24 November 2000.

28 Niagara Institute home page (www.niagarainstitute.com).

29 The origins of the C.D. Howe Institute can be traced to the creation, in 1958, of the Private Planning Association of Canada (PPAC), which was established "to undertake research on educational activities and economic policy issues." In 1973 the PPAC merged with the C.D. Howe Memorial Foundation to become the C.D. Howe Research Institute (HRI). In 1981 the HRI was dissolved and the reconstituted PPAC became the C.D. Howe Institute. See the C.D. Howe Institute home page, "A History of the Institute" (www.cdhowe.org).

30 See chapter 5.

31 The responsibilities varied according to each institute. See Harrison, *The Constitutional Conferences Secretariat,* figure 2 and President of the Privy Council, *News Release.*

32 Ibid., 3.
33 Ibid., 4.
34 Ibid., 5.
35 Harrison, *Constitutional Conferences Secretariat*, 16.
36 Canada West Foundation, *Renewal of Canada*, 1.
37 According to Milne, shortly after Clark invited the institutes to participate in the conferences, the heads of the institutes met and insisted that
their involvement would depend on maintaining their "own independence and control over the organization, management, and final report
of the Conferences, including the manner in which participants would
be selected." Milne, "Innovative Constitutional Processes," 30. While
the institutes developed their own models for recruiting participants,
they still had to satisfy the government's selection criteria.
38 See Abelson, "New Channel of Influence," 849–72.
39 Harrison, *Constitutional Conferences Secretariat*, 8.
40 Atlantic Province's Economic Council, *Annual Report 1992*. In 1998
APEC's entire budget was $593,722.
41 Figures quoted in a press release, "Constitutional Conference Costs,"
issued by the Constitutional Conferences Secretariat.
42 Roger Gibbins is currently president of the Canada West Foundation.
43 For more on the handling of these conferences, see Lindquist, "Citizens, Experts and Budgets."
44 Ibid., 113.

CHAPTER EIGHT

1 See, for instance, Heclo, "Issue Networks."
2 See, Hay, "Letting CIIPS Fall"; Egan, "Science Council"; Bindman,
"Legal Think-Tank"; and Dowling, "Economic Council."
3 Dowling, "Economic Council."
4 Egan, "Science Council." For more on the Science Council, see De La
Mothe, "A Dollar Short."
5 See Abelson and Lindquist, "Who's Thinking about International Affairs?"
6 Some of these issues have undoubtedly been discussed by Canadian
think tanks at their recent Think Link conferences. The first such meeting of think tanks took place in Winnipeg in March 2000.
7 For more on the role of think tanks in emerging democracies, see
Struyk, *Reconstructive Critics*.
8 The relationship between the World Bank and several think tanks is
examined in Stone, *Banking on Knowledge*.
9 Rich, "Perceptions of Think Tanks." A survey was sent to the heads
of government departments in Canada as part of the Policy Research
Initiative, but a more comprehensive survey has not yet been
distributed.

APPENDIX ONE

1 Wall, *Andrew Carnegie*, 898.
2 Ibid.
3 For a history of the Hoover Institution see Duignan, *Hoover Institution*.
4 Mission statement of the Hoover Institution. Available on institute's homepage (www.hoover.stanford.edu).
5 Quoted in "The Good Think-Tank Guide."
6 Several studies have been written on the history of the Council on Foreign Relations. See, for example, Schulzinger, *Wise Men*; Shoup and Minter, *Imperial Brain Trust*; Silk and Silk, *American Establishment*; Perloff, *Shadows of Power*; Council on Foreign Relations, *Twenty-Five Years*; Grose, *The Inquiry*; Santoro, *Diffidence and Ambition*; and Wala, *Council on Foreign Relations*. For a conspiratorial interpretation of the role of the CFR by members of the conservative John Birch Society, see Courtney and Courtney, *Council on Foreign Relations*.
7 Council on Foreign Relations homepage (www.cfr.org).
8 Abelson, *American Think Tanks*, 52.
9 Linden, "Powerhouses of Policy," 102. For an insider's account of the inner workings of the AEI, see Wiarda, *Universities*, chapter 7.
10 CSIS mission statement. For a detailed history of the organization see Smith, *Strategic Calling*.
11 Abelson, *American Think Tanks*, 93.
12 Several articles have been written on the IPS. For example, see Muravchik, "Think-Tank of the Left"; Yoffe, "IPS Faces Life"; and Powell, *Covert Cadre*.
13 Dickson, *Think Tanks*, 222–3.
14 The Urban Institute, *Urban Institute*, 7.
15 Ibid., 9.
16 Ibid., 7.
17 Ibid., 3.
18 cato Institute homepage (www.cato.org)
19 O'Connor and Cohn, "A Baby Boomers' Think Tank," 22.
20 Fialka, "Cato Institute's Influence Grows."
21 For more on the Manhattan Institute's ties to Mayor Giuliani, see Scott, "Intellectuals."
22 Redburn, "Conservative Thinkers."
23 Friedman, "Institute Tied to Clinton."
24 Fineman, "Clinton's Team."
25 Balz, "Moderate, Conservative Democrats."

APPENDIX TWO

1 Canada West Foundation, *Annual Report 1997*, 1.

2 Ibid.
3 Jérôme-Forget, "Institute for Research on Public Policy," 92.
4 Ibid., 87.
5 C.D. Howe Web Site (www.cdhowe.org).
6 Ibid. For a detailed discussion of the C.D. Howe Institute and its various incarnations, see Ernst, "From Liberal Continentalism."
7 C.D. Howe Institute, *1997 Annual Report*, 6.
8 Ibid., 8.
9 North-South Institute, *Prospectus*.
10 For brief commentaries by the NSI's three presidents on the work of the institute, see the NSI's *Annual Report 1996*.
11 Ibid.
12 North South Institute, *The North-South Institute*.
13 Interview, 22 February 2000.
14 Canadian Centre for Policy Alternatives, web site (www.policyalternatives.ca).
15 Ibid., "Statement of Purpose."
16 Mackenzie Institute, "Mission and Description" (www.mackenzieinstitute.com).
17 Public Policy Forum, "History of the Forum" (www.ppforum.com).
18 Ibid.
19 Interview with author, 14 September 1999.
20 Data obtained from survey distributed by author to Canadian policy institutes in the fall of 1997.
21 Interview with author, 16 December 1998.
22 Canadian Policy Research Networks, Inc., *Shared Responsibility: 1997–98 Annual Report*.
23 Canadian Policy Research Networks, Inc., CPRN *Mission and Mandate*, 3.
24 Atlantic Institute for Market Studies, "Introduction," *1995–1996 Annual Report*.
25 Atlantic Institute for Market Studies, "President's Message," *1995–1996 Annual Report*.

Bibliography

WORKS CITED

Abelson, Donald E. "Do Think Tanks Matter? Opportunities, Incentives and Constraints for Think Tanks in Canada and the United States." *Global Society* 14, no. 2 (2000): 213–36.

– "Public Visibility and Policy Relevance: Assessing the Impact and Influence of Canadian Policy Institutes." *Canadian Public Administration* 42, no. 2 (1999): 240–70.

– "Surveying the Think Tank Landscape in Canada." In Martin W. Westmacott and Hugh Mellon, eds., *Public Administration and Policy: Governing in Challenging Times.* Scarborough, ON: Prentice-Hall, 1999: 91–105.

– "Policy Experts and Political Pundits: American Think Tanks and the News Media." *NIRA Review* (summer 1998): 40–3.

– "In Search of Policy Influence: The Strategies of American Think Tanks." *NIRA Review* (spring 1998): 28–32.

– "Think Tanks in the United States." In Diane Stone, Andrew Denham, and Mark Garnett, eds., *Think Tanks across Nations: A Comparative Approach.* Manchester: Manchester University Press, 1998: 107–26.

– *American Think Tanks and their Role in U.S. Foreign Policy.* London and New York: Macmillan and St Martin's Press, 1996.

– "From Policy Research to Political Advocacy: The Changing Role of Think Tanks in American Politics." *Canadian Review of American Studies* 25, no. 1 (1995): 93–126.

– "A New Channel of Influence: American Think Tanks and the News Media." *Queen's Quarterly* 99, no. 4 (1992): 849–72.

Abelson, Donald E., and Christine M. Carberry. "Following Suit or Falling Behind? A Comparative Analysis of Think Tanks in Canada and the United States." *Canadian Journal of Political Science* 31, no. 3 (1998): 525–55.

- "Policy Experts in Presidential Campaigns: A Model of Think Tank Recruitment." *Presidential Studies Quarterly* 27, no. 4 (fall 1997): 679–97.

Abelson, Donald E., and Evert A. Lindquist. "Think Tanks in North America." In R. Kent Weaver and James G. McGann, eds., *Think Tanks and Civil Societies: Catalyst for Ideas and Action.* New Brunswick, NJ: Transaction Publishers, 2000: 37–66.

- "Who's Thinking about International Affairs? The Evolution and Funding of Canada's Foreign and Defence Policy Think Tanks." Paper presented at the Annual Meetings of the Canadian Political Science Association, Ottawa, June 1998.

Achenbach, Joel. "Wonk If You Love Clinton." *Washington Post*, 8 November 1992.

Allen, Charles F., and Jonathan Portis. *The Comeback Kid: The Life and Career of Bill Clinton.* New York: Birch Lane Press, 1992.

Alterman, Eric. *Sound and Fury: The Washington Punditocracy and the Collapse of American Politics.* New York: Harper Collins, 1992.

Anderson, George. "The New Focus on the Policy Capacity of the Federal Government." *Canadian Public Administration* 39, no. 4 (winter 1996): 469–88.

Anderson, Martin. *Impostors in the Temple.* New York: Simon and Schuster, 1992.

- *Revolution.* New York: Harcourt Brace Jovanovich, 1988.

Associations Canada. Toronto: Canadian Almanac and Directory Publishing Company, 1996, 1999.

Atlantic Institute for Market Studies. *1995–1996 Annual Report.* Halifax: Atlantic Institute for Market Studies, 1996.

Atlantic Province's Economic Council. *Annual Report 1992.* Halifax: Atlantic Province's Economic Council, 1992.

Atwood, Thomas C., and Thomas W. Mead. *The Directory of Public Policy Organizations 1998–1999.* Washington, DC: The Heritage Foundation, 1998.

Babington, Charles. "Bush Names Zoellick as Trade Representative." *Washington Post*, 10 January 2000.

Baer, Donald. "A Network for the Nineties: The Retreat That Spawned a Presidency." *U.S. News & World Report*, 23 November 1992.

Baier, Gerald, and Herman Bakvis. "Think Tanks and Political Parties: Competitors or Collaborators?" *Isuma: Canadian Journal of Policy Research* 2, no. 1 (spring 2001): 107–113.

Balz, Dan. "Moderate, Conservative Democrats Buck 'Constraints,' Form Think Tank." *Washington Post,* 30 June 1989.

Bandow, Doug. "New Democrats Lose Think-Tank War." *Wall Street Journal,* 18 March 1993.

Barnes, James A. "Will DLC Be a Lobbying Heavyweight?" *National Journal,* 23 October 1993.

Beers, David. "Buttoned-Down Bohemians." *San Francisco Chronicle,* 3 August 1986.

Beigie, C.E. "Economic Policy Analysis: The Role of the C.D. Howe Research Institute." *Canadian Business Review* 39 (summer 1974): 39–42.

Bentley, Arthur F. *The Process of Government.* Chicago: University of Chicago Press, 1908.

Berman, Edward H. *The Influence of the Carnegie, Ford and Rockefeller Foundations on American Foreign Policy: The Ideology of Philanthropy.* New York: State University of New York Press, 1983.

Bindman, Stephen. "Loss of a Legal Think-Tank," *Ottawa Citizen,* 11 March 1992.

Blumenthal, Sidney. *The Rise of the Counter-Establishment: From Conservative Ideology to Political Power.* New York: Harper and Row, 1988.

Brace, Paul, and Barbara Hinckley. *Follow the Leader: Opinion Polls and the Modern Presidents.* New York: Basic Books, 1992.

Bradford, Neil. *Commissioning Ideas: Canadian National Policy Innovation in Comparative Perspective.* Toronto: Oxford University Press, 1998.

Bremmer, Robert H. *American Philanthropy.* Chicago: University of Chicago Press, 1988.

Brinkley, Douglas. "Jimmy Carter's Modest Quest for Global Peace." *Foreign Affairs* 74, no. 6 (November/December 1995): 90–100.

Brodie, Janine M., and Jane Jenson. *Crisis, Challenge, and Change: Party and Class in Canada.* Toronto: Methuen, 1980.

Brookings Institution. *Annual Report 1998.* Washington, DC: The Brookings Institution, 1999.

Brownstein, Ronald, and Nina Easton. *Reagan's Ruling Class: Portraits of the President's Top One Hundred Officials.* Washington, DC: Presidential Accountability Group, 1982.

Brummett, John. *High Wire: From the Backroads to the Beltway – The Education of Bill Clinton.* New York: Hyperion Press, 1994.

Burch, Philip H. *Research in Political Economy.* Supplement 1, *Reagan, Bush and Right-Wing Politics: Elites, Think Tanks, Power and Policy.* Greenwich, CT: JAI Press, 1997.

Butler, Stewart, M., Michael Sanera, and W. Bruce Weinrod, eds. *Mandate for Leadership II: Continuing the Conservative Revolution.* Washington, DC: Heritage Foundation, 1984.

Campbell, Colin. *Managing the Presidency: Carter, Reagan, and the Search for Executive Harmony.* Pittsburgh, PA: University of Pittsburgh Press, 1986.

Campbell, John L. "Institutional analysis and the role of ideas in political economy." *Theory and Society* 27 (1998): 377–409.

Campbell, Murray. "Wonks." *Globe and Mail,* 2 December 1995.

Canada West Foundation. *Annual Report 1997: 25 Years of Commitment to the West within a Strong Canada.* Calgary, AB: Canada West Foundation, 1997.

– *Conference Report: Renewal of Canada – Institutional Reform.* Calgary, AB: Canada West Foundation, 1992.

Canadian Centre for Philanthropy web site (www.ccp.ca).

Canadian Centre for Policy Alternatives web site (www.policyalternatives.ca).

Canadian Policy Research Networks, Inc. *Shared Responsibility: 1997–98 Annual Report.* Ottawa: CPRN, Inc., 1998.

Carter, Jimmy. *Keeping Faith: Memoirs of a President.* New York: Bantam, 1982.

– *Why Not the Best?* Nashville, TN: Broadman Press, 1975.

C.D. Howe Institute. "A History of the Institute." C.D. Howe Institute web site (www.cdhowe.org).

Center for International Private Enterprise. "Think Tanks as Advocates of Change: An Interview with Phillip Truluck." *Economic Reform Today,* November 1996, 5–8.

Checkel, Jeffrey T. *Ideas and International Political Change.* New Haven, CT: Yale University Press, 1997.

Chisolm, Laura Brown. "Sinking the Think-Tanks Upstream: The Use and Misuse of Tax Exemption Law to Address the Use and Misuse of Tax-Exempt Organizations by Politicians." *University of Pittsburgh Law Review* 51, no. 3 (1990): 577–640.

Coleman, William D., and Grace Skogstad, eds. *Public Policy and Policy Communities in Canada: A Structural Approach.* Toronto: Copp Clark Pitman, 1990.

Commission on U.S.-Latin American Relations. *The United States and Latin America: Next Steps.* New York: Center for Inter-American Relations, 1976.

– *The Americas in a Changing World.* New York: Quadrangle and the Center for Inter-American Relations, 1975.

Conference Board of Canada. "What's in It for you?" The Conference Board of Canada web site (www.conferenceboard.ca).

– "Who We Are: The Conference Board of Canada." Conference Board of Canada web site (www.conferenceboard.ca).

Constitutional Conferences Secretariat. "Constitutions Conference Costs." *Press Release,* 14 January 1992.

Council on Foreign Relations. *A Record of Twenty-Five Years.* New York: Council on Foreign Relations, 1947.

Courtney, Kent, and Phoebe Courtney. *The Council on Foreign Relations: America's Unelected Rulers.* New Orleans, LA: The Conservative Society of America, 1962.

Covington, Sally. *Moving a Public Policy: The Strategic Philanthropy of Conservative Foundations.* Washington, DC: National Committee for Responsive Philanthropy.

Critchlow, Donald T. *The Brookings Institution, 1916–52: Expertise and the Public Interest in a Democratic Society.* DeKalb, IL: Northern Illinois University Press, 1985.

Crowley, Brian Lee. "How Can Think Tanks Win Friends and Influence People in the Media?" *Insider,* no. 264, October 1999.

Culleton Colwell, Mary Anna. *Private Foundations and Public Policy: The Political Role of Philanthropy.* New York: Garland, 1993.

Daalder, Ivo H., and James M. Lindsay. "Bush: Still Needs Work on Foreign Affairs." *Newsday,* 8 December 1999.

Dalby, Simon. *Creating the Second Cold War: The Discourse of Politics.* London: Pinter Publishers, 1990.

Dawson, R. MacGregor. *The Government of Canada.* 5th ed. Toronto: University of Toronto Press, 1947.

De La Mothe, John. "A Dollar Short and a Day Late: A Note on the Demise of the Science Council of Canada." *Queen's Quarterly* 99, no. 4 (1992): 873–86.

Demson, Sandra. *A Brief History of the Canadian Institute of International Affairs.* Toronto: Canadian Institute of International Affairs, 1995.

Denham, Andrew, and Mark Garnett. *British Think-Tanks and the Climate of Opinion.* London: UCL Press, 1998.

Department of Finance. *Supplementary Estimates (C), 1991–92, for the Fiscal Year Ending March 31, 1992.* Ottawa: Government of Canada, 1992.

– Umbrella Group on Policy Management. *Report from the Sub-group on Relations with the External Policy Research Community.* Ottawa: Department of Finance, July 1997.

Dickerson, John F. "Newt Inc." *Time,* 13 February 1995, 28.

Dickson, Paul. *Think Tanks.* New York: Atheneum, 1972.

Dobuzinskis, Laurent. "Trends and Fashion in the Marketplace of Ideas." In Laurent Dobuzinskis, Michael Howlett, and David Laycock, eds., *Policy Studies in Canada: The State of the Art.* Toronto: University of Toronto Press, 1996: 91–124.

Docherty, David C. *Mr. Smith Goes to Ottawa: Life in the House of Commons.* Vancouver: UBC Press, 1997.

Dolny, Michael. "What's in a Label? Right-Wing Think Tanks Are Often Quoted, Rarely Labeled?" *Extra!* May/June 1998.

Domhoff, William G. *The Power Elite and the State: How Policy is Made in America.* New York: Aldine de Gruyter, 1990.

Domhoff, William G., and Thomas R. Dye. *Power Elites and Organizations.* London: Sage, 1987.

Dowling, Deborah. "Closing Down the Economic Council," *Ottawa Citizen,* 10 March 1992.

Duignan, Peter. *The Hoover Institution on War, Revolution and Peace: Seventy-Five Years of Its History.* Stanford, CA: Hoover Institution Press, 1989.

Duignan, Peter, and Alvin Rabushka, eds. *The United States in the 1980s.* Stanford, CA: Hoover Institution Press, 1980.

Edwards, Lee. *The Power of Ideas: The Heritage Foundation at 25 Years.* Ottawa, IL: Jameson Books, 1997.

Egan, Kelly. "Science Council Was Far Ahead of Its Time," *Ottawa Citizen*, 8 March 1992.

Ernst, A. "From Liberal Continentalism to Neoconservatism: North American Free Trade and the Politics of the C.D. Howe Institute." *Studies in Political Economy* 39 (1992): 109–40.

Federal-Provincial Relations Office. *Shaping Canada's Future Together.* Ottawa: Federal-Provincial Relations Office, 1991.

Fialka, John J. "Cato Institute's Influence Grows in Washington As Republican-Dominated Congress Sets Up Shop." *Wall Street Journal*, 14 December 1994.

Fineman, Howard. "Clinton's Team: The Inner Circles." *Newsweek,* 26 October 1994.

Fraser Institute. *Challenging Perceptions: Twenty-Five Years of Influential Ideas: A Retrospective, 1974–1999.* Vancouver: The Fraser Institute, 1999.

Freund, Gerald. *Narcissism and Philanthropy: Ideas and Talent Denied.* New York: Viking, 1996.

Friedman, Thomas L. "Institute Tied to Clinton Issues Policy Proposals." *New York Times,* 7 December 1992.

Gairdner, William, ed. *After Liberalism: Essays in Search of Freedom, Virtue and Order.* Toronto: Stoddart, 1998.

Gellner, Winand. "Think Tanks in Germany." In Diane Stone, Andrew Denham, and Mark Garnett, eds., *Think Tanks across Nations.* Manchester: Manchester University Press, 1998: 82–106.

– "Political Think-Tanks and Their Markets in the u.s.: Institutional Setting." *Presidential Studies Quarterly* 25, no. 3 (summer 1995): 497–510.

Germond, Jack W., and Jules Witcover. *Mad as Hell: Revolt at the Ballot Box, 1992.* New York: Warner Books, 1993.

Gill, Stephen. *American Hegemony and the Trilateral Commission.* New York: Cambridge University Press, 1990.

Goldman, Peter, Thomas M. De Frank, Mark Miller, Andrew Murr, and Tom Matthews. *Quest for the Presidency, 1992.* College Station, tx: Texas A&M University Press, 1994.

Goldstein, Judith, and Robert Keohane, eds. *Ideas and Foreign Policy: Beliefs, Institutions and Political Change.* Ithaca, ny: Cornell University Press, 1993.

– "The Good Think-Tank Guide." *Economist,* 21 December–3 January 1992, 49–53.

Gorman, Siobhan. "Bush's Lesson Plan." *National Journal* 31, no. 32 (7 August 1999): 2230–2.

Gray, Colin S. "Think Tanks and Public Policy." *International Journal* 33, no. 1 (winter 1977–78): 177–94.

Greathead, E.D. "The Antecedents and Origins of the Canadian Institute of International Affairs." In Harvey L. Dyck and Peter Krosby, eds., *Empire and Nations: Essays in Honour of Frederic H. Soward.* Toronto and

Vancouver: University of Toronto Press and University of British Columbia Press, 1969.

Greenberger, Scott S. "CAMPAIGN 2000: Bush's 'Wonks' Sweat Details of His Principles: The Road to the White House." *Atlanta Journal and Constitution,* 6 August 1999.

Greenspan, Edward, and Anthony Wilson-Smith. *Double-Vision: The Inside Story of the Liberals in Power.* Toronto: Doubleday, 1996.

Grose, Peter. *The Inquiry: The Council on Foreign Relations from 1921 to 1996.* New York: Council on Foreign Relations, 1996.

Grove, Lloyd. "Steering His Party toward the Center." *Washington Post,* 24 July 1992.

Guy, John James. *People, Politics and Government.* 3d ed. Scarborough, ON: Prentice-Hall, 1995.

Haas, Peter M., ed. *Knowledge, Power and International Policy Coordination.* Columbia, SC: University of South Carolina Press, 1997.

Hagedorn, Hermann. *Brookings: A Biography.* New York: Macmillan, 1936.

Hager, George. "Bush shops for Advice at California Think Tank: Ex-White House Stars Fill." *Washington Post,* 8 June 1999.

Harrison, Kathryn, and George Hoberg. "Setting the Environmental Agenda in Canada and the United States: The Cases of Dioxin and Radon." *Canadian Journal of Political Science* 24, no. 1 (1991): 3–27.

Harrison, Peter. *The Constitutional Conferences Secretariat: A Unique Response to a Public Management Challenge.* Ottawa: Canadian Centre for Management Development, 1992.

Hay, John. "Letting CIIPS Fall Where It May Has Nothing To Do with Saving Money." *Ottawa Citizen,* 30 March 1992.

Healy, Patrick, and Sara Hebel. "Academics Start to Line Up behind Presidential Candidates." *Chronicle of Higher Education,* 28 May 1999.

Heatherly, Charles L., ed. *Mandate for Leadership: Policy Management in a Conservative Administration.* Washington, DC: The Heritage Foundation, 1981.

Heatherly, Charles L., and Burton Yale Pines, eds., *Mandate for Leadership III: Policy Strategies for the 1990s.* Washington, DC: The Heritage Foundation, 1989.

Heclo, Hugh. "Issue Networks and the Executive Establishment." In Anthony King ed., *The New American* Political System, Washington, DC: The American Enterprise Institute, 1978.

Hellebust, Lynn, ed. *Think Tank Directory: A Guide to Nonprofit Public Policy Research Organizations.* Topeka, KS: Government Research Service, 1996.

Heritage Foundation. *1998 Annual Report.* Washington, DC: The Heritage Foundation, 1998.

Hess, Stephen. *Organizing the Presidency.* Washington, DC: Brookings Institution, 1988.

Higgott, Richard, and Diane Stone. "The Limits of Influence: Foreign Policy Think Tanks in Britain and the USA." *Review of International Studies* 20 (1994): 15–34.

Hohenberg, John. *The Bill Clinton Story: Winning the Presidency.* Syracuse, NY: Syracuse University Press, 1994.

Holmes, John. "The CIIA: A Canadian Institution." *Bout de Papier* 7, no. 4 (1990): 9–10.

Holwill, Richard N. *Agenda '83: A Mandate for Leadership Report.* Washington, DC: Heritage Foundation, 1983.

House Policy Committee. "Congressional Policy Advisory Board Meets with House Leadership." House Policy Committee web site (policy.house.gov/news/releases/1998).

Internal Revenue Code of 1986: 1077–96.

Ivins, Molly, and Lou Dubose. *Shrub: The Short but Happy Political Life of George W. Bush.* New York: Random House, 2000.

Jehl, Douglas. "Clinton, Others Begin 5-Day 'Thinking Party.'" *Los Angeles Times,* 30 December 1992.

Jenson, Jane. "Commissioning Ideas: Representation and Royal Commissions." In Susan D. Phillips, ed., *How Ottawa Spends: Making Change.* Ottawa: Carleton University Press, 1994: 39–71.

Jérôme-Forget, Monique. "Institute for Research on Public Policy." In R. Kent Weaver and James McGann, eds., *Think Tanks and Civil Societies: Catalysts for Ideas and Actions.* New Brunswick, NJ: Transaction Publishers, 2000: 87–102.

Judis, John B. "Taking Care of Business." *New Republic,* 19 August 1999: 24–31.

– "The Japanese Megaphone: Foreign Influences on Foreign Policymaking." In Eugene R. Wittkopf, ed., *The Domestic Sources of Foreign Policy: Insights and Evidence.* 2d ed. New York: St Martin's Press, 1994: 95–106.

Kaiser, Robert G., and Ira Chinoy. "How Scaife's Money Powered a Movement." *Washington Post,* 2 May 1999.

Kaplan, Fred. *The Wizards of Armageddon.* New York: Simon and Schuster, 1985.

Kessler, Glenn. "Economic Adviser Has Knack for Translating Tough Issues." *Washington Post,* 4 January 2001.

Kingdon, John W. *Agendas, Alternatives and Public Policies.* New York: Harper Collins, 1984.

Kitfield, James. "Periphery Is Out: Russia and China, In." *National Journal* 31, no. 32, 7 August 1999: 2293.

Kitschelt, Herbert P. "Political Opportunity Structures and Political Protest: Anti-Nuclear Movements in Four Democracies." *British Journal of Political Science* 16 (1986): 57–85.

Knickerbocker, Brad. "Heritage Foundation's Ideas Permeate Reagan Administration." *Christian Science Monitor,* 7 December 1984.

Kriesi, Hanspeter, Rudd Koopmans, Jan Willem Duyvendak, and Marco G. Guigni. "New Social Movements and Political Opportunities in Western Europe." *European Journal of Political Research* 22 (1992): 219–44.

Kroeger, Arthur. "The Constitutional Conferences of January-March 1992: A View from Within." Speech to the Institute of Public Administration of Canada, University of Victoria Conference, 23 April 1992.

Landers, Robert K. "Think-Tanks: The New Partisans?" *Congressional Quarterly* 1, no. 23 (20 June 1986): 455–72.

Langford, John W., and K. Lorne Brownsey, eds. *Think Tanks and Governance in the Asia-Pacific Region.* Halifax: Institute for Research on Public Policy, 1991.

Lee, Steven. "Beyond Consultations: Public Consultations to Making Foreign Policy." In Fen Osler Hampson and Maureen Appel Molot, eds., *Canada among Nations 1998: Leadership and Dialogue.* Toronto: Oxford University Press, 1998, 55–67.

Linden, Patricia. "Powerhouses of Policy: A Guide to America's Think-Tanks." *Town and Country,* January 1987.

Lindquist, Evert A. "A Quarter-Century of Think Tanks in Canada." In Diane Stone, Andrew Denham, and Mark Garnett, eds., *Think Tanks across Nations: A Comparative Approach.* Manchester: Manchester University Press, 1998, 127–44.

- "Citizens, Experts and Budgets: Evaluating Ottawa's Emerging Budget Process." In Susan D. Phillips, ed., *How Ottawa Spends 1994–95.* Ottawa: Carleton University Press, 1994, 91–128.

- "Think Tanks or Clubs? Assessing the Influence and Roles of Canadian Policy Institutes." *Canadian Public Administration* 36, no. 4 (1993): 547–79.

- "Transition Teams and Government Succession: Focusing on the Essentials." In Donald J. Savoie, ed., *Taking Power: Managing Government Transitions.* Toronto: Institute of Public Administration of Canada, 1993.

- *Behind the Myth of Think-Tanks: The Organization and Relevance of Canadian Policy Institutes.* PHD dissertation, University of California at Berkeley, 1989.

Lipset, Seymour Martin. *Continental Divide.* New York: Routledge, 1990.

- "Canada and the U.S.: The Cultural Dimension." In Charles F. Doran and John H. Sigler, eds., *Canada and the United States.* Englewood Cliffs, NJ: Prentice-Hall, 1985.

Lorinc, John. "Hold the Fries and the Social Programmes." *Saturday Night,* March 1994, 11–15, 61.

McCombs, Phil. "Building a Heritage in the War of Ideas." *Washington Post,* 3 October 1983.

McGann, James. *Think Tanks, Catalysts for Ideas in Action: An International Survey.* Tokyo: National Institute for Research Advancement, 1999.

- *The Competition for Dollars, Scholars and Influence in the Public Policy Research Industry.* Lanham, MD: University Press of America, 1995.

– "Academics to Ideologues: A Brief History of the Public Policy Research Industry." PS: *Political Science and Politics* 24, no. 4 (December 1992): 739–40.

McGann, James G., and R. Kent Weaver. *Think Tanks and Civil Societies: Catalysts for Ideas and Action.* New Brunswick, NJ: Transaction Publishers, 2000.

Mackenzie Institute. "Mission and Description" (www.mackenzieinstitute.com).

Maggs, John. "Tax Cuts, Big and Small." *National Journal* 31, no. 32 (7 August 1999): 2236.

Manley, John F., and Ronald A. Rebholz. "Questioning University's Relationship to Hoover Institution." *Standard [online] Report,* April 1999.

Manny, Carter. "The CIIA, 1928–1939." BA thesis, Harvard University, 1971.

Maraniss, David. "Letter from Never-Never Land: Epiphany and Elbow Rubbing at the Renaissance Weekend." *Washington Post,* 2 January 1993.

– "A Weekend with Bill and Friends, Hilton Head's New Year's Tradition: Name Tags, Networking and Talk, Talk, Talk." *Washington Post,* 30 December 1992.

Marshall, Will, and Martin Schram. *Mandate for Change.* New York: Berkeley Books, 1993.

Meese, Edwin III. *With Reagan: The Inside Story.* Washington, DC: Regnery Gateway, 1992.

– *The Transition to a New Administration.* Stanford, CT: Hoover Institution, 1981.

Melton, R.H. "Closing of Dole's Think Tank Raises Questions about Fund-Raising." *Washington Post,* 18 June 1995.

Menges, Constantine C. *Inside the National Security Council.* New York: Simon and Schuster, 1988.

Merelman, R.M. *Partial Visions.* Madison, WI: University of Wisconsin Press, 1991.

Milne, David. "Innovative Constitutional Processes: Renewal of Canada Conferences, January-March 1992." In Douglas Brown and Robert Young, eds., *Canada: The State of the Federation, 1992.* Kingston, ON: Institute of Intergovernmental Relations, 1992, 27–51.

Minutaglio, Bill. *First Son: George W. Bush and the Bush Family Dynasty.* New York: Time Books, 1999.

Mitchell, Elizabeth. *W: Revenge of the Bush Dynasty.* New York: Hyperion Press, 2000.

Moore, Jim, and Rick Ihde. *Clinton: Young Man in a Hurry.* Fort Worth, TX: Summit Publishing Group, 1992.

Moore, W. John. "Local Right Thinkers." *National Journal,* 1 October 1988.

Morgan, Frank B., ed. U.S. *Department of Education, Degrees and Other Formal Awards Conferred, 1944–95.* Washington, DC: Government Printing Office, 1996.

Morin, Richard, and Claudia Deane. "The Ideas Industry," *Washington Post,* 7 December 1999.

– "The Ideas Industry," *Washington Post*, 8 June 1999.
– "The Ideas Industry: Brookings Aims to Bridge La Difference." *Washington Post*, 17 August 1999.
Mufson, Steven. "For Rice, a Daunting Challenge Ahead." *Washington Post*, 18 December 2000.
Muravchik, Joshua. "The Think-Tank of the Left." *New York Times Magazine*, 27 April 1987.
National Committee for Responsive Philanthropy. *$1 Billion for Ideas: Conservative Think Tanks in the 1990s*. Washington, DC: National Committee for Responsive Philanthropy, 1999.
– *Moving a Public Policy: The Strategic Philanthropy of Conservative Foundations*. Washington, DC: National Committee for Responsive Philanthropy, 1997.
National Institute for Research Advancement. *The World Directory of Think Tanks, 1998*. Tokyo: NIRA, 1998.
Newsom, David D. *The Public Dimension of Foreign Policy*. Bloomington, IN: Indiana University Press, 1996.
Niagara Institute, web site (www.niagarainstitute.com).
North-South Institute. *The North South Institute*. Ottawa: North-South Institute, 1997.
– *Prospectus*. Ottawa: North-South Institute, 1976.
Nossal, Kim Richard. *The Politics of Canadian Foreign Policy*. 3d ed. Scarborough, ON: Prentice-Hall, 1997.
O'Connell, Brian, ed. *America's Voluntary Spirit*. New York: The Foundation Center, 1983.
O'Connor, Colleen, and Bob Cohn. "A Baby Boomer's Think Tank." *Newsweek*, 1 September 1986.
Omang, Joanne. "The Heritage Report: Getting the Government Right with Reagan." *Washington Post*, 16 November 1980.
Orlans, Harold. *The Nonprofit Research Institute: Its Origin, Operation, Problems and Prospects*. New York: McGraw-Hill, 1972.
Osendarp, J.E. "A Decade of Transition: The Canadian Institute of International Affairs, 1928–1939." MA thesis, York University, 1983.
Pal, Leslie A. *Public Policy Analysis: An Introduction*. Toronto: Methuen Press 1987.
Pastor, Robert A. "The Carter Administration and Latin America: A Test of Principle." In John D. Martz, ed., *United States Policy in Latin America: A Quarter Century of Crisis and Challenge*. Lincoln, NE: University of Nebraska Press, 1988: 62–5.
Perloff, James. *The Shadows of Power: The Council on Foreign Relations and the American Decline*. Appleton, WI: Western Islands, 1988.
Peschek, Joseph G. *Policy Planning Organizations: Elite Agendas and America's Rightward Turn*. Philadelphia, PA: Temple University Press, 1987.

Powell, S. Steven. *Covert Cadre: Inside the Institute for Policy Studies*. Ottawa, IL; Green Hill Publishers, 1988.

President Clinton's New Beginning. New York: Donald I. Fine Inc., 1992.

President of the Privy Council and Minister Responsible for Constitutional Affairs. *News Release*, 2 December 1991.

Presthus, Robert, ed. *Cross-National Perspectives*. Leiden: E.J. Brill, 1977.

Pross, A. Paul. *Group Politics and Public Policy*. Toronto: Oxford University Press, 1992.

Public Policy Forum. "History of the Forum" (www.ppforum.com).

RAND. *An Introduction to RAND: The Reach of Reason*. Santa Monica, CA: RAND, 1999.

Reagan, Ronald. *An American Life*. New York: Simon and Schuster, 1990.

Redburn, Tom. "Conservative Thinkers Are Insiders." *New York Times*, 31 December 1993.

Regan, Mary Beth. "A Think Tank with One Idea: The Newt World Order." *Business Week*, 3 July 1995.

Rich, Andrew. "Think Tanks as Sources of Expertise for Congress and the Media." Paper presented at the annual meetings of the American Political Science Association, Boston, September 1998.

– "Perceptions of Think Tanks in American Politics: A Survey of Congressional Staff and Journalists." *Burson-Marstellar Worldwide Report*, December 1997.

Rich, Andrew, and R. Kent Weaver. "Think Tanks, the Media and the Policy Process." Paper presented at the 1997 annual meetings of the American Political Science Association, Washington, DC, August 1997.

– "Advocates and Analysts: Think Tanks and the Politicization of Expertise." In Allan J. Cigler and Burdett A. Loomis, eds., *Interest Groups Politics*. 3d ed. Washington, DC: CQ Press, 1998.

Richardson, Theresa, and Donald Fisher, eds. *The Development of the Social Sciences in the United States and Canada: The Role of Philanthropy*. Stanford, CA: Ablex Publishing Corporation, 1999.

Ritchie, R.S. *An Institute for Research on Public Policy: A Study of Recommendations*. Ottawa: Information Canada, 1971.

Robinson, William H. "Public Think-Tanks in the United States: The Special Case of Legislative Support Agencies." Paper presented at the conference Think Tanks in the USA and Germany, University of Pennsylvania, Philadelphia, 1993.

Rosenbaum, David E. "Torrent of Free Advice Flows into Little Rock." *New York Times*, 15 November 1992.

Russell, Peter H. *Constitutional Odyssey: Can Canadians Become Sovereign People?* Toronto: University of Toronto Press, 1993.

Russo, Robert. "Bush Battling Questions of Brain Power." *London Free Press*, 13 December 1999.

Saloma, John S. *Ominous Politics: The New Conservative Labyrinth*. New York: Hill and Wang, 1984.

Sanders, Jerry W. *Peddlers of Crisis: The Committee on the Present Danger and the Politics of Containment*. Boston: South End Press, 1983.

Santoro, Carlo Maria. *Diffidence and Ambition: The Intellectual Sources of US Foreign Policy*. Boulder, CO: Westview Press, 1992.

Saunders, Charles B. *The Brookings Institution: A Fifty Year History*. Washington, DC: Brookings Institution, 1966.

Schmitt, Eric. "A Cadre of Familiar Foreign Policy Experts Is Putting Its Imprint on Bush." *New York Times,* 23 December 1999.

Schneider, Mark, and Paul Teske. "Toward a Theory of the Political Entrepreneur: Evidence from Local Government." *American Political Science Review* 86 (1992): 737–47.

Schram, Martin. *Running for President: A Journal of the Carter Campaign*. New York: Pocket Books, 1978.

Schulzinger, Robert D. *The Wise Men of Foreign Affairs: The History of the Council on Foreign Relations*. New York: Columbia University Press, 1984.

Scott, Janny. "Intellectuals Who Became Influential: The Manhattan Institute Has Nudged New York to the Right." *New York Times,* 12 May 1997.

Sealander, Judith. *Private Wealth and Public Life: Foundation Philanthropy and the Reshaping of American Social Policy From the Progressive Era to the New Deal*. Baltimore, MD: Johns Hopkins University Press, 1997.

Shoup, Laurence H. *The Carter Presidency and Beyond: Power and Politics in the 1980s*. Palo Alto, CA: Ramparts Press, 1980.

Shoup, Laurence H., and William Minter. *Imperial Brain Trust: The Council of Foreign Relations and the United States Foreign Policy*. New York: Monthly Review Press, 1977.

Silk, Leonard, and Mark Silk. *The American Establishment*. New York: Basic Books, 1980.

Simpson, Glenn R. "New Addition to Gingrich Family Tree: The Progress and Freedom Foundation." *Roll Call,* 12 September 1994.

Sklar, Holly, ed. *Trilateralism: The Trilateral Commission and Elite Planning for World Management*. Boston: South End Press, 1980.

Smith, Bruce L.R. *The Rand Corporation: Case Study of a Nonprofit Advisory Corporation*. Cambridge, MA: Harvard University Press, 1966.

Smith, James A. *Strategic Calling: The Center for Strategic and International Studies 1962–92*. Washington, DC: Center for Strategic and International Studies, 1993.

– *Brookings at Seventy-Five*. Washington, DC: The Brookings Institution, 1991.

– *The Idea Brokers: Think Tanks and the Rise of the New Policy Elite*. New York: The Free Press, 1991.

Splane, Richard. *75 Years of Community Service to Canada: Canadian Council on Social Development, 1920–1995*. Ottawa: Canadian Council on Social Development, 1996.

Stairs, Denis. "Public Opinion and External Affairs: Reflections on the Domestication of Canadian Foreign Policy." *International Journal* 33, no. 1 (winter 1977–78): 128–49.

Statistics Canada. "Earned Doctorates, by Field of Study and Sex, Canada, 1991 to 1995." In *Education in Canada, 1997*. Ottawa: Supply and Services, 1998.

Stone, Diane. *Capturing the Political Imagination: Think Tanks and the Policy Process*. London: Frank Cass, 1996.

– *Banking on Knowledge: The Genesis of the Global Development Network*. London: Routledge, 2000.

Stone, Diane, Andrew Denham, and Mark Garnett, eds. *Think Tanks across Nations: A Comparative Approach*. Manchester: Manchester University Press, 1998.

Struyk, Raymond J. *Reconstructive Critics: Think Tanks in Post-Soviet Bloc Democracies*. Washington, DC: Urban Institute Press, 1999.

Sundquist, James L. "Research Brokerage: The Weak Line." In Laurence E. Lynn, ed., *Knowledge and Policy: The Uncertain Connection*. Washington, DC: The National Academy of Sciences, 1978.

Swanson, J. "Brain Power: Bush Aligns with Hoover Think Tank." *Dallas Morning News*, 11 August 1999.

Taylor, Peter Shawn. "The Idea Peddlers." *National Post Business*, December 2000, 86–90, 92, 94, 96.

Towell, Pat. "DLC Moves into Driver's Seat." *National Convention News: The Daily Newspaper for the 1992 Democratic National Convention*, 13 July 1992.

Troester, Rod. *Jimmy Carter as Peacemaker: A Post-Presidential Biography*. New York: Praeger Publishers, 1996.

Truman, David B. *The Governmental Process: Political Interests and Public Opinion*. New York: Alfred A. Knopf, 1951.

Tupper, Allan. "Think-Tanks, Public Debt, and the Politics of Expertise in Canada." *Canadian Public Administration* 36, no. 4 (1993): 530–46.

Tyman, Kathleen. "A Decade-Long Heritage of Conservative Thought." *Washington Post*, 4 October 1983.

The Urban Institute. *30: The Urban Institute 1968–1998*. Washington, DC: The Urban Institute, 1998.

Van Der Woerd, Nicoline. *World Survey of Strategic Studies Centres*. London: International Institute of Strategic Studies, 1992.

Vanier Institute of the Family Home Page (www.familyforum.com).

Van Slambrouck, Paul. "California Think Tank Acts as Bush 'Brain Trust'." *Christian Science Monitor*, 2 July 1999.

Wala, Michael. *The Council on Foreign Relations and American Foreign Policy in the Early Cold War*. Providence, RI: Berghahn Books, 1994.

Wall, John Frazier. *Andrew Carnegie*. Pittsburgh: University of Pittsburgh Press, 1989.

Wallace, William. "Between Two Worlds: Think-Tanks and Foreign Policy." In Christopher Hill and Pamela Beshoff, eds., *Two Worlds of International*

Relations: Academics, Practitioners and the Trade in Ideas, London: Routledge, 1994, 139–63.

Walker, Michael. "What's Right, Who's Left, and What's Leftover?" In William D. Gairdner, ed., *After Liberalism: Essays in Search of Freedom, Virtue, and Order.* Toronto: Stoddart, 1998.

Weaver, R. Kent. "The Changing World of Think Tanks." *PS: Political Science and Politics* 22, no. 2 (September 1989): 563–78.

Weinraub, Bernard. "Conservative Group's Blueprint for Reagan." *San Francisco Chronicle,* 11 December 1980.

Weisberg, Jacob. "Clincest: Washington's New Ruling Class." *New Republic,* 26 April 1993.

Weiss, Carol H. *Organizations for Policy Analysis: Helping Government Think.* Newbury Park, CA: Sage Publications, 1992.

Weisskopf, Michael. "New Political Landscape Bountiful for Think Tank with Gingrich Ties." *Washington Post,* 5 February 1995.

Wheeler, Charles. "Heritage Chiefs Recall Decade of Growth, Power." *Washington Times,* 29 April 1987.

Whitaker, Ben. *The Foundations: An Anatomy of Philanthropy and Society.* London: Eyre Methuen, 1974.

Wiarda, Howard J. *Universities, Think Tanks and War Colleges: The Main Institutions of American Educational Life: A Memoir.* Philadelphia: Xlibris Corporation, 1999.

Witcover, Jules. *Marathon: The Pursuit of the Presidency 1972–1976.* New York: Viking, 1977.

Wood, Robert C. *Whatever Possessed the President? Academic Experts and Presidential Policy, 1960–1968.* Amherst, MA: University of Massachusetts Press, 1993.

Yee, Albert S. "The Causal Effects of Ideas on Policies." *International Organization* 50, no. 1 (1996): 69–108.

Yoffe, Emily. "IPS Faces Life." *New Republic,* 6–13 August 1977, 16–18.

SELECTED PUBLICATIONS OF AMERICAN THINK TANKS

The American Enterprise Institute

Calfee, John E. *Prices, Markets, and the Pharmaceutical Revolution.* Washington, DC: American Enterprise Institute Press, 2000.

Darga, Kenneth. *Sampling and the Census: A Case against the Proposed Adjustments for Undercount.* Washington, DC: American Enterprise Institute Press, 1999.

Downs, Chuck. *Over the Line: North Korea's Negotiating Strategy.* Washington, DC: American Enterprise Institute Press, 1999.

Golub, Stephen S., *Labour Costs and International Trade*. Washington, DC: American Enterprise Institute Press, 1999.

Hahn, Robert W. *Reviving Regulatory Reform: A Global Perspective*. Washington, DC: American Enterprise Institute Press, 2000.

Hassett, Kevin A., and Glen Hubbard. *The Magic Mountain: A Guide to Defining and Using a Budget Surplus*. Washington, DC: American Enterprise Institute Press, 1999.

Leedeen, Michael A. *Machiavelli on Modern Leadership: Why Machiavelli's Iron Rules Are As Timely and Important Today As Five Centuries Ago*. Washington, DC: American Enterprise Institute Press, 1999.

Long, Clarisa. *Genetic Testing and the Use of Information*. Washington, DC: American Enterprise Institute Press, 1999.

Ornstein, Norman, and Thomas Mann, eds. *The Permanent Campaign and Its Future*. Washington, DC: American Enterprise Institute Press, 2000.

Weaver, Carolyn L. *Social Security and Its Reform*. Washington, DC: American Enterprise Institute Press, 2000.

The Brookings Institution

Aerbach, Joel D., and Bert A. Rockman. *In the Web of Politics: Three Decades of the U.S. Federal Executive*. Washington, DC: Brookings Institution Press, 2000.

Haass, Richard N., and Meagan L. O'Sullivan, eds. *Honey and Vinegar: Incentives, Sanctions and Foreign Policy*. Washington, DC: Brookings Institution Press, 2000.

Kohurt, Andrew, John C. Green, Scott Keeter, and Robert C. Toth. *The Diminishing Divide: Religion's Changing Rules in American Politics*. Washington, DC: Brookings Institution Press, 2000.

Loveless, Tom, ed. *Conflicting Missions? Teachers Unions and Educational Reform*. Washington, DC: Brookings Institution Press, 2000.

O'Hanlon, Michael. *Technological Change and the Future of Warfare*. Washington, DC: Brookings Institution Press, 2000.

Skerry, Perry. *Counting in the Census? Race, Group Identity, and the Evasion of Politics*. Washington, DC: Brookings Institution Press, 2000.

Skocpol, Theda, and Morris Fiorina, eds. *Civic Engagement in American Democracy*. Washington, DC: Brookings Institution Press, 1999.

Sugarman, Steven D., and Frank R. Kemerer, eds. *School Choice and Social Controversy*. Washington, DC: Brookings Institution Press, 1999.

Thurber, James A., and Canice J. Nelson, eds. *Campaign Warriors: Political Consultants in Elections*. Washington, DC: Brookings Institution Press, 2000.

Weaver, Kent R. *Ending Welfare as We Know It*. Washington, DC: Brookings Institution Press, 2000.

The Cato Institute

Carpenter, Ted Galen. NATO's *Empty Victory: A Postmortem of the Balkan War*. Washington, DC: Cato Institute, 2000.

Conrad, Clay S. *Jury Nullification: The Evolution of a Doctrine*. Washington, DC: Cato Institute, 1998.

Goklany, Indur M. *Cleaning the Air: The Real Story on the War on Air Pollution*. Washington, DC: Cato Institute, 1999.

Gwartney, James, and Robert Lawson. *Economic Freedom of the World: 2000 Annual Report*. Washington, DC: Cato Institute, 2000.

Klein, Daniel, ed. *What Do Economists Contribute?* Washington, DC: Cato Institute, 1999.

Milloy, Steven, and Michael Gough. *Silencing Science*. Washington, DC: Cato Institute, 1999.

Posner, Richard. *Natural Monopoly and Its Regulation*. Washington, DC: Cato Institute, 1999.

Simon, Julian L. *Hoodwinking the Nation*. Washington, DC: Cato Institute, 1999.

Singleton, Solveig, and Daniel T. Griswold, eds. *Economic Casualties: How U.S. Foreign Policy Undermines Trade, Growth, and Liberty*. Washington, DC: Cato Institute, 1999.

Vandoren, Peter. *Chemicals, Cancer, and Choices: Risk Reduction through Markets*. Washington, DC: Cato Institute, 1999.

The Carnegie Endowment for International Peace

Abramowitz, Morton I. *China: Can We Have a Policy?* Washington, DC: Carnegie Endowment for International Peace, 1997.

Aleinikoff, Alexander T. *Between Principles and Politics: The Direction of U.S. Citizenship Policy*. Washington, DC: Carnegie Endowment for International Peace, 1998.

Aslund, Anders, and Martha Brill Olcott, (eds) *Russia After Communism*. Washington, DC: Carnegie Endowment for International Peace, 1999.

Edwards, Sebastian, and Moises Naim. *Mexico 1994: Anatomy of an Emerging Market Crash*. Washington, DC: Carnegie Endowment for International Peace, 1998.

Garnett, Sherman W. *Keystone in the Arch: Ukraine in the Emerging Security Environment of Central and Eastern Europe*. Washington, DC: Carnegie Endowment for International Peace, 1997.

Jones, Rodney W., Mark G. McDonough, Toby F. Dalton, and Gregory D. Koblentz. *Tracking Nuclear Proliferation: A Guide to Maps and Charts*. Washington, DC: Carnegie Endowment for International Peace, 1998.

Papademetriou, Demetios G., T. Alexander Aleinikoff, and Deborah Waller Meyers. *Reorganizing the Immigration Function: Toward a New Framework for Accountability.* Washington, DC: Carnegie Endowment for International Peace, 1998.

Rothkopf, David J. *The Price of Peace: Emergency Economic Intervention and the U.S. Foreign Policy.* Washington, DC: Carnegie Endowment for International Peace, 1998.

Shevetsova, Lilia. *Yeltsin's Russia: Myths and Reality.* Washington, DC: Carnegie Endowment for International Peace, 1999.

Zhang, Ming. *China's Changing Nuclear Posture: Reactions to the South Asian Nuclear Tests.* Washington, DC: Carnegie Endowment for International Peace, 1999.

The Center for Strategic and International Studies

Collins, Joseph J., and Gabrielle D. Bowdoin. *Beyond Unilateral Economic Sanctions: Better Alternatives for U.S. Foreign Policy.* Washington, DC: CSIS Press, 1999.

Cossa, Ralph A., ed. *U.S.-Korea-Japan Relations: Building toward a "Virtual Alliance."* Washington, DC: CSIS Press, 1999.

Garrison , William B. Jr, and Peter S. Watson. *National Conformity Assessment Schemes: Nontariff Trade Barriers in Information Technology.* Washington, DC: CSIS Press, 1999.

Gong, Gerrit. W. *Taiwan Strait Dilemmas: China-Taiwan-U.S. Policies in the New Century.* Washington, DC: CSIS Press, 2000.

Goure, Daniel, and Jeffrey M. Ranney. *Averting the Defense Train Wreck in the New Millennium.* Washington, DC: CSIS Press, 1999.

Hausker, Karl. *The Convergence of Ideas on Improving the Environmental Protection System.* Washington, DC: CSIS Press, 1999.

Heath, Jonathon. *Mexico and the Sexenio Curse: Presidential Successions and Economic Crises in Modern Mexico.* Washington, DC: CSIS Press, 1999.

Ikle, Fred C. *Defending the U.S. Homeland Strategic and Legal Issues for DOD and the Armed Services.* Washington, DC: CSIS Press, 1999.

Mazarr, Michael J. *Global Trends 2005.* Washington, DC: CSIS Press, 1999.

Scherer, F.M. *New Perspectives on Economic Growth and Technological Innovation.* Washington, DC: CSIS Press, 1999.

The Hoover Institution on War, Revolution and Peace

Chesher, James E., and Tibor R. Machan. *The Business of Commerce: Examining an Honorable Profession.* Stanford, CA: The Hoover Institution, 1999.

Diamond, Larry, and Doh Chull Shin. *Institutional Reform and Democratic Consolidation in Korea.* Stanford, CA: The Hoover Institution, 1999.

Drell, Sidney D., Abraham D. Sofaer, and George D. Wilson, eds. *The New Terror: Facing the Threat of Biological and Chemical Weapons.* Stanford, CA: The Hoover Institution, 1999.

Edwards, Lee. *The Collapse of Communism*. Stanford, CA: The Hoover Institution, 2000.

King, Charles. *The Moldovans: Romania, Russia, and the Politics of Culture*. Stanford, CA: The Hoover Institution, 2000.

Machan, Tibor R., ed. *Business Ethics in the Global Market*. Stanford, CA: The Hoover Institution, 1999.

Miller, James C. III. *Monopoly Politics*. Stanford, CA: The Hoover Institution, 1999.

Schweizer, Peter, ed. *The Fall of the Berlin Wall*. Stanford, CA: The Hoover Institution, 1999.

Sowell, Thomas. *Barbarians inside the Gates and Other Controversial Essays*. Stanford, CA: The Hoover Institution, 1999.

Wise, David A., ed. *Personal Saving, Personal Choice*. Stanford, CA: The Hoover Institution, 1999.

The Heritage Foundation

Anderson, James H. *America at Risk: The Citizen's Guide to Missile Defense*. Washington, DC: The Heritage Foundation, 1999.

Carter, Samuel Casey. *No Excuses: Seven Principles of Low-Income Schools Who Set the Standard for High Achievement*. Washington, DC: The Heritage Foundation, 1999.

The Heritage Foundation. *A Guide for Congress*. 1999 edition. Washington, DC: The Heritage Foundation, 1999.

Holmes, Kim R., and James J. Przystup, eds. *Between Diplomacy and Deterrence: Strategies for U.S. Relations with China*. Washington, DC: The Heritage Foundation, 1997.

Johnson, Bryan T., Kim R. Holmes, and Melanie Kirkpatrick. *1999 Index of Economic Freedom*. Washington, DC: The Heritage Foundation, 1999.

Rector, Robert E., and Sarah E. Youssef. *The Impact of Welfare Reform: The Trend in State Caseloads, 1985–1998*. Washington, DC: The Heritage Foundation, 1999.

Rees, Nina Shokraii, and Sarah E. Youssef. *School Choice 1999: What's Happening in the States*. Washington, DC: The Heritage Foundation, 1999.

Thierer, Adam D. *The Delicate Balance: Federalism, Interstate Commerce, and Economic Freedom in the Technological Age*. Washington, DC: The Heritage Foundation, 1999.

The Institute for Contemporary Studies

Agrawal, Arun, Charla Britt, and Keshav Kanel. *Decentralization in Nepal: A Comparative Analysis: A Report on the Participatory Development Program*. San Francisco, CA: Institute for Contemporary Studies, 1999.

Bolick, Clint. *Transformation The Promise and Politics of Empowerment*. San Francisco, CA: Institute for Contemporary Studies, 1999.

Chickering, Lawrence A. *Beyond Left and Right: Breaking the Political Stalemate.* San Francisco, CA: Institute for Contemporary Studies, 1999.

Henderson, Carter. *Funny, I Don't Feel Old! How to Flourish after 50.* San Francisco, CA: Institute for Contemporary Studies, 1999.

Holt, Mikel. *Not Yet "Free At Last" The Unfinished Business of the Civil Rights Movement: Our Battle for School Choice.* San Francisco, CA: Institute for Contemporary Studies, 1999.

Jacobs, Joseph. *The Compassionate Conservative Assuming Responsibility and Respecting Human Dignity.* San Francisco, CA: Institute for Contemporary Studies, 1999.

Klitgaard, Robert, Ronald Maclean-Abaroa, and H. Lindsey Parris. *Corrupt Cities: A Practical Guide to Cure and Prevention.* San Francisco, CA: Institute for Contemporary Studies, 1999.

Oakerson, Ronald. *Governing Local Public Economies: Creating the Civic Metropolis.* San Francisco, CA: Institute for Contemporary Studies, 1999.

The Institute for Policy Studies

Barnet, Ann B., and Richard J. Barnett. *The Youngest Minds: Parenting and Genes in the Development of Intellect and Emotion.* Washington, DC: Institute for Policy Studies, 1998.

Bennis, Phyllis, and Michel Moushabeck, eds. *Beyond the Storm: A Gulf Crisis Reader.* Washington, DC: Institute for Policy Studies, 1991.

Honey, Martha. *Ecotourism and Sustainable Development: Who Owns Paradise?* Washington, DC: Institute for Policy Studies, 1999.

– *Hostile Acts: U.S. Policy in Costa Rica in the 1980s.* Washington, DC: Institute for Policy Studies, 1994.

Shuman, Michael. *Going Local: Creating Self-Reliant Communities in a Global Age.* Washington, DC: Institute for Policy Studies, 1998.

RAND

Brooks, Arthur C. *Arts, Markets, and Governments: A Study in Cultural Policy Analysis.* Santa Monica, CA: RAND, 1998.

Clark, W.A.V., and Peter A. Morrison. *Demographic Foundations of Political Empowerment in Multiminority Cities.* Santa Monica, CA: RAND, 1996.

Eiseman, Elisa. *Cloning Human Beings: Recent Scientific and Policy Developments.* Santa Monica, CA: RAND, 1999.

Goldman, Charles A. *Managing Policy toward China under Clinton: The Changing Role of Economics.* Santa Monica, CA: RAND, 1995.

Klitgaard, Robert E. *Including Culture in Evaluation Research.* Santa Monica, CA: RAND, 1998.

Klitgaard, Robert E., and Heather Baser. *Working Together to Fight Corruption: State, Society and the Private Sector in Partnership*. Santa Monica, CA: RAND, 1998.

Longshore, Douglas, Peter Reuter, Jack Derks, Martin Grapendaal, and Patricia A. Ebener. *Drug Policies and Harms: A Conceptual Framework*. Santa Monica, CA: RAND, 1999.

MacCoun, Robert J., and Peter Reuter. *Drug Control*. Santa Monica, CA: RAND, 1998.

Resetar, Susan A., Beth E. Lachman, Robert J. Lempert, and Monica M. Pinto. *Technology Forces at Work: Profiles of Environmental Research and Development at Dupont, Intel, Monsanto, and Xerox*. Santa Monica, CA: RAND, 1999.

Szayna, Thomas, William D. O'Malley, and Preston Niblack. *Assessing Armed Forces' Deficiencies for Peace Operations: A Methodology*. Santa Monica, CA: RAND, 1997.

SELECTED PUBLICATIONS OF
CANADIAN THINK TANKS

The Caledon Institute of Social Policy

Battle, Ken. *Constitutional Reform by Stealth*. Ottawa: Caledon Institute, 1995.

Battle, Ken, and Sherri Torjman. *Ottawa Should Help Build a National Early Childhood Development System*. Ottawa: Caledon Institute, 2000.

Brouwer, Andrew. *Equal Access to Student Loans for Convention Refugees*. Ottawa: Caledon Institute, 2000.

Mendelson, Michael. *Aboriginal People in Canada's Labour Market*. Ottawa: Caledon Institute, 1999.

– *The Price of Prudence*. Ottawa: Caledon Institute, 1999.

Rachlis, Michael. *A Review of the Alberta Private Hospital Proposal*. Ottawa: Caledon Institute, 2000.

Torjman, Sherri. *Employment Insurance: Small Bang for Big Bucks*. Ottawa: Caledon Institute, 2000.

– *The Let-Them-Eat-Cake Law*. Ottawa: Caledon Institute, 1995.

– *Small Technicality, Big Problem*. Ottawa: Caledon Institute, 1994.

The Canada West Foundation

Canada West Foundation. *The Canadian Social Policy Landscape: A Road of Recent Initiatives*. Calgary, AB: Canada West Foundation, 2000.

– *Cities @ 2000: Canada's Urban Landscape – New Trends, Emerging Issues*. Calgary, AB: Canada West Foundation, 2000.

- *Exploring Alternatives: Government Social Service Policy and Non-Profit Organizations.* Calgary, AB: Canada West Foundation, 2000.
- *Ten Years After: Cross-Border Export/Import Trends since the Canada-United States Free Trade Agreement.* Calgary, AB: Canada West Foundation, 2000.
- *Strings Attached: Non-Profits and their Funding Relationships with Government.* Calgary, AB: Canada West Foundation, 1999.
- *Getting Started: An Overview of Youth Employment Issues and Programs.* Calgary, AB: Canada West Foundation, 1998.
- *The State of Gambling in Canada: An Interprovincial Roadmap of Gambling and Its Impact.* Calgary, AB: Canada West Foundation, 1998.
- *Canadian Free-Nets: Surveying the Landscape of the Information Highway.* Calgary, AB: Canada West Foundation, 1997.
- *Renewal of Food Processing in Western Canada.* Calgary, AB: Canada West Foundation, 1997.
- *Interprovincial Trade and Canadian Unity.* Calgary, AB: Canada West Foundation, 1996.

The Canadian Centre for Policy Alternatives

Dobbin, Murray. *Ten Tax Myths.* Ottawa: CCPA, 2000.
Doherty-Delorme, Denise, and Erika Shaker, eds. *Missing Pieces: An Alternative Guide to Canadian Post-Secondary Education.* Ottawa: CCPA, 2000.
Fuller, Colleen. *Caring for Profit: How Corporations Are Taking Over Canada's Health Care System.* Ottawa: CCPA, 2000.
Hackett, Bob, Richard Gruneau, Donald Grutsein, and Timothy A. Gibson. *The Missing New: Filters and Blind Spots in the Canadian Press.* Ottawa: CCPA, 2000.
Jackson, Andrew, David Robinson, Bob Baldwin, and Cindy Wiggins. *Falling Behind: The State of Working in Canada.* Ottawa: CCPA, 2000.
Lee, Mark. *A Primer on Canadian Productivity: Everything You Wanted to Know about Productivity but Were Afraid to Ask.* Ottawa: CCPA, 2000.
Maclean, Brian K., ed. *Out of Control: Canada and the Turmoil in Global Financial Markets.* Ottawa: CCPA, 2000.
Schnenk, Christopher, and John Anderson. *RESHAPING WORK 2.* Ottawa: CCPA, 2000.
Shaker, Erika. *YNN and the Commercial Carpet-Bombing of the Classroom.* Ottawa: CCPA, 2000.
Shrybman, Steven. *The World Trade Organization: A Citizen's Guide.* Ottawa: CCPA, 2000.

The Canadian Institute of Strategic Studies

Blitt, Jessica. OP *Toucan and Beyond: Contradictions in Canadian Policy in East Timor.* Toronto: CISS, 2000.

Covelli, Nick. *The McNaughton Papers.* Vol. 12, *The Political Economy of Canada's Regional Trade Strategy.* Toronto: CISS, 2000.

Fitz-Gerald, Ann. NATO *Enlargement Round I: Problems and Prospects in Implementing the Initial Enlargement.* Toronto: CISS, 1999.

Godefroy, Andrew. *Canada's Strategy for Space, 1985–1999.* Toronto: CISS, 1999.

Henderson, Robert d'A. *Will China Use Force against Taiwan?* Toronto: CISS, 2000.

Jacoby, Tami Amanda. *The 1999 Israeli Elections: Implications for Peace and Security in the Middle East.* Toronto: CISS, 2000.

Jockel, Joseph T. *The Canadian Forces: Hard Choices, Soft Power.* Toronto: CISS, 2000.

Roussel, Stéphane. *Velvet Divorce or Violent Breakup? Political Violence in Quebec: Looking Ahead to the Next Referendum.* Toronto: CISS, 1999.

Rudd, David. *Towards a New Defence White Paper: Can "Human Security" Influence Force Structure?* Toronto: CISS, 2000.

Tarry, Sarah. *A European Security and Defence Identity: Dead on Arrival?* Toronto: CISS, 2000.

The Canadian Policy Research Networks, Inc.

Betcherman, Gordon, Norm Leckie, Kathryn McMullen. *Barriers to Employer-Sponsored Training in Canada.* Ottawa: CPRN Discussion Paper no. W 02, 7 July 1998.

Davidman, Katie, Gordon Betcherman, Michael Hall, and Deena White. *Work in the Nonprofit Sector: The Knowledge Gap.* Ottawa: CPRN Philanthropist. Vol.14, no. 3, September 1998.

Gunderson, Morley. *Government Compensation: Issues and Options.* Ottawa: CPRN Discussion Paper no. W 03, July 1998.

Hayes, Michael, and James Dunn. *Population Health in Canada: A Systematic Review.* Ottawa: CPRN Study no. H 01, March 1998.

Hughes, Karen. *Gender and Self-Employment in Canada: Assessing Trends and Policy Implications.* Ottawa: CPRN Study no. W 04, 1999.

Krashinsky, Michael, and Gordon Cleveland. *Tax Fairness for One-Earner and Two-Earner Families: An Examination of the Issues.* Ottawa: CPRN Discussion Paper no. F 07, 1999.

McMullen, Kathryn. *Skill and Employment Effects of Computer-Based Technological Change: The Results of the Working with Technology Survey III.* Ottawa: CPRN Study no. W 01, January 1997.

Maxwell, Judith. *Investing in Children Should Be Our Next Priority.* Ottawa: CPRN Canadian Business Economics. Vol. 8, no. 1, February 2000.

Peters, Joseph. *An Era of Change: Government Employment Trends in the 1980s and 1990s.* Ottawa: CPRN Study no. W 03, 1999.

Stroick , Sharon M., and Jane Jenson. *What Is the Best Policy Mix for Canada's Young Children*. Ottawa: CPRN Study no. F 09, 2000.

The C.D. Howe Institute

Allen, Douglas W., and John Richards, eds. *It Takes Two: The Family in Law and Finance*. Toronto: C.D Howe Institute Policy Study 33, 1999.

Boothe, Paul, and Derek Hermanutz. *Simply Sharing: An Interprovincial Equalization Scheme for Canada*. Toronto: C.D. Howe Institute Commentary 128, July 1999.

Cameron, David R., ed. *The Referendum Papers: Essays on Secession and National Unity*. Toronto: University of Toronto Press, in association with the C.D. Howe Institute, 1999.

Coulombe, Serge. *Economic Growth and Provincial Disparity: A New View of an Old Canadian Problem*. Toronto: C.D. Howe Institute Commentary 122, March 1999.

Courchene, Thomas J., and Richard G. Harris. *From Fixing to Monetary Union: Options for North American Currency Integration*. Toronto: C.D. Howe Institute Commentary 127, June 1999.

Mintz, Jack M., and Thomas A. Wilson. *Capitalizing on Cuts to Capital Gains Taxes*. Toronto: C.D. Howe Institute Commentary 137, February 2000.

Monahan, Patrick J. *Doing the Rules: An Assessment of the Federal Clarity Act in Light of the Quebec Secession Reference*. Toronto: C.D. Howe Institute Commentary 135, February 2000.

Orr, Dale, and Thomas A. Wilson, eds. *The Electronic Village: Policy Issues of the Information Economy*. Toronto: C.D Howe Institute Policy Study 32, 1999.

Poschmann, Finn, and John Richards. *How to Lower Taxes and Improve Social Policy: A Case of Eating Your Cake and Having It Too*. Toronto: C.D. Howe Institute Commentary 136, February 2000.

Robson, William B.P., Jack M. Mintz, and Finn Poschmann. *Budgeting for Growth: Promoting Prosperity with Smart Fiscal Policy*. Toronto: C.D. Howe Institute Commentary 134, February 2000.

The Conference Board of Canada

Birkbeck, Kimberley. *Allocating the Fiscal*. Ottawa: The Conference Board, 1998.

Birkbeck, Kimberley, Peter Lok, and Hugh Williams. *Managing European Monetary Union: Risks and Opportunities for Canadians*. Ottawa: The Conference Board, 1999.

Iqbal, Mahmood. *Are We Losing Our Minds? Trends, Determinants and the Role of Taxation in the Brain Drain to the United States*. Ottawa: The Conference Board, 1999.

Moser, Catherine, and Pierre Vanasse. *What's New in Debt Financing for Small and Medium-Sized Enterprises*. Ottawa: The Conference Board, 1997.

Roth, Chris. *Crossborder Mergers in the Banking Sector: Real and Perceived Barriers to Entry*. Ottawa: The Conference Board, 1998.

Saus, Josefina Peraire. *Crisis in Euroland*. Ottawa: The Conference Board, 1999.

Shutt, Theresa. *Members' Briefing/Viewpoint: Toward a Comfortable Retirement. Do You Know Where Your Money Is? A Review of Managed Funds*. Ottawa: The Conference Board, 1999.

Williams, Hugh. *At a Crossroads: Financial Sector Reform in Canada*. Ottawa: The Conference Board,1999.

– *Searching for a Vision: Financial Services in Flux*. Ottawa: The Conference Board, 1999.

The Fraser Institute

Adie, Douglas K. *Mail Monopoly: Analysing the Canadian Postal Service*. Vancouver: The Fraser Institute, 1990.

Gibson, Gordon. *Thirty Million Musketeers: One Canada for All Canadians*. Vancouver: The Fraser Institute, 1995.

Globerman, Steven, and Michael Walker, eds. *The Immigration Dilemma*. Vancouver: The Fraser Institute, 1992.

Grady, Patrick. *The Economic Consequences of Quebec Sovereignty*. Vancouver: The Fraser Institute, 1991.

Grubel, Herb, and Michael Walker, eds. *Unemployment Insurance: Global Evidence of Its Effects on Unemployment*. Vancouver: The Fraser Institute, 1978.

Lehrer, Keith. *Landlord as Scapegoat*. Vancouver: The Fraser Institute, 1991.

Palda, Filip, ed. *Provincial Trade Wars: Why the Blockade Must End*. Vancouver: The Fraser Institute, 1994.

Riggs, A.R., and Tom Velk, eds. *Beyond NAFTA*. Vancouver: The Fraser Institute, 1993.

Sarlo, Christopher. *Poverty in Canada*. 2d ed. Vancouver: The Fraser Institute, 1996.

Usher, Dan. *The Uneasy Case for Equalization Payments*. Vancouver: The Fraser Institute, 1995.

The Institute for Research on Public Policy

Aucoin, Peter. *The New Public Management: Canada in Comparative Perspective*. Montreal: IRPP, 1995.

Gibbons, Roger, and Guy Laforest, eds. *Beyond the Impasse: Towards Reconciliation*. Montreal: IRPP, 1998.

Hobson, Paul A.R., and France St-Hilaire, eds. *Urban Governance and Finance: A Question of Who Does What*. Montreal: IRPP, 1997.

Hum, Derek. *Maintaining a Competitive Workforce: Employee-Based Training in the Canadian Economy.* Montreal: IRPP, 1996.

Hutton, Thomas A. *The Transformation of Canada's Pacific Metropolis: A Study of Vancouver.* Montreal: IRPP, 1998.

Jérôme-Forget, Monique, and Claude E. Forget. *Who is the Master? A Blueprint for Canadian Health Care Reform.* Montreal: IRPP, 1999.

Meisel, John, Guy Rocher, Arthur Silver, and IRPP, eds. *As I Recall/Si je me souviens bien.* Montreal: IRPP, 1999.

Sancton, Andrew. *Governing Canada's City-Regions: Adapting Form to Function.* Montreal: IRPP, 1994.

Seidle, F. Leslie. *Rethinking the Delivery of Public Services to Citizens.* Montreal: IRPP, 1995.

Stanbury, W.T. ed., *Perspectives on the New Economics and Regulation of Telecommunications.* Montreal: IRPP, 1996.

The North-South Institute

Cozac, David, and Melanie Gruer. *Don't Shoot the Messenger: A Guide for Canadian Journalists on Promoting Press Freedom.* Ottawa: NSI, 1997.

Culpeper, Roy, and Carolyn McAskie, eds. *Toward Autonomous Development in Africa.* Ottawa: NSI, 1997.

Delahanty, Julie. *From Social Movements to Social Clauses: Grading Strategies for Improving Conditions for Women Garment Workers.* Ottawa: NSI, 1999.

English, Philip E., and Harris M. Mule. *The African Development Bank.* Vol. 1. Ottawa: NSI, 1997.

Gibb, Heather, ed. *Canadian Perspectives on Labour Mobility in APEC.* Ottawa: NSI, 1997.

Hibler, Michelle, and Rowena Beamish. *Canadian Development Report 1998: Canadian Corporations and Social Responsibility.* Ottawa: NSI, 1998.

Morrison, David R. *Aid and Ebb Tide: A History of CIDA and Canadian Development Assistance.* Ottawa and Waterloo: NSI, in association with Wilfrid Laurier University Press, 1998.

Serieux, John E. *Reducing the Debt of the Poorest: Challenges and Opportunities.* Ottawa: NSI, 1999.

Van Rooy, Alison, ed. *Canadian Development Report 1999: Civil Society and Global Change.* Ottawa: NSI, 1999.

Index